The Bankruptcy Claims Handbook

SECOND EDITION

Business Bankruptcy Committee

Monique D. Hayes, Paul R. Hage and Brett D. Fallon
Editors

ABA
AMERICAN BAR ASSOCIATION
Business Law Section

Cover design by Catherine Zaccarine.

Printed in the United States of America.

25 24 23 22 21 5 4 3 2 1

ISBN: 978-1- 63905-019-2

Discounts are available for books ordered in bulk. Special consideration is given to state bars, CLE programs, and other bar-related organizations. Inquire at Book Publishing, ABA Publishing, American Bar Association, 321 N. Clark Street, Chicago, Illinois 60654-7598.

www.shopABA.org

CONTENTS

PREFACE

This second edition of *The Bankruptcy Claims Handbook* has been prepared by Claims and Priorities Subcommittee of the Business Bankruptcy Committee of the ABA's Business Law Section. The purpose of the *Handbook* is to assist attorneys who are unfamiliar with bankruptcy law. The *Handbook* is also intended to serve as a refresher for those experienced in bankruptcy practice. The claims process is where most non-bankruptcy attorneys will be exposed to bankruptcy law. Therefore the *Handbook* is intended to provide insight into bankruptcy analyses and processes for practitioners embarking on identifying, asserting, objecting to and/or defending claims in a bankruptcy case, and evaluating how claims may be treated in a bankruptcy case.

Our sincere gratitude is due to each contributor listed on the *Contributors* page and to the American Bar Association's dedicated staff members who brought the project to fruition. This book would not have happened without This work also builds on the work of writers and contributors of the predecessor text, *The Bankruptcy Claims Handbook*, first edition, published in 2013, produced by the ABA Business Law Section Business Bankruptcy Committee. The driving force behind the first edition was Brett D. Fallon. The first edition helped influence the contents of this work and portions of the texts were adapted or reworked for inclusion in this publication.

We hope you find *The Bankruptcy Claims Handbook* to be useful and welcome your input and suggestions for future editions.

Monique D. Hayes
Goldstein & McClintock LLLP
Miami, Florida

Paul R. Hage
Jaffe Rait Heuer & Weiss, P.C.
Southfield, Michigan

Brett D. Fallon
Faegre Drinker Biddle & Reath LLP
Wilmington, Delaware

1

Introduction

The purpose of this handbook is to provide a general overview of claims in bankruptcy. Claims are defined broadly under title 11 of the U.S. Code, 11 U.S.C. §§ 101, *et seq.* (the "Bankruptcy Code") to include a "right to payment, whether or not such right is reduced to judgment, liquidated, unliquidated, fixed, contingent, matured, unmatured, disputed, undisputed, legal, equitable, secured, or unsecured" or a "right to an equitable remedy for breach of performance if such breach gives rise to a right to payment, whether or not such right to an equitable remedy is reduced to judgment, fixed, contingent, matured, unmatured, disputed, undisputed, secured, or unsecured."[1]

While the issues and topics discussed could fill an entire treatise, the purpose behind this handbook is to provide a starting point for legal analysis, highlight key issues, and, perhaps, answer a few questions. This handbook is designed to be accessible to those who are unfamiliar with or only dabble from time to time in the bankruptcy realm, while still being informative to those who labor regularly in this field.

The substantive discussion of the book begins in Chapter 2 with a summary of the debtor's duties, including the preparation of the debtor's "schedules," a record that should include all of the debtor's assets and liabilities. As explored in greater depth in Chapter 2, practical challenges in the preparation and service of the schedules have led to the development of case law concerning the adequacy of notice and service.

Next, the discussion shifts in Chapter 3 to the life cycle of a claim, from when a claim arises to the contents, effect, timing, and location

1. 11 U.S.C. § 101(5)(A)–(B).

of filing, and concluding with rules regarding amendments to a claim. As will be discussed, the concept of when a claim arises may, at first glance, seem straightforward, but it has resulted in the development of multiple tests adopted by various jurisdictions.

Chapter 4 addresses secured claims, homing in on the valuation and treatment of the collateral-based secured claim, which is the most common type of secured claim, discussing the creation of a secured claim under Sections[2] 506(a) and 553(a) to the extent a creditor has a right to setoff against the debtor, and concluding by touching briefly on the debtor's right to setoff.

Chapter 5 delves into unsecured claims and the priority structure developed for such claims under Section 507(a)(1)–(10). That Section identifies a number of priority unsecured claims including (i) domestic support obligations, (ii) administrative expenses, (iii) gap period claims, (iv) claims for wages, salaries, and commissions, (v) claims for contributions to employee benefit plans, (vi) certain claims of grain producers and fishermen, (vii) claims for consumer deposits, (viii) claims for taxes and customs duties, (ix) commitments to federal depository regulatory agencies, and (x) claims arising from driving under the influence/driving while intoxicated crimes. Chapter 5 goes on to discuss the "super priority" claim under Section 507(b) of the Bankruptcy Code, the equal priority for claims based on erroneous tax refunds under Section 507(c) and, finally, subrogation of claims under Section 507(d).

The category of administrative expenses has, not surprisingly, generated much discussion and case law development due to its higher priority. Accordingly, Chapter 6 is dedicated to various types of administrative expenses, including the process for asserting claims for such expenses, as well as establishing deadlines for presenting such claims. Administrative expenses include expenses that specifically arise from the debtor being in bankruptcy—most prominently, the fees of bankruptcy professionals—but it also includes the normal, worthwhile expenses of a debtor taking care of business post petition. This may include, for example, monthly rent obligations due to a landlord or equipment lessor. If, however, the debtor decides to reject a lease and the rejection is approved by the court, the landlord or lessor will be entitled to file a claim for "rejection damages," a topic covered in more detail in Chapter 8.

Section 503(b)(9) of the Bankruptcy Code grants an administrative expense claim for goods delivered to the debtor within twenty days of the petition date. Since its enactment as part of the Bankruptcy Abuse Prevention and Consumer Protection Act of 2005 (BAPCPA), Section 503(b)(9) has

---

2. Unless otherwise noted, all references to "Section(s)" in this handbook shall be to delineated segments of the Bankruptcy Code.

been the topic of much discussion and resulted in significant case law. Accordingly, this subset of administrative expenses (often referred to as 503(b)(9) claims) warranted their own chapter considering the complexity, significance, and timeliness of the issues surrounding them, and are explored in Chapter 7.

Topics covered in Chapter 7 include when and how such claims are allowed and paid, what constitutes a "good" for purposes of Section 503(b)(9), when goods are "received" by the debtor for purposes of Section 503(b)(9), how "value" is defined, whether Section 503(b)(9) expenses are subject to disallowance under Section 502(d), which acts to temporarily disallow certain claims of a transferee of voidable transfers (often a preferential transfer) against the estate if the transferee has not turned over the property received, and whether the holder of an administrative expense under Section 503(b)(9) can use goods shipped during the days prior to the petition date as new value in defense of a preference action.

As previously noted, Chapter 8 addresses the claims that result from a debtor's postpetition rejection of executory contracts or leases. The discussion begins with an overview of the debtor's right to choose (or the counter party's right to compel), assumption, or rejection of an executory contract or lease. The discussion then shifts to the deadline (or bar date) for asserting damages resulting from the debtor's rejection of an executory contract or lease, how claims for such damages are treated in bankruptcy, and the applicable cap on such damages.

Claims asserted on behalf of unique groups or classes, such as displaced employees or mass tort claimants exposed to products containing asbestos, are discussed in Chapter 9. Despite the Bankruptcy Code's relative silence on such claims, it is important to understand the applicable rules and procedures for filing and seeking allowance of class claims. It is also important to recognize the powerful leverage certain class claimants may wield in a bankruptcy case and the discretion of the bankruptcy court in recognizing class claims.

Chapter 10 discusses the quasi-claim known as a "reclamation" claim, or the right of a vendor to demand the return of certain delivered goods from the debtor, as set forth in Section 546(c) of the Bankruptcy Code and applicable state law, as well as the procedure for making such demands and the limitations thereof (most notably, the fact that such claims are subject to the rights of a secured creditor that holds a lien on the goods or proceeds of the goods sought to be reclaimed).

The various types, categories, and priorities of claims having been addressed in Chapters 4 through 10, Chapter 11 tackles two principles that have the potential to affect the order of distribution or categorization of a claim in bankruptcy, namely: (i) equitable subordination, and (ii) debt recharacterization. Equitable subordination gives the bankruptcy court the power to impose a lower priority on the payment of claims of a debt or equity holder that had otherwise improved its position in the bankruptcy relative to other similar creditors due to some form of inequitable conduct. Debt recharacterization allows a court to reclassify a claim as equity rather than debt. This equitable remedy is generally used in situations where an insider or capital contributor attempts to decrease the investment's risk by labeling a transaction as debt when, in substance, the transaction is more akin to equity.

Continuing the transition into the postpetition realm, Chapter 12 homes in on the effect and process of a debtor's determination that a particular creditor is a critical vendor, and the assistance this provides a debtor attempting to reorganize in convincing certain essential providers of goods and services, who are reluctant to continue to provide credit to a debtor post petition due to the prospect of not receiving payment in full on their pre-petition receivables. Critical vendor status encourages creditors that are critical to the debtor's continued operations to continue to extend credit in exchange for receiving payment in full or in part on such claims prior to confirmation of a plan.

Those at the helm of the decision-making process—namely, the directors and officers of corporations and other entities—are encouraged to make difficult decisions and take worthwhile risks to assist in the reorganization efforts. Companies often promise to indemnify the directors and officers against liabilities for actions taken in their corporate capacities and to advance or reimburse costs incurred by the directors and officers in defending against lawsuits asserting liability for such actions. Chapter 13 explores these indemnification promises and the types, limits, and exclusions of the liability insurance policies that provide the funds to back up those promises. The analysis goes one step further, summarizing frequent issues that arise concerning the treatment of director and officer insurance in bankruptcy.

Chapter 14 of this handbook explores the claims objection process, the grounds for disallowance of a claim, the consequences of disallowance, and the circumstances under which a claim may be temporarily disallowed.

Chapter 15, which is a new addition to the handbook, discusses the intersection of claim dischargeability and the claims process. This chapter begins with an overview of the types of claims that may be excepted from discharge under Section 523. The chapter then details the process by which a creditor may contest a debtor's ability to discharge a particular debt. Because an adversary proceeding (or lawsuit) is necessary to advance the challenge, the chapter specifies the associated deadlines, pleading requirements, and burden of proof.

When you have reached the final page of this handbook, you should, at the very least, have a basic understanding of the claims process, the rights and duties of both debtors and creditors during this process, the priority scheme, the objection process, and grounds for challenging discharge of a particular claim.

2

Debtor's Duties with Respect to the Claims Process

A. Overview

Courts have long recognized transparency as a condition to bankruptcy relief.[3] The Bankruptcy Code and the Federal Rules of Bankruptcy Procedure (the "Bankruptcy Rule(s)") work in tandem to create a framework under which debtors disclose assets and liabilities, reorganize, and obtain relief.[4] Section 521 of the Bankruptcy Code and Bankruptcy Rule 1007 operate as substantive creditor protections to ensure adequate disclosure. Debtors must provide creditors with full disclosure of their financial and operational affairs, including schedules of assets and liabilities, schedules of income and expenditures, as well as statements of financial affairs, "unless the court orders otherwise."[5]

The schedules must also contain the addresses of the debtor's creditors "so that they may have an opportunity to avail themselves of the rights afforded them by the Bankruptcy Code."[6] In theory, these tasks seem as simple as consulting with the debtor and reviewing the debtor's records (surely the

3. Guay v. Burack, 677 F.3d 10, 19 (1st Cir. 2012) (holding that "[a] long-standing tenet of bankruptcy law requires one seeking benefits under its terms to satisfy a companion duty to schedule, for the benefit of creditors, all his interests and property rights.") (quoting Payless Wholesale Distributors, Inc. v. Alberto Culver (P.R.) Inc., 989 F.2d 570, 571 (1st Cir. 1993).
4. Payless Wholesale Distributors, Inc. v. Alberto Culver (P.R.) Inc., 989 F.2d 570, 571 (1st Cir. 1993).
5. 11 U.S.C. § 521(a)(1)(B).
6. *In re Kleather*, 208 B.R. 406, 410 (Bankr. S.D. Ohio 1997) (quoting *In re Frankina*, 29 B.R. 983, 985 (Bankr. E.D. Mich. 1983) (citing Birkett v. Columbia Bank, 195 U.S. 345, 350 (1904)).

debtor knows or has recorded somewhere to whom it owes money, right?) But completing the creditor matrix can be challenging in practice. This is particularly true where the debts are older, leaving ample time for creditors to go out of business, relocate, restructure, or change names. Additionally, integrated business practices of multi-debtor enterprises may result in a more involved analysis to identify the particular debtor entity and creditor entity involved in the transactions at issue.

Ultimately, the claim information contained in the schedules and the creditor list may be critical in determining what claims are to be discharged in bankruptcy. The Debtor has a duty to accurately disclose, and update when necessary, information relative to its financial affairs and the identity of its creditors. This chapter addresses the following aspects of the debtor's duty to file schedules: (i) general introduction to the debtor's scheduling duty, (ii) types of schedules a debtor must file, (iii) contents of schedules, (iv) the effects of failing to list creditors, and (v) notice requirements.

B. Debtor's Duty to File Schedules

As noted above, a debtor has an express duty to "prepare and file schedules and must do so carefully, completely, and accurately."[7] Although there are "no bright-line rules for how much itemization and specificity is required," a debtor is "required to be as particular as is reasonable under the circumstances."[8] Counsel and other professionals aiding the debtor in preparation of schedules should pay close attention to local rules that may expand upon the general duties set forth in Section 521 and Bankruptcy Rule 1007.

Where the debtor's books and records are less than complete or where time constraints exist, preparing accurate and complete schedules may prove difficult. Courts considering the sufficiency of a debtor's schedules look to whether the schedule gives the trustee (or parties in interest) enough

---

7. Cusano v. Klein, 264 F.3d 936, 946 (9th Cir. 2001) (quoting *In re Mohring*, 142 B.R. 389, 394 (Bankr. E.D. Cal. 1992); *In re Jones*, 134 B.R. 274, 279 (N.D. Ill. 1991); *In re Baumgartner*, 57 B.R. 513, 516 (Bankr. N.D. Ohio 1986); *In re Mazzola*, 4 B.R. 179, 182 (Bankr. D. Mass. 1980)). *In re JZ L.L.C.*, 371 B.R. 412, 417 (B.A.P. 9th Cir. 2007) (quoting Cusano v. Klein, 264 F.3d 936, 946 (9th Cir. 2001) (internal quotations omitted); *In re Mohring*, 142 B.R. 389, 394 (Bankr. E.D. Cal. 1992) (holding that "[t]he Official Forms themselves have generally been regarded as subject to a rule of substantial compliance."), *aff'd*, 153 B.R. 601 (B.A.P. 9th Cir. 1993), *aff'd*, 24 F.3d 247 (9th Cir. 1994); *In re Jones*, 134 B.R. 274, 279 (N.D. Ill. 1991); *In re Baumgartner*, 57 B.R. 513, 516 (Bankr. N.D. Ohio 1986); *In re Mazzola*, 4 B.R. 179, 182 (Bankr. D. Mass. 1980).
8. *Cusano*, 264 F.3d at 946 (quoting *In re Mohring*, 142 B.R. at 395).

information about the claim, asset, or interest so he or she can decide if there is something worth pursuing.[9]

Where precise asset values are not available, a debtor should list the "approximate dollar amount" of each asset.[10] It has been suggested that "[i]f faced with a range of values[for an asset,]" a debtor should "choose a value in the middle of the range."[11] Alternatively, where the value of an asset is wholly unknown, "a simple statement to that effect" will suffice.[12]

Debtors also have a duty to meet stringent timing requirements. Bankruptcy Rule 1007 sets forth the deadline by which a debtor must file its schedules and statement of financial affairs. Under Bankruptcy Rule 1007(c), the debtor must file the appropriate schedules in a voluntary case with the petition or within fourteen days after the petition is filed; and in an involuntary case, the schedules must be filed within fourteen days after the order allowing the case to proceed (the "Order for Relief") is entered. The court may, and often does, grant a further extension for cause shown, and on notice to the Office of the U.S. Trustee (the "U.S. Trustee"), trustee, creditors' committee, and any other party as the court may direct.[13]

---

9. ASARCO, LLC v. Montana Res., Inc., 1:12-CV-137, 2016 WL 6781556, at *9 (S.D. Tex. Mar. 3, 2016), *aff'd sub nom.*, ASARCO, L.L.C. v. Montana Res., Inc., 858 F.3d 949 (5th Cir. 2017); Romeo v. FMA All., Ltd., 2016 WL 3647868, at *6 (E.D.N.Y. June 30, 2016*); In re Furlong*, 660 F.3d 81, 87 (1st Cir.2011) ("As investigation is part of the Trustee's duties under § 704, a debtor is required only to do enough itemizing to enable the trustee to determine whether to investigate further." (citations and internal quotation marks omitted)); Eun Joo Lee v. Forster & Garbus LLP, 926 F. Supp. 2d 482, 489 (E.D.N.Y. 2013); *Cf.* Vreugdenhill v. Navistar Int'l Transp. Corp., 950 F.2d 524, 526 (8th Cir.1991) (holding that informal *notice* of a claim to a bankruptcy trustee is insufficient to satisfy the scheduling requirement).
10. ASARCO, LLC v. Montana Res., Inc., 1:12-CV-137, 2016 WL 6781556, at *9 (S.D. Tex. Mar. 3, 2016), *aff'd sub nom.*, ASARCO, L.L.C. v. Montana Res., Inc., 858 F.3d 949 (5th Cir. 2017); Romeo v. FMA All., Ltd., 2016 WL 3647868, at *6 (E.D.N.Y. June 30, 2016*); In re Furlong*, 660 F.3d 81, 87 (1st Cir.2011) ("As investigation is part of the Trustee's duties under § 704, a debtor is required only to do enough itemizing to enable the trustee to determine whether to investigate further." (citations and internal quotation marks omitted)); Eun Joo Lee v. Forster & Garbus LLP, 926 F. Supp. 2d 482, 489 (E.D.N.Y. 2013); *Cf.* Vreugdenhill v. Navistar Int'l Transp. Corp., 950 F.2d 524, 526 (8th Cir.1991) (holding that informal *notice* of a claim to a bankruptcy trustee is insufficient to satisfy the scheduling requirement).
11. *Cusano*, 264 F.3d at 946 (quoting *In re* Wenande, 107 B.R. 770, 772 (Bankr. D. Wy. 1989)).
12. *Cusano*, 264 F.3d at 946 (quoting *In re* Seruntine, 46 B.R. 286, 288 (Bankr. C.D. Cal. 1984)).
13. Fed. R. Bankr. P. 1007(c). A creditors' committee may be elected under Section 705 or appointed under Section 1102 of the Code.

C. Types of Schedules

The Bankruptcy Rules, in conjunction with the Official Forms, offer guidance on what schedules must be filed and their content. The format may differ among jurisdictions, so parties should refer to the applicable court's local rules and forms in preparing or reviewing the schedules. Generally, eleven types of schedules must be filed with the court. These schedules include:[14]

- Summary of Schedules
- Schedule A: Real Property
- Schedule B: Personal Property
- Schedule C: Property Claimed as Exempt
- Schedule D: Creditors Holding Secured Claims
- Schedule E: Creditors Holding Unsecured Priority Claims
- Schedule F: Creditors Holding Unsecured Nonpriority Claims
- Schedule G: Executory Contracts and Unexpired Leases
- Schedule H: Codebtors
- Schedule I: Current Income of Individual Debtor(s)
- Schedule J: Current Expenses of Individual Debtor(s

Liabilities are divided into three schedules: (i) secured claims (Schedule D), (ii) priority unsecured claims (Schedule E), and (iii) general unsecured claims (Schedule F), with various subcategories enumerated on each schedule.

In addition to the standard schedules, certain debtors must file additional data and reports to provide parties in interest adequate information.[15]

D. Contents and Effect of a Listing

Schedule content is crucial in bankruptcy proceedings. While the act and timeline of filing schedules serve as key gating issues, the substance of a debtor's disclosures bears on its ability to achieve a fresh start.[16]

---

14. In addition to Schedules A through J, in Chapter 11 cases, the petition should also be accompanied by a list of the holders of the twenty largest unsecured claims. Fed. R. Bankr. P. 1007(d). This list is required so that a committee of unsecured creditors may be selected under Section 1102 of the Bankruptcy Code.
15. *Compare* 11 U.S.C. § 521(a)(1)(B) *with* 11 U.S.C. § 1187 (citing11 U.S.C. § 1116) (providing that in a case under Subchapter V and in a small business case a trustee must file its most recent balance sheet, statement of operations, and cash flow statement no later than seven days after the date of the order for relief).
16. *In re Cutler*, 291 B.R. 718, 726–27 (Bankr.E.D.Mich.2003).

1. *Required Content in Schedules Concerning Claims*

Bankruptcy Rule 1007(a) requires a debtor to list all creditors who have or may have a claim.[17] Specifically, Bankruptcy Rule 1007(a) provides, in relevant part, that "the debtor shall file with the petition a list containing the *name and address* of each entity included or to be included on Schedules D, E, F, G, and H *as prescribed by the Official Forms*."[18]

a. Listing and Categorizing Claims

Schedules D, E, and F collectively list claims against the bankruptcy estate: (i) secured claims (Schedule D), (ii) priority unsecured claims (Schedule E), and (iii) general unsecured claims (Schedule F) with various subcategories enumerated on each schedule. The Official Form for each schedule sets forth greater detail about the information required to be disclosed. That said, there are certain general guidelines debtors ought to follow in preparing these documents. The Official Forms require debtors to provide "[a] complete list of claims,"[19] and list (by marking a check in the appropriate box on the form) the claim as contingent,[20] unliquidated,[21] and/or disputed.[22]

Section 101(5) defines the term claim to include "the right to payment, whether or not such right is reduced to judgment, liquidated, unliquidated,

---

17. Fed. R. Bankr. P. 1007(a); *In re Hicks*, 184 B.R. 954, 957 (Bankr. C.D. Cal. 1995) (holding that the "obligation to list all creditors' names and addresses is part of the debtor's duty of full disclosure that is the *quid pro quo* for the fresh start provided by the discharge") (emphasis original).
18. Fed. R. Bankr. P. 1007(a) (emphasis added).
19. This list is often required, under local rule, to be provided in the form of a "mailing matrix" that can be used to generate address labels for notices to the creditors.
20. Contingent debt consists of a claim or interest with respect to which liability has not been established as of the date of the bankruptcy filing because certain events must take place prior to a determination of liability. Mazzeo v. United States (*In re Mazzeo*), 131 F.3d 295, 303 (2d Cir. 1997) ("It is generally agreed that a debt is contingent if it does not become an obligation until the occurrence of a future event, but is noncontingent when all of the events giving rise to liability for the debt occurred prior to the debtor's filing for bankruptcy"); *In re Knight*, 55 F.3d 231, 234 (7th Cir. 1995) ("a debt [is] noncontingent as long as all the events that gave rise to the debtor's liability had occurred prior to the filing of the bankruptcy petition"). A right to indemnification from a surety is the classic case of a contingent right to payment. *In re All Media Properties, Inc.*, 5 B.R. 126, 133 (Bankr. S.D. Tex. 1980), *aff'd*, 646 F.2d 193 (5th Cir. 1981).
21. Unliquidated debt is a claim or interest whose liability is uncertain in amount, due to the fact that the actual amount of the liability depends upon a future determination and is not readily calculable. *In re Knight*, 55 F.3d at 235.
22. Disputed debt is a claim or interest, the amount and/or existence of which is disputed by the debtor. *See, e.g.*, *In re Knight*, 55 F.3d at 234–35 (remarking that a debt the State of Indiana claimed was owed by the debtor, the legitimacy of which the debtor challenged based on a previous agreement with the State, was a disputed claim and a debt to be included when calculating the Section 109(e) requirements).

fixed, contingent, matured, disputed, undisputed, legal, secured, or unsecured"; or the "right to an equitable remedy for breach of performance if such breach gives rise to a right to payment, whether or not such right to an equitable remedy is reduced to judgment, fixed, contingent, matured, unmatured, disputed, undisputed, secured, or unsecured."[23]

Whether a claim is contingent or liquidated are related, but still distinct, concepts. A contingent claim, on one hand, contemplates a debt triggered based on a future event within the actual or presumed contemplation of the parties at the onset of the relationship.[24] Liability "relies on an extrinsic event which may never occur…." Accordingly, where all events triggering liability occurred prepetition, the debt is noncontingent.[25]

A liquidated claim, conversely, refers to a readily determinable debt,[26] focusing on the ease with which a claim's value (and size of the corresponding debt) can be ascertained.[27] Generally, a claim with an easily ascertainable value is liquidated, whereas a value dependent on a "future exercise of discretion is unliquidated."[28] Courts generally hold that a debt is liquidated where the claim is determinable by reference to an agreement or by a simple computation, the claim is fixed, certain, or otherwise determined by a specific standard.[29]

The majority of courts hold that the disputed nature of a claim does not automatically render the debt as non-contingent or unliquidated.[30]

b. Creditor Addresses

In addition to listing and categorizing all creditors' claims, debtors must identify the addresses of each creditor. The purpose of this requirement is to ensure parties in interest receive notice of proceedings that may affect their rights. "Whether notice is reasonable depends on the particular circumstances"[31] While the Bankruptcy Code provides no guidance as to what is the proper address of a creditor, the law is clear that such an address

---

23. *Id.* The classic example of an unmatured debt is the full, principal amount owed under a loan that is to be paid out over time. *See In re* St. Vincent's Catholic Med. Centers of NY, 440 B.R. 587, 603 (Bankr. S.D.N.Y. 2010).
24. Pearl-Phil GMT (Far E.) Ltd. v. Caldor Corp., 266 B.R. 575, 580 (S.D.N.Y. 2001)
25. *In re Nesbit,* 2000 WL 294834, at *2 (Bankr. W.D. Pa. 2000).
26. *In re Adams*, 373 B.R. 116, 119 (B.A.P. 10th Cir. 2007).
27. *In re Greenwich Sentry, L.P.*, 484 B.R. 567, 573 S.D.N.Y. 2012), *aff'd*, 534 Fed. Appx. 77 (2d Cir. 2013).
28. *Id.*
29. *See In re Barcal,* 213 B.R. 1008, 1014 (8th Cir. BAP 1997).
30. The majority of courts considering the question have held that merely because a debtor disputes a debt, or has potential defenses or counterclaims that might reduce the creditors' actual collection, the debt is not thereby rendered "contingent" or "unliquidated." *In re Crescenzi*, 69 B.R. 64, 65 (S.D.N.Y. 1986).
31. Tulsa Professional Services, Inc. v. Pope, 485 U.S. 478, (1988).

must be one at which notice or service would be reasonably calculated to comply with constitutional notions of due process."[32]

Due process jurisprudence generally distinguishes between "known creditors," who are entitled to receive direct notice of each stage in the reorganization proceedings, and "unknown creditors," for whom publication notice is sufficient.[33] An "unknown creditor" is one whose "interests are either conjectural or future or, although they could be discovered upon investigation, do not in due course of business come to knowledge [of the debtor]."[34] A "known creditor," by contrast, is one whose claims and identity are actually known or "reasonably ascertainable" by the debtor.[35] A creditor is "reasonably ascertainable" if its claim can be discovered through "reasonably diligent efforts."[36]

If an address is outdated or otherwise inaccurate, a creditor may later assert that it did not receive proper notice of the bankruptcy proceedings. In that situation, courts disagree on which party bears the burden of proof for supporting or challenging the accuracy of the creditor's address.[37]

---

32. *In re Kleather,* 208 B.R. at 410 (citing Ford Motor Credit Co. v. Weaver, 680 F.2d 451, 456 (6th Cir. 1982)); *see also In re Savage*, 167 B.R. 22, 26 (Bankr. S.D.N.Y. 1994) ("Neither the statute nor the rules state that the creditor be listed at a particular address.").
33. *In re Arch Wireless, Inc.*, 534 F.3d 76, 80 (1st Cir. 2008).
34. Mullane v. Cent. Hanover Bank & Trust Co., 339 U.S. 306, 317 (1950); *see also In re XO Commc'ns, Inc.,* 301 B.R. 782, 793 (Bankr. S.D.N.Y. 2003) (describing an "unknown creditor" as one whose claims are "merely conceivable, conjectural or speculative" (internal quotation marks omitted)).
35. Tulsa Prof'l Collection Servs. Inc. v. Pope, 485 U.S. 478, 490 (1988).
36. Mennonite Bd. of Missions v. Adams, 462 U.S. 791, 798 n. 4 (1983). These efforts often include "a careful search of the debtor's own records." *In re Crystal Oil Co.,* 158 F.3d 291, 297 (5th Cir.1998). As such "in order for a claim to be reasonably ascertainable, the debtor must have in his possession ... some specific information that reasonably suggests both the claim for which the debtor may be liable and the entity to whom he would be liable." *Id.* On the other hand, there is no requirement that the debtor have information suggesting the financial magnitude of the claim. *See* 11 U.S.C. § 101(5)(A) (defining "claim" to include both liquidated and unliquidated liabilities).
37. *Compare In re Kleather*, 208 B.R. at 410 (holding that, in the event a "creditor challenges the accuracy of a listed address, the burden should properly fall upon the creditor to establish that the address provided by the debtor was so incorrect as to fall short of this threshold.") (quoting *In re Walker*, 125 B.R. 177, 180 (Bankr. E.D. Mich. 1990) (*citing* Hill v. Smith, 260 U.S. 592, 595 (1923)) *with* Faden v. Ins. Co. of N. Am. (*In re Faden*), 96 F.3d 792, 795 (5th Cir. 1996) ("the burden of proof rests with the debtor to show that a creditor had 'notice or actual knowledge' under Section 523(a)(3).") (citing U.S. Small Bus. Admin. v. Bridges, 894 F.2d 108, 111 (5th Cir. 1990)).

c. Exception to Address Requirement

The requirement that a debtor list a creditor's address in the schedules, though absolute under the language of Bankruptcy Rule 1007, has acquired a narrow exception under the case law for circumstances where the debtor does not know a creditor's address so long as the debtor has *diligently* attempted to locate the address. In the absence of such diligence, however, where "the debtor knows or can ascertain the address and fails to insert it, the discharge will not, in some circumstances, protect the debtor against the claim of that creditor ... unless ... such creditor was not prejudiced by the lack of notice of the case."[38]

d. Accuracy of Address

Courts have addressed the adequacy of listing a creditor at the wrong address in various scenarios, including where the creditor changed its address,[39] where a corporate creditor was not scheduled at its principal place of business,[40] and where a creditor was scheduled in care of an attorney who previously represented the creditor.[41] Some courts have found that if the debtor schedules a debt, the creditor associated with that debt is charged with constructive notice of the case, even if it doesn't receive actual notice of the bankruptcy.[42] Where a known claim is not effectively scheduled,

---

38. *In re Faden*, 96 F.3d 792, 799 (5th Cir. 1996); *In re Walker*, 149 B.R. 511, 514 (Bankr. N.D. Ill. 1992) ("One circumstance to consider in evaluating the sufficiency of notice is whether alleged inadequacies in the notice prejudiced the creditor.")
39. Where a creditor changes its address and the debtor, unaware of the address change, lists the creditor's previous address, the debt should be considered properly scheduled. Zinn v. Hallock, 86 N.Y.S.2d 882 (1949) (holding that debtor's debt was properly discharged where creditor was properly scheduled, even though creditor did not have actual notice of bankruptcy due to moving locations and notice was returned to the referee as undeliverable).
40. "There is no requirement that a corporate creditor be listed at a particular office address or its principal place of business, as long as the address is reasonably calculated to afford adequate notice." 4 COLLIER ON BANKRUPTCY, ¶ 521.06[2][c] (citing Chanute Prod. Credit Ass'n. v. Schicke (*In re Schicke*), 290 B.R. 792 (B.A.P. 10th Cir. 2003); *see also In re Kleather*, 208 B.R. 406 (notice to address given for mailing payments was sufficient, even though it was address of debtor's parent corporation); *In re R.E. Lee & Sons, Inc.*, 95 B.R. 316 (Bankr. M.D. Pa. 1989) (creditor was adequately scheduled even though address listed was post office box for wrong department in creditor's organization).
41. *In re Schicke*, 290 B.R. 792 (10th Cir. 2003) (debtor may schedule a creditor in care of attorney who represented creditor twelve years prior to bankruptcy, provided that the attorney is the creditor's agent in matters related to the Chapter 7 case); *In re Savage*, 167 B.R. 22 (Bankr. S.D.N.Y. 1994) (notice to attorney attempting to collect debt owed by debtor was sufficient).
42. *In re Vega*, 15 B.R. 174 (Bankr. W.D. Okla. 1981). In both situations, the general rule of presumption of notice by mail is rebuttable with evidence of non-receipt by the addressee.

however, the debtor receives no such benefit and, to the contrary, faces a number of disconcerting repercussions.

2. *Effect of Failure to List*

The effects of failing to file timely, thorough schedules can be devastating to a debtor's ability to benefit from its bankruptcy. Though the Bankruptcy Code does not prescribe the procedures and deadlines for filing schedules of assets and liabilities by a Chapter 11 debtor, Sections 707(a)(3), and 1307(c)(9) of the Bankruptcy Code provide that cases filed under Chapters 7 and 13 may be dismissed if the schedules are not filed within fifteen days of the petition, and Section 521(i) provides for automatic dismissal of individual debtor cases filed under Chapters 7 or 13 if the schedules have not been filed within forty-five days of the petition, unless the debtor can show that a good faith effort was made to file them. In an earlier era, a debtor could be adjudged in contempt of court for neglecting to file a schedule when ordered to do so. Today, as detailed below, the potential negative consequences of failing to list a creditor cannot be overstated.

a. Dischargeability

An individual debtor's failure to schedule a debt in his or her schedule may render the debt nondischargeable. For instance, Section 523(a)(3) of the Bankruptcy Code provides that the discharge granted to an individual debtor will not extend to a debt that is "neither listed nor scheduled … in time to permit … timely filing of a proof of claim, unless such creditor had notice or actual knowledge of the case in time for such timely filing."[43] In addition, for debts that a court can determine to be nondischargeable by their nature (such as debts for money or credit obtained by false pretenses, or debts that arose through fraud, embezzlement, or larceny), debts of this nature will not be discharged if the debt was not listed or scheduled in time to permit not only the timely filing of a proof of claim but also a "timely request for a determination of dischargeability" of the debt unless the creditor "had notice or actual knowledge of the case in time for such timely filing and request."[44] In an individual debtor case where, after a discharge has been granted, there is a reversion of certain estate assets to the debtor, the failure to properly schedule an asset, including a cause

43. 11 U.S.C. § 523(a)(3).
44. 11 U.S.C. § 523(a)(3) (providing that debts of a type listed in Sections 523(a)(2), (a)(4), or (a)(6) are not discharged if a debtor fails to list or schedule such debts under Section 521(1) in time to permit a timely filing of a proof of claim and a timely request for a determination of dischargeability of such debt).

of action, will result in a finding that the asset continues to belong to the bankruptcy estate, and will not revert to the discharged bankrupt.[45]

b. Dismissal

With respect to individual debtors under Chapters 7 and 13, the failure to file the documents required by Section 521(a)(1) (list of creditors, schedule of assets, and liabilities, schedule of current income and expenditures, and statement of financial affairs) may lead to dismissal under Section 521(i). Section 521(i) provides for *automatic* dismissal of an individual debtor's voluntary case under Chapter 7 or 13 if the debtor has failed to file all of the required schedules "within 45 days after the date of the filing of the petition," unless the trustee (or debtor) has filed a motion for an extension *before* the expiration of that time period, and unless the court finds that the debtor "attempted in good faith to file all the information required."[46]

Failure to meet filing obligations may be present grounds for dismissal of a Chapter 11 case pursuant to Section 1112(b)(4)(F).[47] Dismissal under 11 U.S.C. § 1112(b) requires a two-step analysis: First, there must be "cause" to act; and second, once a determination of "cause" has been made, a choice must be made between conversion and dismissal based on the "best interests of the creditors and the estate."[48] One of the relevant enumerated factors is an "unexcused failure to satisfy timely any filing or reporting requirement established by this title or by a rule applicable to a case under this chapter."[49]

In short, the Bankruptcy Code does not allow debtors under Chapters 7, 13, and 11 to proceed through bankruptcy without filing their schedules and statements of financial affairs.[50] Irrespective of whether the debtor is

45. Cusano v. Klein, 264 F.3d at 946 (citing Stein v. United Artists Corp., 691 F.2d 885, 893 (9th Cir. 1982) (holding that only property "administered or listed in the bankruptcy proceedings" reverts to the bankrupt); Hutchins v. I.R.S., 67 F.3d 40, 43 (3d Cir. 1995) (observing that "if the tax refund [at issue] were a unique asset that had to be scheduled separately, as the I.R.S. asserts, then the failure to schedule the refund is fatal to Hutchins' claim…[because] [i]t is clear that an asset must be properly scheduled in order to pass to the debtor through abandonment under 11 U.S.C. § 554."); Vreugdenhil v. Navistar Int'l Transp. Corp., 950 F.2d 524, 526 (8th Cir. 1991) (holding that property is not abandoned by operation of law unless the debtor "formally schedule[s] the property before the close of the case.").

46. 11 U.S.C. § 521(i) (emphasis added).

47. 11 U.S.C. § 1112(b)(4)(F) ("[U]nexcused failure to satisfy timely any filing or reporting requirement established by this title or by an rule applicable to a case under this chapter.").

48. Nelson v. Meyer *(In re Nelson)*, 343 B.R. 671, 675 (9th Cir. BAP 2006) (quoting Ho v. Dowell *(In re Ho)*, 274 B.R. 867, 877 (9th Cir. BAP 2002)).

49. 11 U.S.C. § 1112(b)(4)(F).

50. Once schedules have been filed, the adequacy of the information contained in them will require the scrutiny of the trustee, creditors' committee, or other interested party.

an individual or a corporation, the Bankruptcy Code offers many incentives for debtors to file timely, accurate, and complete schedules if they wish to receive the maximum benefit from the bankruptcy process.

c. Notice Requirements

The debtor's obligation with respect to the schedules is to prepare and file them; the Bankruptcy Code does not require a debtor to send notice to all its creditors of how their claims have been scheduled. Bankruptcy Rule 2002 identifies certain proceedings and filings in the bankruptcy case about which the court clerk, or some other person as the court may direct (such as the debtor or the trustee), is required to give notice to various parties.[51] For some of these notices, Official Forms have been prescribed by the Judicial Conference of the United States, and they are to be "observed and used with alterations as may be appropriate."[52]

There are three events requiring notice, which are of particular relevance in the claims process: (i) the meeting of creditors, (ii) the claim filing deadline in Chapter 9 or 11 cases, and (iii) the claim filing deadline in a Chapter 7, 12, or 13 case. First, the debtor, the trustee, and all creditors and indenture trustees must be given notice of the meeting of creditors at least twenty-one days in advance of the meeting of creditors.[53] Second, in chapter 9 or 11 cases, the debtor, the trustee, all creditors, and indenture trustees must be given notice of the "time fixed for filing proofs of claim" at least twenty-one days in advance.[54]

Finally, in Chapter 7, 12, or 13 cases, the debtor, all creditors, and indenture trustees must be given notice of the time allowed for filing claims.[55] However, no notice of the claim-filing deadline need be given in a Chapter 7 case if it "appears from the schedules that there are not assets from which a dividend can be paid." Instead, the notice of the meeting of creditors can specify that it is "unnecessary to file claims" and that if assets become available later, "further notice will be given for the filing of claims."

51. Fed. R. Bankr. P. 2002.
52. Fed. R. Bankr. P. 9009.
53. Fed. R. Bankr. P. 2007(a)(1).
54. Fed. R. Bankr. P. 2007(a)(7).
55. Fed. R. Bankr. P. 3002.

3

Life Cycle of Claims

A. Overview

When a person or entity files for bankruptcy relief, that person or entity—the "debtor"—owes money to creditors. The debtor may also have some property or interest—the "estate"—from which creditors can ultimately receive payment. For a creditor who is owed money from a debtor when the bankruptcy is filed to hope to receive any payment from the estate upon its claim, the claim must first be allowed. In some circumstances, allowance can arise simply from the schedules filed by the debtor, without the need for any further action by the creditor. In other cases, the creditor will need to file what is called a "proof of claim."

Filing a proof of claim begins with filling out a version of the official proof of claim form (Official Form B10) or a substantial equivalent.[56] Once the form is filled out and executed under penalty of perjury, it must be filed in the proper bankruptcy court where the debtor filed its petition. In larger corporate bankruptcies, a "claims agent" may be appointed to facilitate the orderly process of filing claims. In those cases, a creditor will receive notice to file claims with this agent, instead of with the court. After the claim is filed and assigned a number, the claims will then be grouped with similar claims, streamlining the claim objection process for the trustee or the debtor. This chapter explores the steps in this process in more detail.

56. Fed. R. Bankr. P. 3001(a).

B. Entities That Must File

Depending on the type of case and certain other factors, an entity may be required to file a proof of claim or interest in order to have a claim against the estate. For example, in Chapter 7, 12, and 13 cases, an unsecured creditor or an equity security holder *must* file a proof of claim or interest, unless (i) an eligible non-creditor entity filed a claim, or (ii) the creditor already filed a claim in a Chapter 11 case that was subsequently converted to a Chapter 7 case.[57] Pursuant to Bankruptcy Rule 3002(c), the court may enlarge the time for filing the proof of claim under Chapters 7, 12, and 13.

In Chapter 11 as well as Chapter 9 cases, however, if a claim or interest is scheduled by the debtor, so long as it is not marked as being contingent, unliquidated, or disputed, then the scheduled claim will be recognized or allowed; the claim is "deemed filed," and no proof of claim is necessary.[58] But if the creditor's claim is not listed, or is listed for an amount different from what the creditor believes it is owed, or is listed as disputed, contingent, or unliquidated, then a proof of claim must be filed.[59] On the other hand, if a proof of claim or interest is filed, it will "supersede any scheduling of that claim or interest."[60]

If a Chapter 11 case is converted to a Chapter 7 case, a proof of claim will need to be filed even if the claim was listed in the Chapter 11 debtor's schedules, because claims cannot be "deemed filed" in a case under Chapter 7.[61]

C. Presumptive Allowance of Claims

A properly filed proof of claim enjoys prima facie status, meaning it is "deemed allowed," unless a party in interest objects.[62] Official Form B10 sets forth various instructions and requirements for a properly filed proof

57. Fed. R. Bankr. P. 3002(a); *see also* Fed. R. Bankr. P. 3004, 3005, and 1019(3). *See, e.g.*, Zidell, Inc. v. Forsch (*In re Coastal Alaska Lines, Inc.*), 920 F.2d 1428, 1433 (9th Cir. 1990) (Chapter 7); Jones v. Arross, 9 F.3d 79, 81 (10th Cir. 1993) (Chapter 12); United States v. Chavis (*In re Chavis*), 47 F.3d 818, 824 (6th Cir. 1995) (Chapter 13).
58. *See* 11 U.S.C. §§ 925, 1111(a); *In re ATD Corp.*, 278 B.R. 758, 760 (Bankr. N.D. Ohio 2002), *aff'd.*, 352 F.3d 1062 (6th Cir. 2003).
59. Fed. R. Bankr. P. 3003(c)(1), (c)(2).
60. Fed. R. Bankr. P. 3003(c)(4); *In re Pennave Props.* Assocs., 165 B.R. 793, 796 (E.D. Pa. 1994) (In a Chapter 11 case, the undersecured creditor's proof of claim listed only the secured portion of its claim despite debtor's schedules that listed the entire amount of the claim. The court held that the proof of claim superseded the schedules, and the creditor was only entitled to receive the secured portion of the claim. The bankruptcy court was not required to protect the unsecured portion of the claim.).
61. Fed. R. Bankr. P. 1019(3).
62. 11 U.S.C. § 502(a).

of claim. For example, the claim must contain all necessary supporting documentation as well as an amount of the claim (this can become an issue for unliquidated claims where the amount is unknown and will not become ascertainable during the bankruptcy proceeding). If properly filed, the Bankruptcy Code presumes that a claim is valid and shall be allowed absent an objection from a party in interest.

If an objection arises, the objecting party has the initial burden of proof, and the claimant has the ultimate burden of persuasion regarding the validity of its claim.[63] At least one court has found that the burden of proof will fall on whichever party would bear that burden outside of bankruptcy.[64]

D. Jurisdiction and Venue

1. Conceded Jurisdiction

If a proof of claim or interest is filed, the filing party submits itself to the jurisdiction of the bankruptcy court with respect to the claim as well as litigation and other matters pending before the bankruptcy court.[65] This will result in the waiver of the right to a jury trial on the claim.[66]

2. Location of Filing

A proof of claim or interest must be filed with the "clerk in the district where the case … is pending."[67] If a proof of claim or interest was intended to be filed with the bankruptcy court but was erroneously delivered elsewhere, it must be sent to the proper bankruptcy court, and the court has the power to deem the claim "filed with the clerk … as of the date of its original delivery."[68]

---

63. Gran v. Internal Revenue Serv. (*In re Gran*), 964 F.2d. 822, 827 (8th Cir. 1992); *In re Oriental Rug Warehouse Club, Inc.*, 205 B.R. 407, 410 (Bankr. D. Minn. 1997).
64. *In re Pursley*, 451 B.R. 213, 229 (Bankr. M.D. Ga. 2011).
65. *See* Stern v. Marshall, 564 U.S. 462, 131 S. Ct. 2594 (2011).
66. *See, e.g.*, Langenkamp v. Culp, 498 U.S. 42, 44–45 (1990); Altman v. Alternative Debt Portfolios, L.P. (*In re EZ Pay Servs.*), 389 B.R. 278, 284–86 (Bankr. M.D. Fla. 2008); MCI WorldCom Comm'ns, Inc. v. Communications Network Int'l (*In re WorldCom, Inc.*), 378 B.R. 745, 754–55 (Bankr. S.D.N.Y. 2007). In very simple terms, this is because bankruptcy courts were historically regarded as courts of equity, as distinct from courts of law – categories that carry over from the English court system – and jury trials historically were not available in courts of equity.
67. Fed. R. Bankr. P. 5005(a).
68. Fed. R. Bankr. P. 5005(c).

E. When a Claim Arises

The Bankruptcy Code defines "claim" very broadly to include any right to payment, including contingent and unmatured claims, and any right to an equitable remedy for breach of performance.[69] "Claims" that are subject to allowance through a proof of claim are usually debts that arise prepetition.[70] If a claim arose postpetition, it may be treated differently than a prepetition claim, likely through a different process than the filing of a proof of claim. Most of the time, whether a claim arose prepetition or postpetition will be clear-cut. But in some cases, the time that a claim "arose" is not obvious at all, and it can become a greatly disputed matter. Complicating the matter is the act that the courts are split as to how to determine when a claim arises. As a result, a court may apply one of several tests to determine whether something is a cognizable claim in bankruptcy.

1. Conduct Test

The broadest application to disputes over claim status is the conduct test. Under the conduct test, a claim arises when the debtor's conduct that gave rise to the creditor's claim occurred, regardless of when the creditor manifests or discovers its injury.[71] Thus, under this test, a claim may arise prepetition if the conduct that ultimately injured the creditor occurred prepetition, even if the creditor was not actually injured or did not discover its injury until at a much later, postpetition date.[72]

2. Relationship Test

Some courts, regarding the conduct test as overly broad, look not only at the timing of the debtor's conduct, but also at whether there was a prepetition relationship between the creditor and the debtor that gave rise to the injury.[73] Under the relationship test, a claim may arise prepetition if the conduct that ultimately injured the creditor occurred prepetition, and

---

69. 11 U.S.C. 101(5).
70. Although the Bankruptcy Code's definition of "claim" does not specify that it be prepetition, the Code's principal definition of "creditor" is a person that has a claim against a debtor "that arose at the time of or before" the petition date or Order for Relief. 11 U.S.C. § 101(10).
71. *See, e.g.*, Grady v. A.H. Robins Co., Inc., 839 F.2d 198, 199 (4th Cir. 1988) (plaintiff's claim arose "when the acts giving rise to [the defendant's] liability were performed, not when the harm caused by those acts was manifested").
72. *See also* Watson v. Parker (*In re Parker*), 313 F.3d 1267, 1269 (10th Cir. 2002) ("We now adopt the conduct theory as the one more in tune with the plain language and the policy underlying the Bankruptcy Code.").
73. *See, e.g.*, Epstein v. Official Comm. of Unsecured Creditors of the Estate of Piper Aircraft Corp. (*In re Piper Aircraft Corp.*), 58 F.3d 1573, 1576 (11th Cir. 1995).

if there was some sort of prepetition relationship with the debtor, such as the use of the debtor's product or the existence of a contract.[74]

3. *Accrual Test*

The narrowest test, known as the accrual test, which focused on when the creditor's cause of action accrued under applicable nonbankruptcy law.[75] The inquiry concerned whether the creditor had a right to payment that could be enforced.[76] In other words, if all the circumstances had not yet transpired that would allow the creditor to file a lawsuit to enforce the claim, then the creditor did not have a "claim" in the bankruptcy. This test is not now used. The Third Circuit was previously the only jurisdiction that adopted this test, but it has now overruled the accrual test.[77]

4. *Exposure Test*

The Third Circuit uses the exposure test and holds that a claim "arises when an individual is exposed prepetition to a product or other conduct giving rise to an injury, which underlies a 'right to payment' under the Bankruptcy Code."[78] To date, no other jurisdictions have adopted the test from *In re Grossman's, Inc.*

F. Limitations on Prepetition Claims

Determining when a claim arises in bankruptcy has two primary effects. The first is the discharge received by the debtor. In most cases, a successful bankruptcy will result in the debtor receiving a discharge from all claims,

---

74. *See also* Lemelle v. Universal Mfg. Corp., 18 F.3d 1268, 1277 (5th Cir. 1994) (finding that the absence of "any pre-petition contact, privity, or other relationship" between the debtor and creditor "precludes a finding by the district court that the claims asserted" were discharged in bankruptcy proceedings); California Dept. of Health Servs. v. Jensen (*In re Jensen*), 995 F.2d 925, 930–31 (9th Cir. 1993); United States v. LTV Corp. (*In re Chateaugay Corp.*), 944 F.2d 997, 1003–04 (2d Cir. 1991).
75. *See, e.g.*, The Kilbarr Corp. v. Gen. Servs. Admin. Office of Fed. Supply & Servs. (*In re* Remington Rand Corp.), 836 F.2d 825, 830 (3d Cir. 1988); Avellino & Bienes v. M. Frenville Co., Inc. (*In re Frenville Co., Inc.*), 744 F.2d 332, 336 (3d Cir. 1984).
76. *See, e.g., Frenville*, 744 F.2d at 333–37 (finding that claim arose postpetition because, even though debtor's alleged negligent preparation of financial statements occurred prepetition, the plaintiffs only had a right to payment on their claim for contribution or indemnity arising out of the negligence when they filed their suit against the debtor, which happened postpetition).
77. *See, e.g.*, Wright v. Owens Corning, 679 F.3d 101 (3d Cir. 2012).
78. Jeld-Wen, Inc. v. Van Brunt (*In re Grossman's, Inc.*), 607 F.3d 114, 125 (3d Cir. 2010) (court held "that a 'claim' arises when an individual is exposed pre-petition to a product or other conduct giving rise to an injury which underlies a 'right to payment' under the Bankruptcy Code.").

so whether a debt is, in fact, a claim and whether the claim is a prepetition or postpetition claim are important to the creditor's rights.[79] In Chapter 7 cases, the debtor is typically not granted a discharge of claims that arose postpetition.The second effect is that a claim that arises postpetition can potentially receive the elevated treatment of an administrative expense rather than that of a general unsecured claim.

G. Effect of Filing

As noted above, if a proof of claim or interest is filed, the claim will be "deemed allowed" unless a valid objection is brought against it.[80] An allowed claim is entitled to rights to distribution and other rights provided by the Bankruptcy Code, such as the right to vote on proposed bankruptcy plans.[81] A proof of claim filed in compliance with the applicable Bankruptcy Rules will be presumed valid and will constitute prima facie evidence of the validity of both the claim and its amount.[82]

The effect of prima facie validity is that a party objecting to the claim has the burden of introducing evidence sufficient to rebut the presumption of validity.[83] The evidence must show a true dispute and have a probative force equal to the contents of the claim.[84] If such evidence is provided, the burden of proof goes back to the party that would have held it outside of bankruptcy.[85]

---

79. *See, e.g.*, 11 U.S.C. §§ 524(a)(1) and (a)(2) (generally voiding judgments on debts against the debtor and preventing actions to enforce debts against the debtor, with debts defined in Section 101(12) as "liability on a claim"); 11 U.S.C § 727 (discharging debts in a Chapter 7 case); 11 U.S.C. § 1328(a) (discharging all debts provided for by a Chapter 13 plan or otherwise disallowed). *Cf.* 11 U.S.C. § 1141(d)(1)(A) (confirmation of Chapter 11 plan discharges debtor from all debts that arose prepetition and also debts that arose postpetition but before date of confirmation).
80. 11 U.S.C. § 502(a).
81. *See, e.g.*, 11 U.S.C. § 1126 (a) (holder of claim may accept or deny a filed plan of reorganization); 11 U.S.C. § 507 (allowed claims receive distribution in order of priority).
82. Fed. R. Bankr. P. 3001(f); Victoria v. Greenville Hosp. Corp. (*In re Victoria*), 389 B.R. 250, 255 (M.D. Ala. 2008).
83. Chambliss v. Oakwood Acceptance Corp. (*In re Chambliss*), 315 B.R. 166, 169 (Bankr. S.D. Ga. 2004) (citing *In re Pac. Arts Publishing, Inc.*, 198 B.R. 319, 321 (Bankr. C.D. Cal.1996) (citations omitted); *In re Challa*, 186 B.R. 750, 754 (Bankr. M.D. Fla. 1995); *In re Clements*, 185 B.R. 895, 898–99 (Bankr. M.D. Fla. 1995)).
84. *In re Clements,* 185 B.R. at 898-99 (citing *In re VTN, Inc.*, 69 B.R. 1005 (Bankr. S.D. Fla. 1987).
85. *See, e.g.*, *In re Winn-Dixie Stores, Inc.*, 418 B.R. 475, 476 (Bankr. M.D. Fla. 2009); *In re King*, No. 08-13152-SSM, 2009 Bankr. LEXIS 2722, *4–7, 2009 WL 960766 *2–5 (Bankr. E.D. Va. Apr. 8, 2009); *In re Kincaid*, 388 B.R. 610, 613–14 (Bankr. E.D. Pa. 2008).

Proofs of claim must be signed and dated by the person or creditor asserting the claim. The person signing the proof of claim must declare under penalty of perjury that the information contained in the proof of claim is true and correct. The proof of claim form (Official Form B10) cautions a claimant that, by filing a claim, it is subject to a fine or penalty.[86] If a fraudulent claim is filed, the claimant can be subject to a fine of up to $250,000 for an individual or $500,000 for an organization, imprisonment of up to five years, or both.[87] Despite possible criminal liability, courts have found that there is "no private cause of action under 18 U.S.C. § 152(4) for filing a false proof of claim in a bankruptcy proceeding."[88]

H. General Bar Date for Claims

Pursuant to Rule 3002 of the Federal Rules of Bankruptcy Procedure, a proof of claim must be filed within seventy days after the order for relief (i.e., the petition date) in cases under Chapters 7, 12, and 13. Fed. R. Bankr. P. 3002 (c). In practice, however, in Chapter 7 cases, the trustee will set a deadline for filing a proof of claim if the trustee determines that there will be a distribution to creditors. In cases under Chapter 9 and 11, the deadline for filing a proof of claim is set by the court. The court sets the time upon the debtor's motion or the motion of another party in interest to establish the bar date for filing proofs of claims.

Once the court grants the motion and sets a bar date, the debtor sends a notice to all creditors and parties in interest of the last day to timely file a proof of claim and with instructions on where to file the claim. The notice of the bar date may instruct a creditor to send the proof of claim to a bankruptcy claims agent, if applicable, or require that the proof of claim be filed electronically via ECF filing with the respective bankruptcy court. Practitioners should review the notice and order carefully and follow those instructions for filing the claim. Claims that have been properly filed in a Chapter 11 case are deemed to be already filed in the same case that is subsequently converted to a Chapter 7 case. Bankruptcy Rule 1019(3). However, claims deemed allowed pursuant to section 1111(a) of the Bankruptcy Code must be physically filed in the Chapter 7 case.

86. 18 U.S.C. § 152.

87. *See* 18 U.S.C §§ 152 and 3571; *see also* Wood v. United States (*In re Wood*), 341 B.R. 804, 812 (Bankr. S.D. Fla. 2006).

88. Heavrin v. Boeing Capital Corp., 246 F. Supp. 2d 728, 731 (W.D. Ky. 2003), *aff'd. sub nom.*, Heavrin v. Nelson, 384 F.3d 199 (6th Cir. 2004).

I. Amendment of Claims

1. Permissive Amendment Prior to the Bar Date

Although the Bankruptcy Code and the Bankruptcy Rules do not address amendment of claims, the courts generally freely permit amendment of a proof of claim prior to the bar date. Generally speaking, amendments to already existing proofs of claim are allowed unless the amendment creates a new claim altogether.[89] "It is a well settled principle that, absent contrary equitable considerations or prejudice to the opposing party, amendments to proofs of claim should be freely permitted."[90]

2. Post-Bar-Date Amendments

While amended proofs of claim are treated liberally prior to the bar date, post-bar-date amendments receive a closer scrutiny to ensure that the amended claim is not an attempt to assert a new claim after the bar date.[91] Post-bar date, most courts use a "nexus test," which requires that "amendment of a claim be freely allowed where its purpose is to cure a defect, provide a more particular description of the claim, or plead a new theory of recovery based upon facts stated in the original claim."[92]

The nexus test "seeks to determine whether the amendment to the proof of claim is based on the same underlying legal claim or whether it is in fact a new claim for which the creditor missed the proof-of-claim bar date."[93] Courts have held that the examination must also "take into account various equitable considerations, including whether other creditors may be unfairly prejudiced or ... surprised; whether the efficiency of administering the estate will be compromised; whether excusable neglect or inattentiveness exist on behalf of the claimant; whether the

89. Highlands Ins. Co., Inc. v. Alliance Operating Corp. (*In re Alliance Operating Alliance Corp.*), 60 F.3d 1174 (5th Cir. 1995) (amendment of claim from unsecured status to a priority claim was deemed to create a new claim rather than a permissive amendment).

90. *In re Edison Bros. Stores, Inc.*, 2002 WL 999260 (Bankr. D. Del. May 15, 2002).

91. Brown v. Ameriquest Funding II, LLC (*In re Brown*), 431 B.R. 309, 314 (Bankr. D. Mass. 2010).

92. *See* Clamp-All Corp., 235 B.R. at 140; *see also In re Maxon Eng'g. Servs.*, 2006 Bankr. LEXIS 4271, 2006 WL 3909972 *1–2 (Bankr. D.P.R. Jan. 25, 2006); *In re Callery*, 274 B.R. 51 (Bankr. D. Mass. 2002); *In re Winn-Dixie Stores, Inc.*, 381 B.R. 804, 808 (Bankr. M.D. Fla. 2008) *aff'd. in part*, 414 B.R. 764 (M.D. Fla. 2009); Toyota Motor Credit Corp. v. Rodriguez (*In re Rodriguez*), 2010 WL 1838286 (M.D. Fla. May 3, 2010).

93. *In re Lehman Fin. Group, LLC*, 2006 Bankr. LEXIS 2152, *3–4, 2006 WL 2640210 at 1 (Bankr. N.D. Ill. Sept. 11, 2006); *In re Full Gospel Assembly of Delray Beach, Inc.*, 2007 WL 1423613 (Bankr. S.D. Fla. May 9, 2007); *In re Tel. Co.*, 308 B.R. 579, 582 (Bankr. M.D. Fla. 2004); *In re George*, 426 B.R. 895, 899 (Bankr. M.D. Fla. 2010).

debtor-in-possession had knowledge or notice of the claim before the deadline; whether essential documents were available; whether the debtor hindered computation of the claim; and whether the amending creditor has engaged in any bad faith, retaliatory, or dilatory conduct."[94]

Other courts have supplanted the nexus component with a streamlined two-prong "equitable" analysis to determine whether it is appropriate to allow post-bar-date amendments.[95] Under this analysis, the court must first assess whether there was a "timely assertion of a similar claim or demand evidencing an intention to hold the estate liable."[96] If the first prong of the test is satisfied, then the court must then determine "whether it would be equitable to allow the amendment."[97]

94. *In re Lehman Fin. Group, LLC*, 2006 Bankr. LEXIS 2152, at *3–4, 2006 WL 2640210 at *1.

95. *See In re Sneijder*, 407 B.R. 46, 54 (Bankr. S.D.N.Y. 2009); *In re J.S. II, LLC*, 389 B.R. 563, 567 (Bankr. N.D. Ill. 2008).

96. *In re Enron Creditors Recovery Corp.*, 370 B.R. 90, 95 (Bankr. S.D.N.Y. 2007).

97. *Id.*

4

Secured Claims

A. Overview

Secured claims generally receive better treatment in bankruptcy than unsecured or administrative expense claims. A debtor's bankruptcy petition filing does not abrogate a secured creditor's prepetition lien or setoff rights, but the filing does operate to delay lien or setoff enforcement actions pending administration of the case. Whether a lien or setoff right survives bankruptcy depends on many factors. While a debtor may discharge personal monetary liability for a debt through bankruptcy, there is no *per se* extinguishment of liens in a bankruptcy case.

B. Secured Claim Defined

A secured creditor in a bankruptcy case is a creditor who holds a claim against a debtor that is secured by a lien on property that the debtor owned as of the petition date (i.e., the creditor's collateral is property of the bankruptcy estate). A distinction must be made between collateral owned by the debtor and collateral owned by others. If none of a creditor's collateral is owned by the debtor, then the creditor's claim is unsecured as to the debtor, even though it is a secured claim against the collateral owner. For example, a bank may hold a claim secured by a blanket lien on all assets owned by a limited liability company. If the sole member of the company guaranteed the bank's claim but did not grant any liens on the member's other assets to secure the guaranty, then in a bankruptcy case filed by the member, the bank will hold an unsecured claim.

A creditor also holds a secured claim in a bankruptcy case when it has a valid right to setoff the amount of a claim the creditor has against the debtor by the amount of a claim the debtor has against the creditor. For example, a bank should be treated as a secured creditor if the bank has a right to setoff or reduce the balance the debtor owes to the bank on a promissory note by the balance maintained in the debtor's deposit account at the bank.[98]

A claim is secured only up to the value of the collateral or the amount subject to setoff. If any part of a claim exceeds the value of the creditor's interest in property of the estate or exceeds the amount subject to setoff, that portion of the claim is an unsecured claim. An otherwise secured creditor who holds an unsecured claim for such excess amount is called an "undersecured" creditor. Regardless of the extent to which a claim is secured, a claim that has been filed or scheduled in accordance with Bankruptcy Code requirements will be treated as an "allowed claim" as long as no objection to the claim is sustained by the bankruptcy court.[99]

If the value of the collateral is greater than the amount of the creditor's claim, then the creditor is "oversecured." An oversecured creditor's claim may include interest and "any reasonable fees, costs, or charges provided for under the agreement or State statute under which such claim arose."[100] Thus, an oversecured creditor can collect postpetition interest on its claim and its reasonable attorneys' fees (if allowed by the terms of the prepetition agreement with the debtor), whereas such interest and fees would generally be disallowed for unsecured creditors.[101]

C. Impact of Automatic Stay on Secured Claims

A claim can be secured "by a lien on the property in which the estate has an interest"—i.e., collateral.[102] A lien is a "charge against or interest in property to secure payment of a debt or performance of an obligation."[103] A lien can be created by agreement, statute, common law, equity, or judicial process.

The automatic stay created by the Bankruptcy Code goes into effect when the bankruptcy case is commenced. The automatic stay prohibits a secured creditor from foreclosing on its collateral or exercising setoff rights without obtaining prior permission from the bankruptcy court. The stay also precludes "any act to create, perfect, or enforce any lien against property

98. *See infra* Part H.
99. 11 U.S.C. § 502 ("(a) A claim or interest…is deemed allowed, unless a party in interest, including a creditor of a general partner in a partnership that is a debtor in a case under chapter 7 of this title, objects.").
100. 11 U.S.C. § 506(b).
101. 11 U.S.C. § 502(b)(2).
102. 11 U.S.C. § 506(a)(1).
103. 11 U.S.C. § 101(37).

of the estate."[104] Under certain circumstances set forth in the Bankruptcy Code, a secured creditor may obtain an order granting it relief from the stay and allowing foreclosure on the collateral by filing a motion, subject to notice, objection, and a hearing.

Under every bankruptcy chapter, a secured creditor is entitled to recover the value of the creditor's interest in the collateral owned by the debtor. If another secured creditor has a higher priority lien on the same collateral, then the value of the second priority secured creditor's claim is limited to any value in excess of the first priority secured creditor's claim. If the debt is secured by property owned solely by an individual or entity who is not the debtor, then the claim as to the bankrupt debtor is unsecured.

The debtor may provide value to a secured creditor (or "adequate protection" of the secured creditor's interest in the collateral) through cash payments or through a sale of the collateral and distribution of sale proceeds. If a secured creditor's lien is not avoided or invalidated during the course of the case, the Bankruptcy Code permits bankruptcy plans to modify (with limitations) how secured claims are treated.

D. Valuing a Secured Claim

Courts determine the collateral's value "in light of the purpose of the valuation and of the proposed disposition or use of such property."[105] If the collateral is to be sold, courts typically look at the liquidation value, or the estimated net sale proceeds that the collateral would generate in an auction or forced sale. If the debtor elects to retain and continue to use the property, the collateral is valued using a going concern or fair market value (the price a willing seller and a willing buyer would agree upon after the property has been on the market for a reasonable time).[106]

If the debtor is an individual debtor in a Chapter 7 or Chapter 13 case, the value of personal property securing an allowed claim is determined by looking at "replacement value," which means "the price a retail merchant would charge for property of that kind considering the age and condition of the property at the time value is determined."[107]

When disputes arise over valuation, the bankruptcy court conducts an evidentiary hearing to evaluate competing opinions of value. Each party

104. 11 U.S.C. § 362(a)(4).

105. 11 U.S.C. § 506(a)(1).

106. *See* In re Heritage Highgate, Inc., 679 F.3d 132, 142 (3rd Cir. 2012) ("The proper measure under § 506(a) [for property being retained and used is] the collateral's fair market value because it is most respectful of the property's anticipated use."). *See also* In re Winthrop Old Farm Nurseries, 50 F.3d 72, 75 (1st Cir. 1995) ([T]he present value of the income stream would be equal to the collateral's fair market value.").

107. 11 U.S.C. § 506(a)(2).

advocating a particular value must present proof of value using the relevant standard (e.g., liquidation or fair market value). Proof may be offered by various means including the debtor's own testimony, leading market indices (such as the NADA guide for vehicles), or testimony by experts like real estate appraisers or business valuation professionals. Litigation over valuation can be time consuming and very costly.

In cases where a secured creditor needs to file a proof of claim in the debtor's bankruptcy case, careful consideration should be given to the property value the creditor states in the claim. Another party might later argue that the value stated in the creditor's proof of claim is a binding admission that the claim is undersecured or oversecured, which can have significant consequences. For example, an undersecured creditor might be entitled to stay relief or adequate protection payments during the bankruptcy case, but not entitled to recover postpetition interest and attorneys' fees. Conversely, an oversecured creditor may be entitled to recover postpetition interest and attorneys' fees through payments from the debtor over time, but may not be entitled to adequate protection payments prior to confirmation of the debtor's bankruptcy plan.

E. Treatment of Secured Claims in Chapter 7

In a Chapter 7 case, the trustee is required to "dispose of any property in which an entity other than the estate has an interest, such as a lien" prior to the final distribution of property of the estate.[108] Distribution in a Chapter 7 case is generally covered by Sections 507, 510, 725, and 726 of the Bankruptcy Code.

The trustee may dispose of property subject to liens by selling or abandoning the property. If there is sufficient value to realize equity above the amount of liens, sale costs, and the debtor's property exemptions, then the trustee is likely to sell property that is subject to a lien unless the secured creditor obtains relief from the automatic stay so it can foreclose. The trustee may abandon the bankruptcy estate's interest in property when the property has insufficient value to generate significant net proceeds from sale.

When the trustee sells property "free and clear of liens," the purchaser takes title free of liens, but the secured creditor's liens transfer to the sale proceeds. The trustee must then pay secured creditors from the net sale proceeds in the same order of priority as their liens attached to the collateral before sale.[109] If the collateral sold by the trustee was a creditor's only security for its claim, then the remaining balance due on the creditor's

108. 11 U.S.C. § 725.
109. 11 U.S.C. § 726(a)(1).

claim after applying the net sale proceeds will be treated as an unsecured deficiency claim.

For example, assume a Chapter 7 debtor owns a car worth $30,000 and subject to a lender's secured claim in the amount of $15,000. Also assume that the debtor has an enforceable right to claim a $4,000 exemption in any equity resulting from the sale of the car, and the trustee's fees and expenses to sell the car are $1,200. If the gross sale proceeds are $30,000, the trustee would distribute the proceeds as follows: first $1,200 to pay sale costs, then $15,000 to the lienholder, then $4,000 to the debtor, and the remaining $9,800 to the bankruptcy estate for distribution to unsecured creditors in accordance with the priority scheme of the Bankruptcy Code.

In an individual Chapter 7 case, a debtor wishing to extinguish a lien on consumer goods that are either exempt under Section 522 or abandoned under Section 544 of the Bankruptcy Code may do so only by "redeeming" the property, *i.e.*, by paying the secured creditor the full amount of its allowed secured claim. Redemption is governed by Section 722 of the Bankruptcy Code.[110] Subject to court approval, a Chapter 7 debtor may choose to use exempt funds or seek financing to pay the secured creditor a lump sum equal to the current market value of an asset like a vehicle in exchange for clear title.

F. Treatment of Secured Claims in Chapter 13

In a Chapter 13 case, distributions to creditors will be determined by the court's confirmation of a plan. Distributions generally are governed by Sections 507, 510, 1122, 1322, and 1325 of the Bankruptcy Code. While the plan may modify the rights of creditors, the ability of a plan to modify the rights of secured creditors is limited.

The court will confirm a Chapter 13 plan only if:

(a) each secured creditor has accepted the plan,[111]

(b) the debtor surrenders the collateral to the secured creditor,[112] or

(c) the plan contains all of the following provisions:

(i) the secured creditor must "retain the lien securing [the secured] claim" until the earlier of "the payment of the underlying debt under nonbankruptcy law" or the date the debtor is granted a discharge; in addition, if the Chapter 13 case is dismissed or converted before completion of the plan, the "lien shall ... be

110. 11 U.S.C. § 722.
111. 11 U.S.C. § 1325(a)(5)(A).
112. 11 U.S.C. § 1325(a)(5)(C).

retained [by the secured creditor] to the extent recognized by applicable nonbankruptcy law,"[113]
(ii) "[t]he value, as of the effective date of the plan, of property to be distributed under the plan on account of [the secured] claim is not less than the allowed amount of such claim,"[114] and
(iii) if property to be distributed to the creditor is in the form of periodic payments, such payments shall be in equal monthly amounts, and if the claim is secured by personal property, the amount of such payments shall not be less than an amount sufficient to provide to the claim holder adequate protection during the plan period.[115]

Normally, under Section 506(a) of the Bankruptcy Code, the "allowed amount" of a secured claim is the amount of the creditor's interest in the collateral. Because a Chapter 13 plan can modify the rights of secured creditors, the plan can reduce the "allowed amount" of an undersecured creditor's secured claim to the value of the collateral—a procedure known as "lien stripping." The remaining unsecured portion of the claim will be classified as a general unsecured claim for plan distribution purposes.[116] When a Chapter 13 plan proposes to strip a secured creditor's lien and the plan is confirmed, the process is known as a "cramdown."[117]

Chapter 13, however, contains exceptions to the ability to reduce the allowed amount of the secured claim. The plan cannot modify the rights of a claim secured solely by the debtor's primary residence.[118] Additionally, a "hanging paragraph" below Section 1325(a)(9) provides that cramdown will not apply to any secured creditors who hold a purchase money security interest in: (a) a motor vehicle acquired for personal use, if the debt was incurred within 910 days (roughly 2½ years) before the filing of the petition, or (b) any other collateral, if the debt was incurred within the one-year period prior to filing the petition.[119]

---

113. 11 U.S.C. § 1325(a)(5)(B)(i).
114. 11 U.S.C. § 1325(a)(5)(B)(ii).
115. 11 U.S.C. § 1325(a)(5)(B)(iii).
116. *See, e.g.*, *In re Brown*, 746 F.3d 1236, 1241 (11th Cir. 2014) ("Surrender would satisfy the creditor's secured claim, not the entire debt. If a creditor holds an undersecured claim, the creditor would still have an unsecured claim to the extent the debt exceeds the collateral's judicially-determined replacement value.").
117. *See, e.g.*, Assocs. Commercial Corp. v. Rash, 520 U.S. 953, 957, 117 S. Ct. 1879, 1882–83 (1997) ("Under the cram down option, the debtor is permitted to keep the property over the objection of the creditor; the creditor retains the lien securing the claim . . . and the debtor is required to provide the creditor with payments, over the life of the plan, that will total the present value of the allowed secured claim, i.e., the present value of the collateral.").
118. 11 U.S.C. § 1322(b)(2).
119. 11 U.S.C. § 1325(a)(9).

G. Treatment of Secured Claims in Chapter 11

In a Chapter 11 case, distributions to creditors will be determined by a plan that is confirmed by the court. The plan must create categories or classes of claims. Only "impaired" classes of claims (so called because the plan changes their legal, equitable, or contractual rights) are entitled to vote on the plan. Classes that consist of secured or priority creditors are entitled to better treatment than classes of unsecured nonpriority creditors. Distribution in a Chapter 11 case generally is governed by Sections 507, 510, 1122, 1123, 1126, and 1129 of the Bankruptcy Code.

In order to be confirmable, a Chapter 11 plan must make distributions to classes of claims and interests in accordance with the provisions of Section 1129. Normally, under Section 1129(a)(8), a Chapter 11 plan can be confirmed only if each class of claims and interests either accepts the plan or is not impaired under the plan.[120] However, the Bankruptcy Code allows the debtor to seek confirmation over the objection of an impaired class of claims under the cramdown provision in Section 1129(b) if all confirmation requirements are met except for Section 1129(a)(8) and "the plan does not discriminate unfairly, and is fair and equitable, with respect to each class of claims or interests that is impaired under, and has not accepted, the plan."[121]

To be "fair and equitable," the plan must provide one of the following three alternative treatments for each class of secured claims:

(i) the holders of such claims retain their liens to the extent of the allowed amount of their secured claims, and receive "on account of such claim deferred cash payments totaling at least the allowed amount of such claim, of a value, as of the effective date of the plan, of at least the value of such holder's interest in the estate's interest in such property,"[122]

(ii) if the collateral is sold free and clear of the creditor's lien, the lien must "attach to the proceeds of such sale,"[123] or

(iii) the holders of such claims must be given the "indubitable equivalent" of their secured claims.[124]

An undersecured creditor in a Chapter 11 case can elect to have its entire claim treated as a secured claim.[125] Making this choice is called an "1111(b) election." An undersecured creditor who makes this election

120. 11 U.S.C. § 1129(a)(8).
121. 11 U.S.C. § 1129(b)(1).
122. 11 U.S.C. § 1129(b)(2)(A)(i).
123. 11 U.S.C. § 1129(b)(2)(A)(ii).
124. 11 U.S.C. § 1129(b)(2)(a)(iii).
125. 11 U.S.C. § 1111(b).

agrees to waive the unsecured deficiency claim that would ordinarily be created through the bifurcation of the claim into its secured and unsecured parts under Section 506(a)(1) of the Bankruptcy Code.[126] In exchange, the debtor's plan must provide the creditor with deferred cash payments that: (i) total the allowed amount of the entire claim, and (ii) have a value on the effective date of the plan equal to the value of the lien.[127]

For example, assume a creditor has an allowed claim of $1 million, but the value of the collateral securing the claim is only $600,000. Without an 1111(b) election, the claim will be bifurcated into a secured claim of $600,000 and an unsecured claim of $400,000. With an 1111(b) election, the debtor must make payments to the creditor that add up to $1 million over time and have a present value of at least $600,000. If the debtor cannot prove that making such payments is feasible, the debtor may be unable to obtain confirmation of a plan and may be compelled to liquidate.

H. Creditor's Right to Setoff

The Bankruptcy Code does not create a federal right of setoff. Instead, the Code permits a creditor to use any setoff rights existing under applicable state or other federal law.[128] Setoff rights generally exist when there are mutual debts between two parties. Pursuant to the Bankruptcy Code, a creditor can "offset a mutual debt" that the creditor owed to the debtor before the bankruptcy petition date against a claim that the debtor owed to the creditor before the petition date, but cannot setoff a prepetition claim against a postpetition claim.[129] The Bankruptcy Code also provides that a claim that is subject to setoff under Section 553 is a secured claim "to the extent of the amount subject to setoff."[130] The right to setoff is not mandatory, but permissive.[131]

A creditor will not have a right to setoff in bankruptcy if the following circumstances are present:

(i) the creditor's claim is disallowed,

(ii) the claim was transferred by a nondebtor entity to the creditor

(a) after the commencement of the bankruptcy case, or

126. 11 U.S.C. § 506(a)(1).
127. 11 U.S.C. § 1129(b).
128. *See* Citizens Bank of Maryland v. Strumpf, 516 U.S. 16, 18-19 (1995).
129. 11 U.S.C. § 553(a).
130. 11 U.S.C. § 506(a).
131. Cumberland Glass Mfg. Co. v. DeWitt & Co., 237 U.S. 447, 455 (1915) ("The provision is permissive rather than mandatory, and does not enlarge the doctrine of set-off, and cannot be invoked in cases where the general principles of set-off would not justify it. . .. The matter is placed within the control of the bankruptcy court, which exercises its discretion in these cases upon the general principles of equity.").

(b) within the ninety days prior to the filing of the petition while the debtor was insolvent, or

(iii) the creditor incurred its debt to the debtor within the ninety days prior to the filing of the petition, while the debtor was insolvent, and for the purpose of obtaining a right to setoff against the debtor.[132]

The debtor is presumed to be insolvent within the ninety days prior to the filing of the petition.[133] If a setoff is taken within the ninety days prior to the filing of the petition, it may be deemed preferential and can be recovered by the trustee.[134] The setoff can be avoided to the extent that there was a reduction in the amount by which the debt owed by the creditor to the debtor was greater than the amount owed by the debtor to the creditor.[135]

The automatic stay initially prevents a creditor from exercising the right to setoff during the bankruptcy because it prohibits "the setoff of any debt owing to the debtor that arose before the commencement of the case under this title against any claim against the debtor."[136] As a result, a postpetition setoff cannot be done without first obtaining relief from the automatic stay under Section 362(d) of the Bankruptcy Code.

Confirmation of a Chapter 11 plan generally bars collection of the debtor's prepetition debts except as they are required to be paid under the plan.[137] Accordingly, it can be argued that if a creditor attempts to setoff a debt after confirmation, no setoff right would exist because the debtor would no longer owe a debt to the creditor. The courts have split as to whether a creditor's right to setoff survives confirmation of a Chapter 11 plan.[138]

I. Debtor's Right to Setoff

Section 558 of the Bankruptcy Code provides that the estate "shall have the benefit of any defense available to the debtor as against any entity other than the estate, including statutes of limitation, statutes of frauds, usury, and other personal defenses."[139] Using this section, courts have permitted

132. 11 U.S.C. § 553(a).
133. 11 U.S.C. § 553(c).
134. 11 U.S.C. § 553(b).
135. *Id.*
136. 11 U.S.C. § 362(a)(7).
137. 11 U.S.C. § 1141(d).
138. *Compare In re De Laurentiis Entm't Group, Inc.*, 963 F.2d 1269, 1277 (9th Cir. 1992) (holding that a creditor's right to setoff survives plan confirmation), *with* I.R.S. v. Driggs, 185 B.R. 214, 215 (D. Md. 1995) (affirming denial of IRS's setoff motion because debtor's confirmed reorganization plan prohibited setoff and the IRS failed to object to the plan).
139. 11 U.S.C. § 558.

debtors to exercise any applicable state law right to setoff against debts owed to creditors.[140]

Unlike with a creditor's setoff under Section 553, courts have held that a debtor may set off prepetition claims against postpetition claims.[141] Thus, the debtors can set off against prepetition claims and administrative claims.[142]

Just as with the creditor's right to setoff under Section 553, there must be mutuality between the parties—"the estate must seek to set off a debt it owes to the creditor against a debt the creditor owes to the estate."[143]

140. *See, e.g.*, *In re PSA, Inc.*, 277 B.R. 51, 53–54 (Bankr. D. Del. 2002).

141. *See In re Women First Healthcare, Inc.*, 345 B.R. 131, 134 (Bankr. D. Del. 2006).

142. *See In re PSA*, 277 B.R. at 53; *see also In re 1701 Commerce, LLC*, No. 12-41748-DML-11, 2014 WL 4657314, at *13 (Bankr. N.D. Tex. Sept. 17, 2014); *In re Circuit City Stores, Inc.*, No. 08–35653, 2009 WL 4755253, at *3 (Bankr. E.D. Va. Dec. 3, 2009).

143. *See, e.g.*, *In re Women First Healthcare*, 345 B.R. at 134–35.

5

Unsecured Claims

A. Overview

This chapter focuses on the priorities detailed in Section 507 of the Bankruptcy Code, according to which distributions from the bankruptcy estate are made.

Section 507 of the Bankruptcy Code contains four subparts, (a) through (d). Section 507(a) sets forth ten categories of claims that, if allowed, are entitled to payment priority in bankruptcy cases. In Chapter 7 cases, the ten categories are entitled to payment in the order listed (*i.e.*, category 1 gets paid in full before any payment goes to category 2, and so on). In Chapter 11 cases, a requirement of plan confirmation is that all allowed priority claims will be paid. These ten categories reflect the judgment of Congress that certain types of claims should be given precedence in receiving payment, though in some instances priority claims may be limited by a statutory cap on the claim's amount.

Section 507(b) authorizes the priority level and payment of a form of "super priority" payment to secured creditors.[144] It provides a priority over every other claim allowed under Section 507(a) (except domestic support obligations) to a claimant whose claim is secured by a lien on

144. 11 U.S.C. § 507(b). As this provision indicates, other sections of the Bankruptcy Code—in particular, Sections 362, 363, and 364—are interrelated to this provision, insofar as they can allow the bankruptcy court to grant secured creditors super priority on payment ahead of all the categories listed in Section 507(a).

the debtor's property and who also has a claim under Section 507(a)(2) arising from either:

(i) the stay of action due to the automatic stay (Section 362),

(ii) the use, sale, or lease of property (Section 363), or

(iii) the granting of a lien in connection with postpetition financing provided to a debtor in possession (Section 364(d)).

"Super priority" claims may arise in a variety of contexts, including a Section 364(c)(1) claim for creditors who provide postpetition financing,[145] an adequate protection claim that proves inadequate to protect the creditor's security interest under 507(b), and a claim of an unsecured utility provider for adequate assurance of future payment.[146] Other provisions of the Bankruptcy Code may impact the timing of payment.[147]

Section 507(c) addresses the priority level of a claim of a governmental unit arising from an erroneous refund or tax credit. Section 507(d) provides that an entity that is subrogated to the rights of a holder of certain Section 507(a) claims is not entitled to the same level of priority as the claimant to which the entity is subrogated.[148]

B. Priority Categories Under Section 507(a)

1. First Priority—507(a)(1)—Domestic Support Objections

A first priority is available to claims for "domestic support obligations." The 2005 amendments to the Bankruptcy Code as part of BAPCPA moved domestic support obligations from the seventh to the first priority.[149] This reflects a clear congressional intent to promote the payment of such claims in bankruptcy cases. Domestic support obligations are defined by the

---

145. *See* 11 U.S.C. § 364(c)(1).

146. *See* 11 U.S.C. § 366(c).

147. For example, the interim compensation provisions for professionals in bankruptcy cases under Section 331 direct that those individuals receive payment at various intervals in a case, ahead of estate creditors. *See* 11 U.S.C. § 331. Section 1114 may require the debtor to "timely pay" and "not modify any retiree benefits." *See* 11 U.S.C. § 1114(e)(1). Section 365(d)(3) requires the trustee to "timely perform" the obligations of the debtor in any nonresidential real property lease of the debtor until the lease is assumed or rejected. *See* 11 U.S.C. § 365(d)(3). In addition, in a case that has converted from Chapter 11 to Chapter 7, a Chapter 7 administrative expense gets priority over a Chapter 11 administrative expense. Section 726(b) provides that when a case converts from Chapter 11 to Chapter 7, the administrative expenses incurred in the Chapter 7 will come ahead of the administrative expenses incurred while the debtor was in Chapter 11. *See* 11 U.S.C. § 726(b).

148. 11 U.S.C. § 507(d).

149. 11 U.S.C. § 507(a)(1).

Bankruptcy Code.[150] The determination of whether a debt is a domestic support obligation is a matter of federal law.[151] Provided that the obligation qualifies as a domestic support obligation, Section 507(a)(1) then designates the claim among two subpriorities: (i) first priority is afforded to obligations owed to a spouse, former spouse, or child of the debtor,[152] and (ii) second priority is owed to a qualifying governmental unit that is an assignee of a domestic support obligation.[153] However, the two subpriorities are junior in priority to a bankruptcy trustee's right to payment for expenses incurred in administering assets of the bankruptcy estate.[154]

2. *Second Priority—507(a)(2)—Administrative Expenses*

Section 507(a)(2) provides a second priority to administrative expenses allowable under Section 503(b) of the Bankruptcy Code, unsecured claims of any Federal Reserve bank related to certain loans authorized under the Federal Reserve Act, and fees and charges assessed against the estate including filing fees and fees assessed by the U.S. Trustee.[155] Section 503(b) provides that certain administrative expenses may be allowed following notice and a hearing, provided that the alleged administrative expense is an actual, necessary cost or expense of preserving the estate. Examples of allowable administrative expenses include, inter alia, wages, salaries, and commissions earned after the commencement of the case, taxes other than those covered by Section 507(a)(8), and compensation of estate professionals including the debtor's attorney.

Chapter 123 of Title 28 of the U.S. Code contains provisions authorizing the federal courts to charge certain fees to litigants and parties. Finally, Section 507(a)(2) of the Bankruptcy Code includes claims for certain loans made by Federal Reserve Banks under the Federal Reserve Act.[156]

---

150. *See* 11 U.S.C. § 101(14A).

151. *In re Cummings*, 244 F.3d 1263, 1265 (11th Cir. 2001) ("Whether a given debt is in the nature of support is an issue of federal law. Although federal law controls, state law does provide guidance in determining whether the obligation should be considered support under § 523(a)(5).") (internal citations and quotations omitted).

152. *See* 11 U.S.C. § 507(a)(1)(A).

153. *See* 11 U.S.C. § 507(a)(1)(B).

154. *See* 11 U.S.C. § 507(a)(1)(C).

155. Section 507(a)(2) does not specifically mention fees charged by the U.S. Trustee; rather, it includes "any fees and charges assessed against the estate under Chapter 123 of title 28." 11 U.S.C. § 507(a)(2). But Chapter 123 includes Section 1930, and that provision covers fees that may be charged in bankruptcy cases, including filing fees and fees assessed by the U.S. Trustee. 4 Collier on Bankruptcy ¶ 507.04.

156. 11 U.S.C. § 507(a)(2).

3. *Third Priority—507(a)(3)—Gap Period Claims*

A third priority is available to holders of claims specifically arising under Section 502(f) of the Bankruptcy Code. Section 502(f) is only applicable in an involuntary bankruptcy case where the debtor incurs obligations in the ordinary course of business or financial affairs between the time the involuntary petition is filed and the Order for Relief is entered.[157] The priority of claims incurred during this "gap period" is designed to encourage creditors to continue to do business with an alleged debtor. Assuming the claim is incurred in the ordinary course of the alleged debtor's business or financial affairs during the gap period, a third priority is available to holders of most, if not all, such claims.[158] Claims by attorneys for fees incurred in representing an alleged debtor during the gap period typically are not entitled to priority under this section since the fees are not related to the debtor's "ordinary course of business."[159]

4. *Fourth Priority—507(a)(4)—Wages, Salaries, and Commissions*

Section 507(a)(4) provides a fourth priority for claims against the debtor for wages, salaries, and commissions (including vacation, severance, sick leave pay, and bonus compensation) or sales commissions earned by independent contractors up to a limit that is currently set at $13,650 per claimant, but is subject to periodic adjustment based on the Consumer Price Index.[160] This priority is available to lessen the impact of a bankruptcy on a business's employees.

---

157. 11 U.S.C. § 301(b) ("The commencement of a voluntary case under a chapter of this title constitutes an order for relief under such chapter.").
158. 11 U.S.C. § 502(f); 11 U.S.C. § 303 (concerning involuntary cases).
159. *See In re Commonwealth Sprinkler Co., Inc.*, 295 B.R. 852, 855 (Bankr. E.D. Va. 2003) (disallowing attorney's fees since they were "related to defending against the involuntary petition and the trustee's motion, . . . [and] were not in the ordinary course of debtor's business."); *In re Baab Steel, Inc.*, 495 B.R. 530, 534 (D. Col. 2013) (denying attorney's fees during gap period because not in the ordinary course of business); *In re Manufacturer's Supply Co.*, 132 B.R. 127, 129 (N.D. Ohio 1991) (claim for funds loaned to debtor to pay counsel fees during gap period not incurred in the ordinary course of business); *In re Hanson Indus, Inc.*, 90 B.R. 405, 416 (Bankr. D. Minn. 1988) (attorneys' fees incurred in gap period only entitled to priority for services relating to general corporate advice, not for defending involuntary petition). *But see* Amtel, Inc. v. Sun Spec Indus., Inc. (*In re Sun Spec. Indus., Inc.*), 3 B.R. 703, 706 (Bankr. S.D.N.Y. 1980) (commenting, in dicta, that gap period attorneys' fees may be entitled to priority).
160. 11 U.S.C. § 104; Revision of Certain Dollar Amounts in the Bankruptcy Code Prescribed Under Section 104(a) of the Code, 84 Fed. Reg. 3,488, 3,488 (Feb. 12, 2019). Adjustment occurs every three years.

The Bankruptcy Code provides that the applicable period for the fourth priority claim is the time beginning 180 days before the earlier of either the date the debtor ceased doing business or the debtor's bankruptcy petition date. The Bankruptcy Code further provides that in order to qualify for priority, the wage must have been "earned" by the individual claimant.

Because Section 507(a)(4) covers claims for unused vacation time earned during the 180-day period, issues can arise concerning when the claim is earned, especially if an individual's employment contract provides that vacation time vests at an interval that does not lend itself to easy proration. Some courts have devised a pro rata accrual approach for calculating vacation benefits that accrue in this manner.[161]

Section 507(a)(4) also covers claims for severance benefits that are earned during the 180-day period. Often, an employer will have a severance policy or an employment contract that provides for specific severance rights. The intricacies of such policies or agreements will affect the treatment of the claim in bankruptcy. As with wages and bonuses, courts appear to focus on the time that the benefit is actually earned (as opposed to the time the benefit is payable) in determining the claimant's eligibility for priority under Section 507(a)(4).[162]

Similarly, claims under the Worker Adjustment and Retraining Notification Act (WARN Act) may be compensable as a priority claim for severance benefits under Section 507(a)(4).[163] A priority claim for these wages can sometimes have a serious impact on a debtor's ability to reorganize as certain courts have held that payment of damages under the WARN Act are eligible for priority if termination occurs during the

161. *See, e.g.*, Northwest Eng'g. Co. v. United Steelworkers, 863 F.2d 1313, 1316–17 (7th Cir. 1988) (vacation pay deemed earned continuously throughout the year regardless of vesting schedule); *accord In re Ground Round, Inc.*, 316 B.R. 423, 428 (Bankr. D. Mass. 2004); Roeder v. United Steelworkers (*In re Old Electralloy Corp.*), 167 B.R. 786, 798 (Bankr. W.D. Pa. 1994); *In re Crouthamel Potato Chip Co.*, 52 B.R. 960 (E.D. Pa. 1985), *rev'd. on other grounds*, 786 F.2d 141 (3d Cir. 1986).

162. *Compare* Matson v. Alarcon (*In re Landamerica Fin. Group, Inc.*), 651 F.3d 404, 409 (4th Cir. 2011) (an individual "earns" a priority claim for severance pay, within the meaning of 507(a)(4), on the date the individual becomes entitled to receive such compensation subject to satisfaction of any contingencies in the applicable severance plan) *with In re Roth Am., Inc.*, 975 F.2d 949, 958 (3d Cir. 1992) (severance benefits earned pro rata over the period of the employee's employment and priority claim available for that portion of the benefits deemed to have accrued during the 180-day period) and *In re Golden Distribs. Inc.*, Ltd., 134 B.R. 760, 763–64 (Bankr. S.D.N.Y. 1991) *aff'd.* 152 B.R. 35 (S.D.N.Y. 1992) (full amount of severance pay for employees discharged after bankruptcy entitled to administrative priority).

163. *See* 29 U.S.C. §§ 2101–09.

180-day period prior to the bankruptcy.[164] An employer who violates the WARN Act's provisions by ordering a plant closing or mass layoff without providing appropriate notice is liable to each aggrieved employee for an amount including back pay and benefits for the period of violation, up to sixty days.[165]

5. Fifth Priority—507(a)(5)—Contributions to Employee Benefit Plans

Section 507(a)(5) provides a fifth priority to allowed unsecured claims for contributions to an employee benefit plan for services rendered within the same 180-day period.[166] The amount of allowed fifth priority claims are subject to a statutory cap for each employee benefit plan. The limit is a function of the number of the debtor's employees covered by the plan multiplied by $13,650, then reduced by (a) the amount of wage priority claims paid to all employees under Section 507(a)(4), plus (b) the amount paid on behalf of the employees to any other employee benefit plan.[167] Consequently, the amount of fourth priority claims under Section 507(a)(4) must be determined before the amount of fifth priority claims under Section 507(a)(5) can be calculated.

Although the term "employee benefit plan" is not defined in the Bankruptcy Code, legislative history indicates that pension plans, health insurance plans, and life insurance plans are intended to be covered by the provision.[168] While one court found that 401(k) plans are also covered, courts typically hold that employee contributions receive priority treatment while employer contributions may be dischargeable.[169] However, the specific plan's details must be analyzed to determine how the employer contributions

164. *See* Henderson v. Powermate Holding Corp. (*In re Powermate Holding Corp.*), 394 B.R. 765, 778 (Bankr. D. Del. 2008); Int'l Board of Teamsters v. Kitty Hawk Int'l, Inc. (*In re Kitty Hawk Int'l, Inc.*), 255 B.R. 428, 438 (Bankr. N.D. Tex. 2000).
165. *See* 29 U.S.C. § 2104.
166. *See* Falcon Creditor Trust v. Blue Cross Blue Shield (*In re Falcon Prods., Inc.*), 372 B.R. 474, 482–83 (Bankr. E.D. Mo. 2007).
167. 11 U.S.C.A. § 507(a)(5)(B)(ii).
168. *See* H.R. Rep. No. 595 (1977).
169. *See, e.g., In re C & S Cartage & Leasing Co.*, 204 B.R. 565, 565–66 (Bankr. D. Neb. 1996) (considering 401(k) plans covered); *In re Hemmeter*, 242 F.3d 1186 (9th Cir. 2001) (finding unpaid employer contributions to be a technical trust and thus nondischargeable); *In re Dombek*, No. 11-40894, 2012 WL 4959442, at *1 (Bankr. N.D. Ill. Oct. 16, 2012) (The Dept. of Labor argued that bankruptcy does not terminate fiduciary duty and liability, and an employer not funding a 401(k) is not dischargeable and is an ERISA violation.). *But see* ITPE Pension Fund v. Hall, 334 F.3d 1011, 1013 (11th Cir. 2003) ("[T]he proper rule, developed by case law, is that employer's contributions are not assets of fund unless the agreement between the fund and the employer specifically and clearly declares otherwise.")

are treated. The applicable definitions of employee benefit plans contained within the Employee Retirement Income Security Act of 1974 (ERISA) may not necessarily be used to define the term.[170] However, the U.S. Supreme Court found that claims arising from workers' compensation programs are not eligible for priority treatment since they are related to the employer's liability rather than employees' wages.[171] Claims arising from pension plans present unique issues, the outcome of which often depends upon the characteristics of the underlying plan and also whether or not the plan is a "defined benefit" or "defined contribution" plan. The term "contributions" is also undefined in the Bankruptcy Code but is commonly understood to cover payments to be made to employees under a debtor's self-insured program and payments owed to employees by virtue of a contract between the debtor and a third-party benefits provider.[172]

The Bankruptcy Code and decisional law provide little guidance on when services are rendered in order to qualify for priority under this section. Decisions concerning retired and terminated employees indicate conflicting results.[173]

6. *Sixth Priority—507(a)(6)—Grain Producers and U.S. Fishermen*

Section 507(a)(6) provides a sixth priority to grain producers and fishermen. The provision initially states that it is applicable to "persons" engaged in the production of grain or as fishermen; and "persons" is a defined term under the Bankruptcy Code which includes individuals, partnerships, and corporations.[174] But then the provision states that this priority claim is limited to $6,725 "for each such individual."[175] It is thus unclear whether Section 507(a)(6) was intended to cover only natural persons or entities as well.

With respect to Section 507(a)(6)(A), Section 557 of the Bankruptcy Code covers a variety of issues specific to cases involving a "grain storage facility," including definitions of "grain storage facility" and "grain"

170. *See* Howard Delivery Serv., Inc. v. Zurich Am. Ins. Co., 547 U.S. 651, 661–62 (2006).

171. *Id.* at 668, 653.

172. *See* 5 Collier on Bankruptcy, ¶ 507.07[4][a].

173. *Compare* Consolidated Freightways, Inc. v. Aetna, Inc. (*In re Consolidated Freightways, Inc.*), 564 F.3d 1161, 1167–68 (9th Cir. 2009) (holding claim of retired employees not entitled to priority because no services provided during the 180-day period) *with* Ivey v. Great-West Life & Annuity Co. (*In re J.G. Furniture Group, Inc.*), 405 F.3d 191, 193 (4th Cir. 2005) (holding that claims of employees terminated prior to the 180-day period still entitled to priority because the services rendered by the benefit plan were rendered within the 180-day period).

174. *See* 11 U.S.C. § 101(41).

175. 11 U.S.C. § 507(a)(6); Revision of Certain Dollar Amounts in the Bankruptcy Code Prescribed Under Section 104(a) of the Code, 84 Fed. Reg. at 3,488.

itself.[176] A claim under this section will not be entitled to priority unless it is a claim for "grain or the proceeds of grain." Courts have held that this means that a holder of a claim for money owed following the sale of grain will not be entitled to priority.[177]

Section 507(a)(6)(B) covers claims of fishermen who sold "fish or fish produce" to a "fish produce storage or processing facility." The Bankruptcy Code does not define the terms used in this subpart, so courts must examine the facts supporting particular claims asserted in this category to make a determination regarding priority treatment.[178]

7. Seventh Priority—507(a)(7)—Consumer Deposits

A seventh priority is available to holders of allowed unsecured claims, up to $3,025 per individual, for prepetition deposits, for undelivered purchases, leases or rentals of property, or the sales of services for personal, family, or household use.[179] One court held that the purpose of this provision is to protect consumers who make payment, whether partial or full, with the expectation that the recipient of funds will hold those funds until the goods or services are provided, and that the funds remain the consumers' property until goods and services are provided.[180] Legislative history states that "the purpose of this priority is to protect consumers who leave a deposit to lay merchandise away, and who does [sic] not receive the merchandise from the retailer who files a petition."[181]

While some divergent results exist, cases have generally construed this priority broadly, applying it, for example, to advance payments in

---

176. *See* 11 U.S.C. § 557.

177. *See In re Mickelson*, 205 B.R. 190, 195-96 (D.N.D. 1996); *In re Esbon Grain Co.*, 55 B.R. 308, 314 (Bankr. D. Kan. 1985), *aff'd.*, 72 B.R. 528 (D. Kan. 1987).

178. *See In re Voliva*, 2012 WL 2871798 *__ (Bankr. E.D.N.C. July 12, 2012) (finding that a debtor whose business practices included separating fish based on quality, then packing, icing and labeling fish for transport was operating a fish processing facility, but a debtor who merely transported fish that had already been packed on ice in styrofoam crates by another company was not operating a fish produce storage or processing facility.)

179. 11 U.S.C. § 507(a)(7); Revision of Certain Dollar Amounts in the Bankruptcy Code Prescribed Under Section 104(a) of the Code, 84 Fed. Reg. at 3,488.

180. *In re Palmas del Mar Country Club, Inc.*, 443 B.R. 569, 574–75 (Bankr. D.P.R. 2010).

181. *Id.* (citing H.R. Rep. No. 95-595, at 188 (1977)).

full for goods and services,[182] partial receipt of goods or services,[183] and gift certificates.[184]

8. *Eighth Priority—507(a)(8)—Taxes and Customs Duties*

Section 507(a)(8) provides an eighth priority to a governmental unit for an unsecured claim arising from a prepetition tax. The term "governmental unit" is broadly defined in the Bankruptcy Code to include federal, state, and local governments and agencies.[185] Six varieties of prepetition tax claims are categorized by Section 507(a)(8) plus related penalties specified in a seventh category. Income and gross receipts taxes, property taxes, trust fund taxes, employment taxes, excise taxes, and customs duties are each entitled to priority under this section.[186] The seventh category covers penalties related to the foregoing categories provided it is "in compensation for actual pecuniary loss."[187] Finally, the Code provides an extension of any applicable time periods within Section 507(a)(8) if the debtor appeals any collection action for a tax for the period of such appeal plus ninety days, or if a taxing authority is prohibited from collecting a tax due to a stay from a prior bankruptcy case of the debtor or confirmed plan for the duration of such prior stay or confirmed plan, plus ninety days.

The numerous issues attendant to whether or not a particular tax qualifies under one of the subcategories of Section 507(a)(8) are beyond the scope of this handbook. However, general consideration should be given to whether a claim relates to an actual tax. While the Bankruptcy Code does not define the term "tax," some cases do address the issue. The U.S. Supreme Court, in *United States v. Reorganized CF&I Fabricators of Utah, Inc.*, stated "[A] tax is a pecuniary burden laid upon individuals or property for the purpose of supporting the Government."[188] A tax is different from a penalty because the "tax is an enforced contribution to

---

182. *See, e.g.*, Salazar v. McDonald (*In re Salazar*), 430 F.3d 992, 997 (9th Cir. 2005).
183. *See, e.g., In re Tart's T.V., Furniture & Appliance Co.*, 165 B.R. 171 (Bankr. E.D.N.C. 1994).
184. *See, e.g., In re WW Warehouse, Inc.*, 313 B.R. 588, 594-95 (Bankr. D. Del. 2004). *But see In re City Sports, Inc.*, 554 B.R. 329, 338 (Bankr. D. Del. 2016) (holding that § 507(a)(7) did not include gift cards since "the transaction is complete once those instruments are issued."); *In re Util. Craft, Inc.*, No. 06-10816, 2008 WL 5429667, at *4 (Bankr. M.D.N.C. Dec. 29, 2008) (holding that § 507(a)(7) did not include store credit).
185. *See* 11 U.S.C. § 101(27).
186. *See* 11 U.S.C. § 507(a)(8)(A) – (F).
187. *See* 11 U.S.C. § 507(a)(8)(G).
188. United States v. Reorganized CF&I Fabricators of Utah, Inc., 518 U.S. 213, 224 (1996).

provide for the support of government; a penalty ... is an exaction imposed by statute as punishment for an unlawful act."[189]

9. Ninth Priority—507(a)(9)—Commitments to Federal Depository Regulatory Agencies

Section 507(a)(9) provides a ninth priority to allowed unsecured claims for any capital maintenance commitment to a "Federal depository institution regulatory agency."[190] The Bankruptcy Code defines "Federal depository institutions regulatory agency" broadly to include federal banking agencies, including those that are acting as a receiver or conservator of a failed bank.[191]

10. Tenth Priority—507(a)(10)—Claims Arising from DUI/DWI

A tenth priority is granted to allowed unsecured claims for death or personal injury arising from the operation of a motor vehicle or vessel while intoxicated.[192] One case interpreting this provision construed it broadly, holding that a claim against an intoxicated passenger was eligible for priority under this section because the passenger gave instructions to operate the vehicle which led to injury.[193]

C. The 507(b) "Super Priority" and Related Issues

Section 507(b) provides that if a secured creditor is granted "adequate protection" as defined in Section 361 of the Bankruptcy Code and, if after receiving such adequate protection the creditor suffers a diminution in its secured claim, it is entitled to an administrative expense under 507(a)(2) arising from either: (i) the automatic stay against the creditor's efforts under Section 362,[194] (ii) the use, sale, or lease of the creditor's collateral pursuant to Section 363,[195] or (iii) the granting of a lien to the creditor

---

189. *Id.*
190. 11 U.S.C. § 507(a)(9).
191. *See* 11 U.S.C. § 101(21B).
192. 11 U.S.C. § 507(a)(10).
193. *In re Loader*, 406 B.R. 72, 78–79 (Bankr. D. Idaho 2009).
194. *See, e.g.*, Grundy Nat'l Bank v. Rife, 876 F.2d 361, 363–64 (4th Cir. 1989).
195. *See, e.g.*, Bank of N.Y. Trust Co. N.A. v. Pac. Lumber Co. (*In re Scopac*), 624 F.3d 274, 284 (5th Cir. 2010); *In re DeSardi*, 340 B.R. 790, 801 (Bankr. S.D. Tex. 2006); *In re Mendez*, 259 B.R. 754, 756 (Bankr. M.D. Fla. 2001) (awarding superpriority for value of vehicle debtor totaled).

under Section 364(d).[196] The claim is given priority over all other holders of allowed Section 507(a)(2) claims.

Although claims arising under this section are commonly referred to as "super priority" claims, these claims are still junior in right of payment to claims arising under Section 507(a)(1). Furthermore, other sections in the Bankruptcy Code may entitle holders of claims to a senior right to payment. For example, Section 364(c)(1) of the Bankruptcy Code provides that under certain circumstances, the court may authorize the debtor to obtain credit entitled to repayment with a priority that is senior in right of payment to all claims arising under Sections 503(b) and 507(a). Finally, cases that convert from Chapter 11 to Chapter 7 may also result in the subordination of preconversion administrative expenses and priority claims to the rights to payment of postconversion administrative expenses.[197]

D. 507(c) Equal Priority for Claims Based on Erroneous Tax Refunds

Section 507(c) establishes that a governmental unit that erroneously overpays a taxpayer shall have an eighth priority claim for the repayment of the refund vis-à-vis Section 507(a)(8). This section has the goal of returning the debtor and the governmental unit to the same position that they were in prior to payment of the erroneous refund.

196. However, the creditor must prove a loss, and debtor's actions may create adequate protection. *See, e.g.*, *In re Ralar Distribs., Inc.*, 166 B.R. 3 (Bankr. D. Mass 1994) *decision aff'd.* 182 B.R. 81 (D. Mass. 1995) *judgment aff'd.* 69 F.3d 1200 (1st Cir. 1995) (denying superpriority status where selling inventory resulted in greater proceeds to creditor than would have been achieved through a liquidation sale).

197. *See, e.g.*, Citibank v. Transamerica Commercial Fin. Corp. (*In re Runner Marine*, Inc.), 134 B.R. 4, 7 (B.A.P. 9th Cir. 1991); *In re Flynn's Constr., Inc.*, 166 B.R. 1, 3 (Bankr. D. Me. 1994).

E. 507(d): Subrogation

Under Section 507(d), a claim entitled to priority under the sections listed therein loses such priority in the hands of a subrogee.[198] It is important to distinguish subrogees from assignees. In this context, a subrogee is either liable on the original obligation or had a duty to the original claim holder to pay the obligation in question. On the other hand, an assignee merely succeeds in the claim from the original holder. Assignees are not mentioned in Section 507(d) and, therefore, appear to be entitled to assert the same priority as the original holder of the claim.[199]

198. *See, e.g.*, *In re Mid-American Travel Serv., Inc.*, 145 B.R. 969, 972–73 (Bankr. E.D. Ark. 1992) (credit card company that was found to be subrogee of cardholders' claims when it reversed charges made by debtor on customers' account was not entitled to customers' 507(a)(7) priority claims).

199. *See In re Missionary Baptist Found. of Am., Inc.*, 667 F.2d 1244, 1246–47 (5th Cir. 1982) (unless it is a subrogee, entity that holds a claim is entitled to assert the priority status the claim would receive if it was asserted by the original holder).

6

Administrative Expenses

A. Introduction

Section 503 of the Bankruptcy Code governs what claims may be allowed and paid as "administrative expenses" of the bankruptcy estate. With a few notable exceptions, administrative expenses are those incurred by the estate *after* the filing of a bankruptcy petition. Administrative expenses are accorded priority in payment above most prepetition claims[200] and, in Chapter 11 cases, typically must be paid in full on or before the effective date of any confirmed plan.[201]

"The policy underlying administrative expense priority is that 'the estate as a whole is benefited if general creditors subordinate their pre-bankruptcy claims in order to secure goods and services *necessary* to an orderly and economical administration of the estate after the petition is filed.'"[202] Because of this scrutiny into necessity, this means that a creditor could be owed money from the debtor as a result of a postpetition transaction, yet not get paid if the court does not regard the transaction as necessary.

200. 11 U.S.C. § 507(a)(2).

201. 11 U.S.C. § 1129(a)(9)(A) provides: "Except to the extent that the holder of a particular claim has agreed to a different treatment of such claim, the plan provides that—with respect to a claim of a kind specified in Section 507(a)(2) … on the effective date of the plan, the holder of such claim will receive on account of such claim cash equal to the allowed amount of such claim."

202. Christian Life Center Litig. Defense Comm. v. Silva (*In re Christian Life Center*), 821 F.2d 1370, 1373 (9th Cir. 1987) (quoting Yermakov v. Fitzsimmons (*In re Yermakov*), 718 F.2d 1465, 1470 (9th Cir. 1983)).

Generally speaking, an expense qualifies as an administrative expense under Section 503(b)(1) if it satisfies a two-part test.[203] First, the expense must arise from a transaction with the bankruptcy estate.[204] Second, the expense must result in a direct and substantial benefit to the estate.[205] The burden of demonstrating that an expense is entitled to administrative priority belongs to the party "asserting such priority."[206]

The provisions of Section 503(b) are strictly construed because of the overarching goal to keep administrative expenses at a minimum, thereby preserving the estate for the benefit of all creditors.[207]

B. Types of Administrative Expenses

Section 503(b) of the Bankruptcy Code provides a nonexclusive list of the types of claims that, after notice and a hearing, shall be allowed as administrative expenses, namely,

(1) the actual, necessary costs and expenses of preserving the estate;[208]

---

203. *In re Mid-Am. Waste Sys., Inc.*, 228 B.R. 816, 821 (Bankr. D. Del. 1999); *In re Women First Healthcare, Inc.*, 332 B.R. 115, 121 (Bankr. D. Del. 2005); *In re New Century TRS Holdings, Inc.*, 446 B.R. 656, 661 (Bankr. D. Del. 2011).

204. *In re Mid-Am. Waste Sys., Inc.*, 228 B.R. at 821; *In re Women First Healthcare, Inc.*, 332 B.R. at 121; *In re New Century TRS Holdings, Inc.*, 446 B.R. at 662. *See also* Hopkins v. Idaho State Univ. Credit Union (*In re Herter*), 464 B.R. 22, 32 (Bankr. D. Idaho 2011) (creditor not entitled to allowance of an administrative expense where there is no evidence of a transaction with the Chapter 7 trustee or the estate); *In re Bender Shipbuilding & Repair, Co., Inc.*, 2011 WL 671904 (Bankr. S.D. Ala. Feb. 17, 2011) (a claim is not entitled to administrative expense priority when it arises from prepetition injuries, regardless of whether payment was to be made postpetition).

205. *In re Mid-Am. Waste Sys., Inc.*, 228 B.R. at 821; *In re Women First Healthcare, Inc.*, 332 B.R. at 121. *See also In re Herter*, 464 B.R. at 32 (Bankr. D. Idaho 2011) (creditor not entitled to allowance of an administrative expense when preservation of an asset confers only an incidental benefit to the bankruptcy estate); *In re Eckberg*, 446 B.R. 909, 916–17 (Bankr. C.D. Ill. 2011) (creditor is not entitled to an administrative expense when there is no quantifiable benefit to the estate).

206. *In re Marcal Paper Mills, Inc.*, 650 F.3d 311, 315 (3d Cir. 2011) (citing *In re O'Brien Envtl. Energy, Inc.*, 181 F.3d 527, 533 (3d Cir.1999)). *See also In re Glebe, Inc.*, 455 B.R. 111 (Bankr. W.D. Va. 2011) (creditors must provide supporting evidence demonstrating that costs and expenses provided an actual benefit to the estate and that such costs and expenses were necessary to preserve the value of the estate in order to be entitled to an administrative expense under Section 503(b)(1)(A)(i)); *In re Illuminations, Inc.*, 2011 WL 3503099 (Bankr. D. Neb. 2011, Aug. 10, 2011) (debtor in Chapter 7 case does not have standing to move for allowance of an administrative expense claim on behalf of a nondebtor landlord).

207. *See* Zurich American Insurance Co. v. Lexington Coal Co., LLC (*In re HNRC Dissolution Co.*), 371 B.R. 210, 224 (E.D. Ky. 2007) (quoting *In re Patch Graphics*, 58 B.R. 743, 745 (Bankr. W.D. Wi. 1986)); *In re Collins & Aikman Corp.*, 384 B.R. 751, 759 (Bankr. E.D. Mich. 2008).

208. 11 U.S.C. § 503(b)(1).

(2) professional compensation and reimbursement awarded under Section 330(a) of the Bankruptcy Code;[209]
(3) the actual, necessary expenses certain participants incurred in a bankruptcy proceeding;[210]
(4) reasonable compensation for certain professional services rendered by attorneys and accountants;[211]
(5) reasonable compensation for services rendered by an indenture trustee in making a substantial contribution in a case under Chapter 9 or 11;[212]
(6) the fees and mileage payable under Chapter 119 of title 28;[213]
(7) the claim of a landlord when a nonresidential real property lease is first assumed, then rejected;[214]
(8) the actual, necessary costs and expenses of closing a healthcare business which are incurred by a trustee or by various governmental agencies;[215] and
(9) the value of any goods received by the debtor within twenty days before the date of commencement of a case under the Bankruptcy Code in which the goods have been sold to the debtor in the ordinary course of such debtor's business.[216]

Each of the referenced categories is summarized below.

---

209. 11 U.S.C. § 503(b)(2).
210. 11 U.S.C. § 503(b)(3).
211. 11 U.S.C. § 503(b)(4).
212. 11 U.S.C. § 503(b)(5).
213. 11 U.S.C. § 503(b)(6).
214. 11 U.S.C. § 503(b)(7). *See In re PMC Marketing Corp.*, 447 B.R. 71 (Bankr. D.P.R. 2011) (landlord entitled to an administrative expense for both prepetition and postpetition arrears upon the assumption of a nonresidential lease agreement, regardless of whether such agreement is subsequently rejected prior to confirmation).
215. 11 U.S.C. § 503(b)(8).
216. 11 U.S.C. § 503(b)(9).

1. "Actual, Necessary" Expenses – Section 503(b)(1)

Administrative expenses under Section 503(b)(1)(A) include the "actual, necessary costs and expenses of preserving the estate."[217]

"[W]ages, salaries, and commissions for services rendered after the commencement of the case" are a category of "actual, necessary costs and expenses of preserving the estate."[218] Despite this broad grant of administrative priority for wages, salaries, and commissions, there are some limitations on payments of postpetition bonuses or severance payments, as discussed below. In addition, postpetition wages owed pursuant to a judicial proceeding, such as a determination of a WARN Act violation, are awarded administrative priority.[219] There is a conflict in the courts as to whether a judicial award entered postpetition for *prepetition* wages is an administrative expense entitled to priority, or is a general unsecured claim.[220]

In addition, all taxes incurred postpetition by the estate, secured or unsecured, including property taxes, as well as fines or penalties related to such taxes, are also awarded administrative priority under this category.[221] Unlike other entities seeking the allowance and payment of an administrative expense, a governmental unit is not required to file a request for payment of an administrative expense.[222]

2. Compensation for Estate Professionals – Section 503(b)(2)

Under Section 327 of the Bankruptcy Code, the trustee is authorized, with court approval, to employ certain named professionals including "attorneys,

---

217. *In re UTEX Communic'ns Corp.*, 457 B.R. 549, 569 (Bankr. W.D. Tex 2011) (incumbent local exchange carrier was entitled to an administrative expense under Section 503(b)(1)(A) for debtor's continued use of creditor's services postpetition, but was not entitled to immediate payment); *see also In re Resource Technology Corp.*, 662 F.3d 472 (7th Cir. 2011) (claimant was not entitled to an administrative expense under the *Reading* exception, which provides an exception to the requirements of administrative expense priority under Section 503(b)(1)(A), because the debtor tortfeasor was "not operating in any meaningful sense" at the time the tort occurred); *In re Illuminations, Inc.*, 2011 WL 3503099 (Bankr. D. Neb. Aug. 10, 2011) (landlord was not entitled to an administrative expense because it failed to demonstrate that the amounts sought were equal to the actual and necessary costs and expenses for preservation of the estate).
218. 11 U.S.C. § 503(b)(1)(A)(i).
219. 11 U.S.C. § 503(b)(1)(A)(ii).
220. *See, e.g.*, First Magnus Financial Corp., 390 B.R. 667 (Bankr. D. AZ. 2008), Henderson v. Powermate Holding Corp. (*In re Powermate Holding Corp.*), 394 B.R. 765 (Bankr. D. Del. 2008), *In re Phila. Newspapers, LLC*, 433 B.R. 164 (Bankr. E.D. Pa. 2010).
221. 11 U.S.C. § 503(b)(1)(B).
222. 11 U.S.C. § 503(b)(1)(D).

accountants, auctioneers, or other professional persons."[223] Compensation and reimbursement awarded to a trustee or other professional whose employment was approved under Section 327 of the Bankruptcy Code is an administrative expense.[224] In general, bankruptcy courts are reluctant to approve payment to professionals for any services rendered before the court approves their retention on behalf of the estate.[225]

Estate professionals must file detailed records of their services, and all parties are given the opportunity to object after a noticed hearing.[226] Compensation will be awarded based on the reasonable value of services provided, which may or may not be the amount they actually billed the estate.[227] In addition, the bankruptcy court may reduce the award of compensation and require the return of any excess paid to the professional.[228]

3. *Reimbursement to Various Entities, Creditors and Their Attorneys, or Accountants – Section 503(b)(3), (4)*

Creditors will be awarded administrative expense priority for "actual" and "necessary" expenses in connection with: (i) filing an involuntary petition against the debtor, (ii) recovering for the benefit of the estate, after obtaining court approval, property transferred or concealed by the debtor, or (iii) providing assistance with the prosecution of a criminal offense related to the case or to the business or property of the debtor.[229]

---

223. 11 U.S.C. § 327(a).
224. *See In re Copeland*, 2011 WL 2460852 (Bankr. D.S.C. June 16, 2011) (attorneys' fees and expenses incurred in connection with a class action settlement were not entitled to treatment as an administrative expense under Section 503(b)(1) or (2) because the attorney was not retained by the Chapter 7 trustee); *see also* Brill v. Brill Media Co., LLC, 2011 WL 1113548 *2 (S.D. Ind. Mar. 24, 2011) (compensation and reimbursement under Section 503(b)(2) requires employment pursuant to Section 327(a)).
225. *See In re Garden Ridge Corp.*, 326 B.R. 278, 280–81 (Bankr. D. Del. 2005) ("The purpose of the rule requiring prior court authorization of a professional's appointment is to eliminate volunteerism and thus aid the court in controlling estate administrative expenses."); *see also* Silverio v. McHale (*In re Luxury Ventures, LLC*), 2011 WL 2746728 (M.D. Fla. July 14, 2011) (attorneys were not entitled to an administrative expense for postconfirmation fees because attorneys failed to obtain necessary approval of the bankruptcy court and the liquidating trustee).
226. 11 U.S.C. § 330; Fed. R. Bankr. P. 2016.
227. 11 U.S.C. § 330(a)(1)(A), (2).
228. 11 U.S.C. § 330(a)(2), (5).
229. 11 U.S.C. § 503(b)(3)(A), (B), (C).

Custodians, that is, receivers and assignees for the benefit of creditors, who are superseded by a trustee are entitled to actual and necessary expenses, including compensation.[230]

Members of an official committee incurred in performance of his or her duties will be awarded reimbursement of their actual and necessary expenses as an administrative expense.[231]

Finally, expenses may be allowed for a creditor, an indenture trustee, an equity security holder, unofficial committees, and perhaps other entities, who provide a "substantial contribution" in a case under Chapter 9 or 11.[232] Such expenses can even be allowed for prepetition expenses that provide a substantial contribution to the estate.[233] The issue of whether a creditor has made a substantial contribution is a question of fact, with the moving party bearing the burden of proof.[234] Most courts narrowly construe what constitutes a substantial contribution and most have taken the position that substantial contribution claims, like other Section 503(b) claims, should be strictly construed.[235] The principal test is that there must be "actual and demonstrable benefit" to the estate and creditors, and a creditor seeking such a claim must present compelling evidence to the court of such benefit.[236] Actions that were duplicative of the debtor's own actions will not meet this criterion. If tangible, demonstrable benefits were provided to

---

230. 11 U.S.C. § 503(b)(3)(E).
231. 11 U.S.C. § 503(b)(3)(F).
232. 11 U.S.C. § 503(b)(3)(D). *See In re S & Y Enterprises, LLC,* 480 B.R. 452, 455–56 (Bankr. E.D.N.Y. 2012) (holding that an unsuccessful bidder had standing to seek an administrative expense for substantial contribution, but finding the entity was unable to meet the requisite standard); *but see In re Mountain Creek Resort, Inc.*, 616 B.R. 45, 55 (Bankr. D. N.J. 2020) (declining to expand the categories of entities entitled to seek an administrative expense for substantial contribution). Note the distinction: for members of an official committee appointed by the court pursuant to Section 1102 of the Bankruptcy Code, all expenses incurred in the performance of their duties are reimbursable, but for members of unofficial committees, or creditors or equity holders not acting as part of an official committee, a determination must be made that there was a "substantial contribution" to the estate before expenses constitute an administrative claim. 11 U.S.C. § 503(b)(3)(D).
233. Lebron v. Mechem Fin. Inc., 27 F.3d 937, 944 (3d Cir. 1994).
234. *In re Jack Winter Apparel, Inc.*, 119 B.R. 629, 632 (Bankr. E.D. Wis. 1990) ("an applicant must meet its burden of persuading the court by a preponderance of the evidence that it rendered services that made a substantial contribution to the Chapter 11 reorganization.").
235. *In re S & Y Enterprises, LLC*, 480 B.R. 452, 459 (Bankr. E.D.N.Y. 2012) ("Payment from the debtor's estate of a creditor's or other entity's counsel fees and expenses based on a substantial contribution in the bankruptcy case should be the exception, not the rule, because any allowed administrative expense diminishes the assets that are available for the debtor's plan of reorganization."); *see also In re KiOR, Inc.*, 567 B.R. 451, 458–59 (D. Del. 2017).
236. Haskins v. United States (*In re Lister*), 846 F.2d 55, 57 (10th Cir. 1988).

the bankruptcy estate, actions primarily taken to benefit a creditor's own self-interest may establish a claim for substantial contribution, even if the self-interested creditor would have undertaken the same actions even without anticipating possible reimbursement by the estate.[237] Indenture trustees are also eligible for compensation for their services that provide a substantial contribution in a Chapter 9 or 11 case,[238] but duties that are routine or are of no quantitative value to the estate are not compensable.[239]

Attorneys or accountants of a creditor or other entity noted above who is entitled to reimbursement can also receive administrative expense priority for their services if such services provided a benefit to the estate.[240]

4. Postpetition Rent and Rejection Lease Payments – Section 503(b)(1), (7)

Postpetition rent obligations are considered an actual and necessary cost of preserving the estate and afforded administrative expense status to the extent they provide value to the estate.[241] Debtors with long-term real property leases have the option of either assuming such leases, and accepting all the rent obligations as obligations of the estate, or rejecting such leases and relinquishing the property. Debtors can use the ability to reject a lease to negotiate with landlords to modify the terms of long-term leases. If a debtor assumes a lease of nonresidential real property, and subsequently elects to reject it, the landlord is entitled to priority treatment as an administrative expense under Section 503(b)(7) of the Bankruptcy Code with respect to all monetary obligations due for the period of two years after the rejection (or turnover of premises, whichever is later), with the balance of amounts due under the rejected lease to be allowed as a general unsecured claim.[242]

---

237. *In re* AmFin Financial Corp., 468 B.R. 827, 832–34 (Bankr. N.D. Ohio 2012); 4 Collier on Bankruptcy P 503.10 (16th 2020).
238. 11 U.S.C. § 503(b)(5).
239. *See In re W.T. Grant Co.*, 85 B.R. 250, 269 (Bankr. S.D.N.Y. 1988), *aff'd. in part, rev'd. in part sub nom*. United States Trust Co. v. Pardo (*In re W.T. Grant*), 119 B.R. 898 (S.D.N.Y. 1990).
240. 11 U.S.C. § 503(b)(4).
241. "Value" does not necessarily require that the estate actually use the property. *See* Kimzey v. Premium Casing Equip., LLC, No. 16-CV-01490, 2018 WL 1321971, at *5–6 (W.D. La. Mar. 14, 2018) (determining that administrative expense was warranted because debtor's "unfettered access" to leased equipment provided an intangible benefit to the estate); *see also* Matter of Whistler Energy II, LLC, 931 F.3d 432, 443–47 (5th Cir. 2019).
242. 11 U.S.C. § 503(b)(7).

5. Closing a Healthcare Business – Section 503(b)(8)

Actual and necessary costs of closing a healthcare business incurred by a trustee, federal agency, or a department or agency of a State (or political subdivision thereof) receive administrative priority under Section 503(b)(8) of the Bankruptcy Code. This grant of administrative expense priority is particularly relevant for medical records, as many states require long-term maintenance of medical records that may extend past the closing of the estate. This provision of the Bankruptcy Code provides an administrative priority for costs associated with the disposal of patient records in accordance with Section 351 of the Bankruptcy Code,[243] as well as the cost of transferring patients to another healthcare facility as an administrative expense.[244]

6. Goods Received by Debtor Within 20 Days of Petition – Section 503(b)(9)

Section 503(b)(9) of the Bankruptcy Code provides administrative expense status to certain prepetition debt. Specifically, Section 503(b)(9) grants administrative expense priority for:

> the value of any goods received by the debtor within 20 days before the date of commencement of a case under [title 11] in which the goods have been sold to the debtor in the ordinary course of such debtor's business.[245]

Despite the fact that this type of expense does not arise from a creditor doing business with the bankruptcy estate, it is given priority over unsecured claims, and shares priority with other administrative expenses.

Chapter 7 of this manual discusses in detail the procedure of how to assert an administrative expense for this type of claim, as well as issues giving rise to litigation.

C. Restrictions on Retention and Severance Payments to Insiders – Section 503(c)

Section 503(c) was also enacted as part of BAPCPA. The statute imposes a variety of restrictions on the compensation that can be paid to insiders and other employees of companies that are in bankruptcy. Most agree that the Congress added this section to cure a perceived problem that

243. 11 U.S.C. § 503(b)(8)(A).
244. 11 U.S.C. § 503(b)(8)(B).
245. 11 U.S.C. § 503(b)(9).

existed in some large pre-BAPCPA cases, namely the granting of excessive compensation packages to executives of a debtor in bankruptcy where employees lost their jobs, unsecured creditors received only pennies on the dollar, and shareholders' interests were wiped out.[246]

Section 503(c) attempts to attack excessive executive compensation practices in bankruptcy in three significant ways. First, subsection (c) (1) of Section 503 provides that there shall neither be allowed, nor paid:

> (1) a transfer made to, or an obligation incurred for the benefit of, an insider of the debtor for the purpose of inducing such person to remain with the debtor's business, absent a finding by the court based on evidence in the record that—
>
> (A) the transfer or obligation is essential to retention of the person because the individual has a bona fide job offer from another business at the same or greater rate of compensation;
>
> (B) the services provided by the person are essential to the survival of the business; and
>
> (C) either—
>
> (i) the amount of the transfer made to, or obligation incurred for the benefit of, the person is not greater than an amount equal to ten times the amount of the mean transfer or obligation of a similar kind given to nonmanagement employees for any purpose during the calendar year in which the transfer is made or the obligation is incurred; or
>
> (ii) if no such similar transfers were made to, or obligations were incurred for the benefit of, such nonmanagement

246. *See e.g., In re Nellson Nutraceutical, Inc.*, 369 B.R. 787, 800 (Bankr. D. Del. 2007) ("[I]t is widely acknowledged that the amendment was a response to perceived abuses of the bankruptcy system by 'the executives of giant companies … who lined their own pockets, but left thousands of employees and retirees out in the cold.'"); *In re Velo Holdings, Inc.*, 2012 WL 2015870 at *5 (Bankr. S.D.N.Y. June 6, 2012) ("The intent of Section 503(c) is to 'limit the scope of key employee retention plans and other programs providing incentives to management of the debtor as a means of inducing management to remain employed by the debtor.'"); *In re Journal Register Co.*, 407 B.R. 520, 535 (Bankr. S.D.N.Y. 2009) (the intent of the statute was to curtail payments to insiders without factual and circumstantial justification); *In re Mesa Air Group, Inc.*, 2010 WL 3810899 at *2 (Bankr. S.D.N.Y. Sept. 24, 2010); *In re Global Home Prods., LLC,* 369 B.R. 778, 784–85 (Bankr. D. Del. 2007).

> employees during such calendar year, the amount of the transfer or obligation is not greater than an amount equal to 25 percent of the amount of any similar transfer or obligation made to or incurred for the benefit of such insider for any purpose during the calendar year before the year in which such transfer is made or obligation is incurred[247]

Subsection (c)(1) took aim at so-called key employee retention plans that were common practice in larger, pre-BAPCPA, Chapter 11 cases. KERPs, as they came to be known, were sometimes given to executives for staying with a debtor through the bankruptcy process. Subsection (c)(1) prohibits the allowance and payment of sums to an insider for "the purpose of inducing such person to remain" with the business "absent a finding by the court based on the evidence in the record" that: (i) the payment is "essential to retention" of the individual "because the individual has a *bona fide* job offer from another business at the same or greater rate of compensation," and (ii) the services of that individual are "essential to the survival of the debtor's business."[248] Moreover, the statute also limits retention bonuses for insiders by linking them to multiple bonuses available to non-management employees.[249] Because of these onerous restrictions, insider retention programs have all but disappeared in Chapter 11 bankruptcy cases since the enactment of Section 503(c)(1).

Second, subsection (c)(2) places similar restrictions on "a severance payment." Section 503(c)(2) provides that there shall neither be allowed, nor paid:

> (2) a severance payment to an insider of the debtor, unless—
>
> (A) the payment is part of a program that is generally applicable to all full-time employees; and
>
> (B) the amount of the payment is not greater than 10 times the amount of the mean severance pay given to nonmanagement employees during the calendar year in which the payment is made.250

247. 11 U.S.C. § 503(c)(1).
248. 11 U.S.C. § 503(c)(1).
249. 11 U.S.C. § 503(c)(1).
250. 11 U.S.C. § 503(c)(2).

Thus, in order to obtain approval of an insider severance payment or plan, the debtor must establish that the proposed payment or plan is part of a program that applies to all full-time employees and the amount of the payment must be limited relative to the amounts paid to such employees. Courts strictly interpret the limitations set forth in Section 503(c)(2).[251] For example, in *In re Forum Health*,[252] the court denied a severance payment to the debtor's former chief executive officer, holding, "[d]ebtors' severance program, although generally applicable to all full-time non-union employees, is not generally applicable to all full-time employees."

Finally, subsection (c)(3) serves as a catch all by placing limitations on non-ordinary course of business transfers or obligations that are not covered by subsections (1) or (2) in that it prohibits:

> (3) other transfers or obligations that are outside the ordinary course of business and not justified by the facts and circumstances of the case, including transfers made to, or obligations incurred for the benefit of, officers, managers, or consultants hired after the date of the filing of the petition.[253]

Some courts have held that the requirement that transfers or obligations be "justified by the facts and circumstances of the case" is the same standard as the business judgment rule developed by courts to analyze a debtor's business decisions under section 363(b).[254] Other courts, however, have held that the standard for approval under section 503(c)(3) is higher than the business judgment rule, reasoning that if payments to employees outside the ordinary course were only subject to the business judgment standard,

251. *See e.g., In re Dana Corp.*, 351 B.R. 96 (Bankr. S.D.N.Y. 2006).

252. *In re Forum Health,* 427 B.R. 650, 655 (Bankr. N.D. Ohio 2010); *see also In re Robb & Stucky Ltd., LLP,* 2011 WL 3948805 (Bankr. M.D. Fla. Sept. 7, 2011).

253. *See* 11 U.S.C. § 503(c)(3).

254. *See e.g., In re Alpha Natural Resources, Inc.*, 546 B.R. 348, 356 (Bankr. E.D. Va. 2016) ("a majority of courts ... agree that the 'facts and circumstances' test of § 503(c)(3) is identical to the business judgment test under § 363(b)(1)"); *In re Patriot Coal Corp.*, 492 B.R. 518, 530–31 (Bankr. E.D. Mo. 2013) (non-ordinary course transfers "must be justified by the facts and circumstances of the case, which ordinarily means that the business judgment standard of Section 363(b) applies"); *In re Borders Group, Inc.*, 453 B.R. 459, 473 (Bankr. S.D.N.Y. 2011) ("[T]he legal standard under 363(b) is no different than section 503(c)(3)..."); *In re Velo Holdings, Inc.*, 2012 WL 2015870 at *9 (Bankr. S.D.N.Y. June 6, 2012); *In re Mesa Air Group,* 2010 WL 3810899 at *4 (Bankr. S.D.N.Y. Sept. 24, 2010); *In re Global Home Prods., LLC,* 369 B.R. 778, 783 (Bankr. D. Del. 2007); *In re Nobex Corp.,* 2006 WL 4063024 at *2 (Bankr. D. Del. Jan. 19, 2006); *In re Dana Corp.,* 358 B.R. 567, 576-77 (Bankr. S.D.N.Y. 2006).

then the "justified by the facts and circumstances of the case" language of Section 503(c)(3) would ostensibly be rendered meaningless.[255]

To date, the majority of the opinions addressing Section 503(c) deal with subsections (c)(1) and (c)(3). Courts interpreting these provisions have generally made a distinction between compensation packages that are *incentive*-based (commonly referred to as a KEIP) and KERPs, which are made "for the purpose of inducing" an employee "to remain with the debtor's business." One court described this analysis as follows:

> Congress added Section 503(c) to the Bankruptcy Code in 2005 to "eradicate the notion that executives were entitled to bonuses simply for staying with the Company through the bankruptcy process." A court "must examine a proposed [incentive plan] ... and determine whether the proposed targets are designed to motivate insiders to rise to a challenge or merely report to work." A plan that does not require affirmative action beyond that contemplated prepetition is not incentive, but is retentive and cannot be approved under the more lenient standards for incentive plans. A court must determine whether the debtor has proposed a retentive plan disguised as an incentive plan in order to circumvent the requirements of Section 503(c)(1). "Although a purported [incentive plan] may contain some retentive effect, that does not mean that the plan, overall, is retentive rather than incentivizing in nature."[256]

In light of the clear restrictions on KERPs under Section 503(c)(1), "a Court must be vigilant when analyzing the terms of a [payment or plan] and be sure the [payment or plan] is not a disguised KERP that is primarily intended to reward its participants for retaining their positions

255. *See e.g., In re Pilgrim's Pride Corp.,* 401 B.R. 229, 236–37 (Bankr. N.D. Tex. 2009) (section 503(c)(3) sets a higher standard of review and should not be equated to the business judgment rule as applied under Section 363; to do so would render 503(c)(3) redundant); GT Advanced Technologies, Inc. v. Harrington, 2015 WL 4459502 (D. N.H. July 21, 2015) (bankruptcy courts are required under Section 503(c)(3) to make their own independent determination about whether a KERP is appropriate under the "facts and circumstances" of each particular case.); *see also* United Mine Workers of America 1974 Pension Plan and Trust v. Alpha Natural Resources, Inc., 553 B.R. 556, 565 (E.D. Va. 2016) (noting that bankruptcy courts have adopted two different tests but affirming because the bankruptcy court had evaluated the proposed incentive plan under both standards).

256. *In re Patriot Coal Corporation,* 492 B.R. 518, 531 (Bankr. E.D. Mo. 2013) (internal citations omitted).

with the debtor."[257] This can be a challenging factual analysis.[258] The burden of proof rests with the plan proponent to prove by a "preponderance of the evidence that the [payment or plan] is primarily incentivizing and not primarily retentive."[259]

Arguably, if a payment or plan is found by the court to be incentive-based, Section 503(c)(1) is not triggered and the propriety of such payment or plan can be analyzed under the more lenient "justified by the facts and circumstances of the case" standard set forth in Section 503(c)(3). In determining whether a proposed payment or plan is "justified by the facts and circumstances" of the case, courts generally consider the following factors, sometimes referred to as the *Dana* factors, which were first established by Judge Burton Lifland in *In re Dana Corporation*:

— Is there a reasonable relationship between the plan proposed and the results to be obtained, *i.e.,* will the key employee stay for as long as it takes for the debtor to reorganize or market its assets, or, in the case of a performance incentive, is the plan calculated to achieve the desired performance?
— Is the cost of the plan reasonable in the context of the debtor's assets, liabilities, and earning potential?
— Is the scope of the plan fair and reasonable; does it apply to all employees; does it discriminate unfairly?
— Is the plan or proposal consistent with industry standards?
— What were the due diligence efforts of the debtor in investigating the need for a plan; analyzing which key employees need to be incentivized;

257. *In re Alpha Natural Resources, Inc.*, 546 B.R. 348 (Bankr. E.D. Va. 2016).

258. *See e.g., In re Global Home Prods., LLC,* 369 B.R. 778, 786 (Bankr. D. Del. 2007) (finding that proposed incentive plans were "primarily incentivizing and only coincidentally retentive" and noting, "The fact that ... all compensation has a retention element" did "not reduce the Court's conviction" that the debtors' primary goal in approving the incentive plans was "to create value by motivating performance."); *In re Velo Holdings, Inc.*, 472 B.R. 201, 2018 (Bankr. S.D.N.Y. 2012) (finding that a purported KEIP will not be deemed retentive simply because it contains "some retentive effect").

259. *In re Residential Capital, LLC (Residential Capital I),* 478 B.R. 154, 170 (Bankr. S.D.N.Y. 2012); *see also In re Hawker Beechcraft, Inc.*, 479 B.R. 308, 313 (Bankr. S.D.N.Y. 2012) ("[t]he proponent of the KEIP bears the burden of proving that the plan is not a retention plan governed by § 503(c)(1)").

what is available; what is generally applicable in a particular industry?

— Did the debtor receive independent counsel in performing due diligence and in creating and authorizing the incentive compensation?[260]

In developing an incentive-based plan, debtors and their professionals should use performance metrics that require key employees to stretch.[261] Such metrics (usually financial metrics such as EBITDA, cash flow, operating income, liquidity, or target-driven metrics, such as timely completing a sale or liquidation) should coincide with the company's goals and objectives, and employee compensation should be tied to meeting or exceeding such metrics. Payments usually take the form of cash bonuses, and are often expressed as a percentage of each employee's base salary. Payments are distributed throughout the corporate transition period, with the final (and typically largest) payment generally linked to either a successful reorganization, sale, or liquidation.[262]

A road map for obtaining court approval of incentive or retention plans has developed in the case law over the years since the enactment of BAPCPA. First, in order to avoid the strict limitations of Section 503(c)(1) of the Bankruptcy Code, debtors and their professionals characterize compensation plans to insiders as incentive-based plans, tying payment to the achievement of designated, challenging, benchmarks that are aligned with the goals of the bankruptcy case.[263]

---

260. *In re Dana Corporation,* 358 B.R. 567, 576–77 (Bankr. S.D.N.Y. 2006).

261. *See e.g.,* United Mine Workers of America 1974 Pension Plan and Trust v. Alpha Natural Resources, Inc., 553 B.R. 556, 560 (E.D. Va. 2016); *In re American Eagle Energy Corporation,* 2016 WL 3573952 (Bankr. D. Colo. June 23, 2016); *In re Global Home Prods.,* 369 B.R. 778, 786 (Bankr. D. Del. 2007).

262. *See* Cumberland & Ivy, *The World of Bankruptcy Compensation for Key Employees,* American Bankruptcy Institute Journal, 38-JAN Am. Bankr. Inst. J. 46 (2019).

263. *See e.g., In re Residential Capital, LLC,* 491 B.R. 73, 8687 (Bankr. S.D.N.Y. 2013) ("the Court concludes that the Debtors have established by a preponderance of the evidence that the KEIPs are properly characterized as performance-based incentive compensation plans, and are not retention plans for insiders subject to the requirements of § 503(c)(1)."); *In re Patriot Coal Corporation,* 492 B.R. 518, 534 (Bankr. E.D. Mo. 2013) ("The [KEIP] is primarily incentive and as such, the appropriate standard is that of Section 503(c)(3)."); *In re Borders Group, Inc.,* 453 B.R. 459, 471 (Bankr. S.D.N.Y. 2011) ("The Court finds that the Debtors have met their burden of establishing that the KEIP is incentivizing, thereby alleviating the need for a section 503(1)(1) analysis."); *In re Nellson Nutraceutical, Inc.,* 369 B.R. 787, 804 (Bankr. D. Del. 2007) (holding that, because bonus plan's primary motivation was not retentive, Section 503(c)(1) did not apply and business judgment standard was to be used to assess plan); *In re Global Home Prods., LLC,* 369 B.R. 778, 787 (Bankr. D. Del. 2007) (same).

Alternatively, plans that do not contemplate payments to insiders are not subject to section 503(c)(1). An insider for a corporation is generally defined in the Bankruptcy Code as a director of the debtor, an officer of the debtor, a person in control of the debtor or a relative of someone who itself is an insider. Additionally, if the debtor is a partnership, an insider is a general partner of the debtor, a relative of a general partner in, general partner of, or person in control of the debtor.[264] Although any person holding an officer or director's title is presumptively an insider, that presumption can be, and often is, rebutted.[265]

Once the court determines that a proposed plan is not subject to Section 503(c)(1) of the Bankruptcy Code, debtors need only establish that the proposed plan is "justified by the facts and circumstances of the case" to pass muster under Section 503(c)(3). Debtors must then submit evidence to show that they can satisfy the *Dana* factors.

D. Procedure for Allowance and Payment of Administrative Expenses

1. *Filing of Request*

Administrative expense claimants "may timely file a request for payment of an administrative expense, or may tardily file such request if permitted by the court for cause."[266]

An entity may file a request, via motion or application, for allowance and payment of administrative expenses not paid in the ordinary course of business. The form used by prepetition creditors for filing proof of claims should not be used for filing requests for payment of administrative expenses. However, a bankruptcy court may approve a specialized claim form to be used as a request for administrative expense, in lieu of filing a motion. Regardless of whether the form of the request is a motion,

264. *See* 11 U.S.C. § 101(31)(B).

265. *See e.g., In re Foothills Texas, Inc.,* 408 B.R. 573, 574–75 (Bankr. D. Del. 2009) ("[a] party seeking to rebut that presumption must present evidence sufficient to establish that the person holds the title of an officer in name only and, in fact, does not meet the substantive definition of the same, *i.e.,* he or she is not taking part in the management of the debtor."); *In re Global Aviation Holdings, Inc.,* 478 B.R. 142, 148 (Bankr. E.D.N.Y. 2012) (finding that director-level employees were not insiders because none of them were members of board, participated in corporate governance, attended board meetings or reported to the board); *In re Borders Group, Inc.,* 453 B.R. 459, 469 (Bankr. S.D.N.Y. 2011) (employees in retention plan were not insiders because none of them had authority to implement company policy, did not report to board of directors, and were subordinate to actual officers).

266. 11 U.S.C. § 503(a).

application, or specialized form, the claimant must show that the claim is entitled to administrative expense priority.[267]

Professionals employed by the bankruptcy estate seeking allowance or payment of compensation as administrative expenses must file an application with the court, attaching detailed records of the time expended and services provided in order to obtain approval of their fees and reimbursement of expenses.[268] The attorneys or accountants of creditors seeking administrative expenses under Section 503(b)(4) should file an application that provides similar detail for the court to evaluate the time, nature, extent, and value of services provided.[269]

2. *Bar Dates*

The deadline to file administrative expense claims is usually set by the bankruptcy court after a request is made by a debtor. The debtor is then required to provide notice to any potential administrative expense claimants. In a Chapter 11 case, the request to set an administrative expense bar date is usually set in conjunction with confirmation of a plan of reorganization. Even if no administrative expense bar date is established, claimants should file requests prior to the closing of a case. Government entities are not required to file requests for payment, and their administrative expenses are not subject to any bar date.[270]

3. *Notice and Hearing*

Absent any court-approved special procedure, approval of the allowance, or payment, of an administrative expense requires notice and a hearing.[271] The burden of proof at any such hearing is on the claimant.[272] However, if no party objects, the court may allow the claim without holding the hearing.[273]

267. *See* Toma Steel Supply Inc. v. TransAmerican Natural Gas Corp. (*In re TransAmerican Natural Gas Corp.*), 978 F.2d 1409, 1415-16 (5th Cir. 1992).
268. *See* 11 U.S.C. § 330; Fed. R. Bankr. P. 2016.
269. 11 U.S.C. § 503(b)(4).
270. 11 U.S.C. § 503(b)(1)(d).
271. 11 U.S.C. § 503(b).
272. Merry-Go-Round Enterprises v. Simon DeBartolo Group (*In re Merry-Go-Round Enterprises, Inc.*), 180 F.3d 149, 157 (4th Cir. 1999); *In re Goody's Family Clothing Inc.*, 401 B.R. 131, 133 (Bankr. D. Del. 2009); *In re HNRC Dissolution Co.*, 343 B.R. at 843.
273. 11 U.S.C. § 102(1).

4. *Special Procedures for Resolving Administrative Expenses*

Debtors often request a court to establish special procedures for asserting administrative expenses. This has become particularly common in cases with numerous Section 503(b)(9) administrative expenses. In such cases, dealing with motions and hearings on an expense-by-expense basis would be administratively inefficient and burdensome on courts and bankruptcy estate. Furthermore, debtors often want to know the extent of their 503(b)(9) obligations at the onset of a case, rather than waiting for creditors to file administrative expenses at the end of a case.

In such cases, many debtors have sought court approval for a procedure that involves setting an early bar date for administrative expenses and providing notice to all potential creditors of that bar date. The bar date notice can contain a specialized form for claimants to complete which eliminates the need for filing a motion or application. In some cases, the debtor proposes a form that allows the creditor to submit the information for any general prepetition claims as well as administrative expenses on the same document to be filed at the same time. Although not within the precise dictates of the Bankruptcy Rules, courts have generally been receptive to such efforts to minimize inefficiencies and reduce costs for the debtors.

7

Administrative Expenses Under Section 503(b)(9)

A. Overview

Section 503(b)(9) grants certain creditors administrative expense priority for:

> the value of any goods received by the debtor within 20 days before the date of commencement of a case under [title 11] in which the goods have been sold to the debtor in the ordinary course of such debtor's business.[274]

Section 503(b)(9) elevates a group of trade creditors, who typically held only general unsecured claims, ahead of priority unsecured creditors and all other general unsecured creditors. Although Section 503(b)(9) generally applies to unsecured creditors, at least one court has held that a secured creditor can be granted an administrative expense under the statute also.[275]

Section 503(b)(9) was intended to work in conjunction with Section 546(c) for sellers who have valid reclamation claims.[276] As one court stated, it "provides a supplemental remedy for those sellers who would be preferred reclamation sellers, but for a minor disqualification under section 546(a)."[277]

---

274. 11 U.S.C. § 503(b)(9).
275. Brown & Cole Stores, LLC v. Assoc. Grocers, Inc. (*In re Brown & Cole Stores, LLC*), 375 B.R. 873, 878 (B.A.P. 9th Cir. 2007).
276. Ningbo Chenglu Paper Products Mfg. Co. Ltd. v. Momenta, Inc. (*In re Momenta, Inc.*), 2012 WL 3765171 at *4 (D. N.H. Aug. 29, 2012).
277. *Id.*

B. Allowance and Payment

The text of Section 503(b)(9) does not specifically identify how or when such administrative expenses must be asserted, nor does it identify how or when such administrative expenses must be paid.

1. How Are Section 503(b)(9) Claims Asserted?

Congress elected to grant those vendors who sell a debtor goods within twenty days prior to the bankruptcy filing an administrative expense by placing these claims in Section 503 of the Bankruptcy Code, as opposed to Section 507(a) (which sets forth certain unsecured "priority" claims). Section 503(a) provides that "Any entity may timely file a request for payment of an administrative expense."[278] While the statute does not define the term "request," Bankruptcy Rule 9013 suggests that a request shall be made by written motion, unless alternative procedures are promulgated by local bankruptcy rules.[279] Accordingly, most courts require Section 503(b)(9) claimants to file a motion seeking allowance and payment.[280]

That said, in larger Chapter 11 cases, in particular, it is fairly common for courts to approve procedures orders early in the case specifically identifying how Section 503(b)(9) administrative expenses are to be asserted (i.e., by motion or, alternatively, by a modified proof of claim form) and, moreover, establishing a bar date for doing so.[281] Additionally, at least two courts have established local rules governing the timing and method for asserting administrative expenses under Section 503(b)(9).[282]

The lack of consistency among the courts about how and when such claims are asserted can lead to confusion and, in some cases has resulted in Section 503(b)(9) claimants having to seek allowance of an untimely request pursuant to Bankruptcy Rule 9006(b) and the doctrine of "excusable

---

278. 11 U.S.C. § 503(a).

279. Fed. R. Bankr. P. 9013.

280. *See, e.g.*, *In re Richfield Equities, LLC*, 556 B.R. 313 (Bankr. E.D. Mich. 2016) (holding that section 503(b) plainly requires that a motion be filed in order to assert a creditor's entitlement to an administrative expense, including an administrative expense under section 503(b)(9), because of its usage of the language "after notice and a hearing.").

281. *See, e.g.*, *In re SemCrude, L.P.*, 416 B.R. 399 (Bankr. D. Del. 2009); *In re Chrysler, LLC*, 45 B.R. 2004 (Bankr. S.D.N.Y. 2009); Lawrence v. Motors Liquidation Co. (*In re Motors Liquidation Co.*), 2010 WL 4966018 (Bank. S.D.N.Y. June 1, 2009); *In re Metaldyne Corp.*, 409 B.R. 671 (Bankr. S.D.N.Y. 2009); *In re Noble Int'l, Ltd.*, 2009 WL 1607704 (Bankr. E.D. Mich. July 22, 2009); *In re Cooper-Standard Holdings, Inc.*, et al., No. 09-12743 (PJW) (Bankr. D. Del. Oct. 26, 2009).

282. *See* D. Mass. Local Bankr. R. 3002-1; E.D. Mich. Local Bankr. R. 3003-1.

neglect."[283] In most cases, it appears that courts are willing to excuse an untimely or improperly filed administrative expense under Section 503(b)(9) absent a showing of some prejudice to the debtor.[284]

2. *When Are Section 503(b)(9) Claims Paid?*

Because they are administrative expenses, Section 503(b)(9) claims are entitled to payment in full on or before the effective date of any confirmed plan under Section 1129(a) of the Bankruptcy Code.[285] While courts agree that the effective date is the outside date for payment of administrative expenses under Section 503(b)(9),[286] vendors have, on occasion, sought immediate payment of such administrative expenses.

For example, in *In re Global Home Products, LLC*,[287] the holder of a Section 503(b)(9) claim filed a motion seeking immediate payment. In denying immediate payment on the claim, the court first noted that Section 503 "does not specify a time for payment of these expenses."[288] As such, the timing of payment is left to the discretion of the court.[289] The court indicated that one of the chief factors courts consider is "bankruptcy's goal of an orderly and equal distribution among creditors and the need to prevent a race to the debtor's assets."[290] As such, according to the court:

> Distributions to administrative creditors are generally disallowed prior to confirmation if there is a showing that the bankruptcy estate may not be able to pay all of the administrative expenses in full. Courts will also consider the particular needs of each administrative

---

283. *See, e.g., In re Dana Corp.*, 2007 WL 1577763 (Bankr. S.D.N.Y. May 30, 2007) (citing *In re Pioneer Investment Services Co. v. Brunswick Associates L.P.*, 507 U.S. 380, 382-83 (1993)); *In re DFI Proceeds, Inc.*, 2009 Bankr. LEXIS 4296 at *2 (Bank. N.D. Ind. Dec. 21, 2009).

284. *See, e.g., In re Bridgeview Aerosol, LLC*, 2010 WL 2465401 at *4 (Bankr. N.D. Ill. June 16, 2010); *In re Modern Metal Prods. Co.*, 2009 WL 2969762 at *1-2 (Bankr. N.D. Ill. Sept. 16, 2009).

285. Section 1129(a)(9)(A) provides:

> Except to the extent that the holder of a particular claim has agreed to a different treatment of such claim, the plan provides that—with respect to a claim of a kind specified in Section 507(a)(2) … on the effective date of the plan, the holder of such claim will receive on account of such claim cash equal to the allowed amount of such claim.

286. *In re Arts Dairy, LLC*, 414 B.R. 219, 221 (Bankr. N.D. Ohio 2009).

287. *In re Global Home Prods., LLC*, 2006 Bankr. LEXIS 3608 (Bankr. D. Del. Dec. 21, 2006).

288. *Id* at *3.

289. *Id.*

290. *Id.*

claimant and the length and expense of the case's administration.[291]

The court then considered various factors from the case law for determining the timing of payment of an administrative expense pursuant to Section 503(a), including: (i) the prejudice to the debtors, (ii) the hardship to the claimant, and (iii) the potential detriment to other creditors.[292] After weighing these factors, the court concluded that the prejudice to the debtors that would result from an order requiring immediate payment of the Section 503(b)(9) claim far outweighed any hardship the creditor might suffer on account of waiting until the effective date of the plan of reorganization.[293] Accordingly, the court denied immediate payment on the claim.

In *In re Bookbinders' Restaurant, Inc.*,[294] the court likewise held that the timing of the payment of an administrative expense allowed under Section 503(b)(9) was within the discretion of the bankruptcy court. Although the court denied the creditors' request for immediate payment, it did concede that "there may be circumstances in which it would be inequitable or inappropriate to permit a debtor to pay certain administrative expenses [i.e., ordinary course postpetition administrative expenses and professional fees] but not others."[295]

Most courts now adopt the analysis set forth in *In re Global Home Products, LLC* and *In re Bookbinders' Restaurant, Inc.* and hold that vendors are not entitled to immediate payment on their administrative expenses under Section 503(b)(9) of the Bankruptcy Code absent extraordinary circumstances.[296]

---

291. *Id.* (citing *In re HQ Global Holdings, Inc.*, 282 B.R. 169 (Bankr. D. Del. 2002) (citations omitted)).
292. *Id.* at *4 (citing *In re Garden Ridge Corp.*, 323 B.R. 136, 143 (Bankr. D. Del. 2005)).
293. *Id* at *5.
294. *In re Bookbinders' Rest., Inc.*, 2006 Bankr. LEXIS 3749 (Bankr. E.D. Pa. Dec. 28, 2006).
295. *Id.*
296. *See, e.g., In re Arts Dairy, LLC*, 414 B.R. at 222 (Bankr. N.D. Ohio 2009) (denying immediate payment); S. Polymer, Inc. v. TI Acquisition, LLC (*In re TI Acquisition,* LLC), 410 B.R. 742, 743 (Bankr. N.D. Ga. 2009) (denying immediate payment); *In re* Modern Metal Prods. Co., 422 B.R. 118, 125 (Bankr. N.D. Ill. 2009); *In re Fashion Shop of Ky., Inc.*, 364 B.R. 283, 284-85 (Bankr. W.D. Ky. 2007) (overruling objection to pay administrative expense of retained postpetition financial advisor before payment of 503(b)(9) administrative expenses); *but see In re Humboldt Creamery, LLC*, 2009 WL 2820552 at *1 (Bankr. N.D. Cal. April 23, 2009) (allowing immediate payment because vendors could neither "be expected to finance the debtor's operations … [nor] afford to wait for payment.").

C. What Is a "Good" for Purposes of Section 503(b)(9)?

An issue that has repeatedly come before the courts is what constitutes a "good" within the scope of the statute. This issue is very relevant because the administrative expense granted under Section 503(b)(9) is expressly limited to the value of "goods received" by the debtor. Claims for services and claims for personal property other than goods are outside the scope of the statute and, thus, are not entitled to priority in payment. The term "goods," though used throughout the Bankruptcy Code, is not defined anywhere within the statute.

1. Most Courts Adopt the UCC Definition of "Goods"

Because the Bankruptcy Code does not define the term "goods," courts typically adopt the definition of the term set forth in Section 2-105(1) of the Uniform Commercial Code (UCC),[297] which defines "goods" as "all things ... which are movable at the time of identification to the contract for sale..."[298] Adopting the UCC definition is logical for a variety of reasons. First, the UCC has been adopted by nearly every state and, thus, it provides as close to a universal definition of the term as is possible.[299] Second, the UCC's definition is consistent with the term's ordinary and common usage.[300] Third, there is ample case law regarding reclamation of goods, a related creditor remedy, which itself originates in the UCC.[301]

---

297. *In re Escalera Resources Co.*, 563 B.R. 336 (Bankr. D. Col. 2017); *In re NE Opco*, 501 B.R. 233, 256 (Bankr. D. Del. 2013); *In re S. Mont. Elec. Generation and Transmission Coop. Inc.*, 2013 WL 85162, at *5 (Bankr. D. Mont. Jan. 8, 2013); GFI Wis., Inc. v. Reedsburg Util. Comm'n. (*In re Grede Foundries, Inc.* II), 440 B.R. 791 (W.D. Wis. 2010) (noting that every bankruptcy court that has addressed the issue has adopted the UCC definition for the term "goods"); *In re Erving Indus., Inc.*, 432 B.R. 354, 368 (Bankr. D. Mass. 2010); *In re Pilgrim's Pride Corp.*, 421 B.R. 231, 240 (Bankr. N.D. Tex. 2009); *In re Samaritan Alliance, LLC*, 2008 WL 2520107, at *4 (Bankr. E.D. Ky. June 28, 2008); *but see In re PMC Marketing Corp.*, 501 B.R. 17 (Bankr. D. P.R. 2013) (rejecting UCC definition as controlling in the section 503(b)(9) context); Hudson Energy Services, LLC v. The Great Atlantic & Pacific Tea Company, Inc. (*In re The Great Atlantic & Pacific Tea Company, Inc.*), 538 B.R. 666, 673 (S.D.N.Y. 2015).

298. UCC § 2-105(1) (2004).

299. *See, e.g., In re Circuit City Stores, Inc.*, 432 B.R. 225, 228 (Bankr. E.D. Va. 2010); *In re SemCrude, L.P.*, 416 B.R. 399, 405 (Bankr. D. Del. 2009); *In re Pilgrim's Pride Corp.*, 421 B.R. 231 (Bankr. N.D. Tex. 2009). With some minor variations, Article 2 of the UCC, governing the sales of goods, has been adopted by the legislatures of 49 states and the District of Columbia. Louisiana did not adopt Article 2 of the UCC.

300. *In re Circuit City Stores, Inc.*, 416 B.R. 531, 536 (Bankr. E.D. Va. 2009).

301. *Id.*

Nevertheless, the UCC definition of the term goods is sufficiently ambiguous such that courts still often struggle with the issue of whether a vendor provided goods or, alternatively, services. For example, courts have held that costs associated with inspecting, ticketing, and repackaging clothing apparel,[302] removing garbage and sewage,[303] processing the debtors' raw materials into finished parts and, thereafter, shipping the parts back to the debtors,[304] freight services,[305] and advertising in a creditor's phonebook[306] all do not involve the sale of goods.

Conversely, courts have found that vendors who: (i) sold salt and chloride de-icer to the debtors in conjunction with snow removal at their plants, (ii) turned the debtors' own postindustrial scrap into plastic pellets that were subsequently sold back to them to make automotive bumpers and facia panels, and (iii) sold parts for engine testing while inspecting, repairing, and cleaning electric motors for a debtor sold goods.[307] Courts have also held that the provision of gas, oil, and water constitutes a sale of a good.[308]

2. *Electricity as a "Good"*

While courts seem to agree that the term "goods" as used in Section 503(b)(9) of the Bankruptcy Code is defined by reference to the definition of that term set forth in the UCC, the provision of electricity is just one example of how complex the application of that definition to a particular vendor can be. A number of courts have addressed this issue and, as discussed below, there is a split in the law. The first two bankruptcy courts to address the issue in the context of section 503(b)(9) were *In re Samaritan Alliance, LLC*[309] and *In re Pilgrim's Pride Corp.*[310] Those courts determined that the sale of electricity was not a sale of a "good"

302. *In re Goody's Family Clothing, Inc.*, 401 B.R. 131, 136–37 (Bankr. D. Del. 2009).
303. *In re Pilgrim's Pride Corp.*, 421 B.R. at 237.
304. *In re Modern Metal Prods. Co.*, 422 B.R. 118, 125 (Bankr. N.D. Ill. 2009).
305. *In re Pilgrim's Pride Corp.*, 421 B.R. at 536.
306. *In re Deer*, 2007 Bankr. LEXIS 4676 (Bankr. S.D. Miss. June 14, 2007).
307. *In re Plastech Engineered Prods., Inc.*, 397 B.R. 828, 838–39 (Bankr. E.D. Mich. 2008).
308. *In re Pilgrim's Pride Corp.*, 421 B.R. at 536.
309. *In re Samaritan Alliance, LLC*, 2008 WL 2520107 at *4 (Bankr. E.D. Ky. June 20, 2008) (electricity not a good because "electricity provided is more properly characterized as a 'service'").
310. *In re Pilgrim's Pride Corp.*, 421 B.R. at 237–39 (electricity not a good because "[o]nce [it] has been 'identified' by measurement at the meter, it has already been consumed by the end user;" "[i]t [would be] impossible for the consumer to return electricity to the provider after it has passed the meter point;" and "[i]t is difficult to imagine how electricity to be delivered could be identified at all before transmission to the customer.").

but, rather, the provision of a service. The courts in those cases concluded that electricity is analogous to intellectual property, telecommunications services, and cable television as opposed to being a "good." A primary rationale for the courts' conclusion was that electricity is neither tangible nor reclaimable once delivered.[311]

Thereafter, the court in *In re Erving Industries, Inc.*[312] issued a thoughtful opinion in which it determined that the supply of electricity to a debtor does in fact constitute a sale of "goods" within the scope of Section 503(b)(9). In that case, the court focused on the physical nature of electricity itself, and the process for distributing and selling such electricity. The court noted: "In some ways, the issue before the Court requires the impossible—the explication of electrical energy, when even great physicists tell us its essential nature remains unknown."[313] Addressing the earlier opinions on the issue, the court held that there is a marked difference between electricity and intangibles such as television, radio, telephone, and internet signals.[314] The court noted:

> Telecommunications signals are properly considered services because they are mechanisms by which other non-goods—intellectual property, ideas, sounds, music, images, and words—are sent from one location to another. Electricity, in contrast, is not merely a medium of delivery, but is *the thing* the customer seeks to purchase.[315]

As such, the court held, "although its ultimate nature may be mystifying to most, electricity *is* tangible and *does* possess physical properties."[316] Although it may not have its own shape and is not easily observed, "electricity really is some *thing,* something that can be felt (although we are loath to) and something that can be created, measured and stored."[317]

Turning to the UCC definition of the term "goods," the court found that electricity is both movable and identifiable. Electricity, the court explained, is unquestionably movable since it moves through a huge

311. *In re Pilgrim's Pride Corp.*, 421 B.R. at 237.
312. *In re Erving Indus., Inc.*, 432 B.R. 354, 370 (Bankr. D. Mass. 2010) (electricity is a good because "[it] does not simply reach a customer's meter and simultaneously cease to exist" but rather "*passes through* the meter" so that "it is literally moving [at the time it is identified to the contract], *and* it remains movable for some period of time … through the customer's electrical wiring until it is ultimately put to use").
313. *Id.*
314. *Id.* (citing *In re Pilgrim's Pride Corp.*, 421 B.R. at 239).
315. *Id.* (emphasis in original).
316. *Id.* (emphasis in original).
317. *Id.* (emphasis in original).

network of transmission and distribution systems before ultimately reaching the consumer's location.[318] Moreover, electricity is identifiable "because it can be measured at the point it passes through the meter."[319]

Subsequently, in *In re Grede Foundries, Inc.,* both the bankruptcy court[320] and, thereafter, the district court[321] adopted the reasoning set forth in *In re Erving Industries* and concluded that electricity does, in fact, constitute "goods." Building on these opinions, the bankruptcy courts in *In re Southern Montana Electric Generation and Transmission Cooperative, Inc.,*[322] *In re Wometco de Puerto Rico, Inc.,*[323] and *In re Escalera Resources Co.,* 563 B.R. 336 (Bankr. D. Col. 2017)[324] likewise found that electricity is a "good" for purposes of Section 503(b)(9).

Conversely, two of the country's busiest business bankruptcy courts, the District of Delaware and the Southern District of New York, have both held that electricity is not a "good" for purposes of Section 503(b)(9). In Delaware, while the bankruptcy court agreed in *In re NE OPCO, Inc.*[325] that the meaning of goods under Section 503(b)(9) "is primarily informed by the meaning of goods under the UCC," it disagreed with those courts that found that electricity is a "good," reasoning that "the period between identification and consumption must be meaningful," and the "infinitesimal delay" between those acts in the case of electricity makes it unidentifiable and, thus, not a "good."[326] The court explained:

> In order for something to be a good under the UCC and, thus, section 503(b)(9) of the Bankruptcy Code, it must be movable at the time of identification to the contract for sale. Electricity is identified as it passes through a meter but it is almost immediately consumed. Indeed,

318. *Id.*
319. *Id.* at 370 (citing Puget Sound Energy, Inc. v. Pac. Gas & Elec. Co. (*In re Pac. Gas & Elec. Co.*), 271 B.R. 626, 640 (N.D. Cal. 2002)).
320. *In re Grede Foundries, Inc.*, 435 B.R. 593 (Bankr. W.D. Wis. 2010).
321. GFI Wisconsin, Inc. v. Reedsburg Utility Comm'n. (*In re Grede Foundries, Inc. II*), 440 B.R. 791 (W.D. Wis. 2010) (electricity is a good because "an electric current is literally moving through the transmission network and continues to move until it is delivered to a customer at the time it is metered and consumed;" "metering satisfies the identification requirement of the UCC and the movement is sufficient to satisfy the movability requirement, even if it reaches the speed of light;" and "there is no principled distinction to be made" between electricity and natural gas or water, which are considered goods under the UCC definition).
322. *In re Southern Montana Electric Generation and Transmission Cooperative, Inc.*, 2013 WL 85162 (Bankr. D. Mont. Jan. 8, 2013).
323. *In re Wometco de Puerto Rico, Inc.*, 2016 WL 155393 (Bankr. D.P.R. Jan. 12, 2016).
324. *In re Escalera Resources Co.*, 563 B.R. 336 (Bankr. D. Col. 2017).
325. *In re NE Opco, Inc.*, 501 B.R. 233 (Bankr. Del. 2013).
326. *Id.* at 251.

> the delay between identification and use is measured in microseconds. In order to do justice to the definition of a good, however, the separation of identification and consumption must be meaningful and, in the case of electricity, that infinitesimal "gap" is too short to establish that electricity is moveable at the time of identification. It is not and, as such, electricity is not a good.[327]

Similarly, the District Court for the Southern District of New York held in *In re The Great Atlantic & Pacific Tea Company, Inc.*[328] that electricity does not qualify as a "good" under the UCC definition because it is not moveable at the time it is identified to the contract (i.e., when the meter registers it) due to the fact that it has already been consumed at the time of such identification.[329] The court reasoned that the time between identification and consumption of a "good" must be "meaningful," and that any such time with respect to electricity could not be "because the flow through the meter, the consumption and the registration of the measurement all happened at 'the speed of light.'"[330] The court further reasoned, "Given the 'metaphysical' and 'ultimately unresolvable nature of this dispute,' the principle that administrative priority claims should be narrowly construed" dictated that electricity should not be deemed to be a good for purposes of Section 503(b)(9).[331]

3. Mixed Goods and Services: The Predominant Purpose Test

Frequently, a vendor provides both goods *and* services to a debtor. In such cases, parties have argued as to whether a predominant purpose test (granting an administrative expense only if the "predominant purpose" of the relationship is the provision of goods) or an allocation approach (bifurcating a vendor's claim by that portion which relates to the provision of services and that portion which relates to the sale of goods and granting an administrative expense solely for the latter) is more appropriate.

To date, only one court has adopted the predominant purpose test. In *In re Circuit City Stores, Inc.*,[332] the court noted that a number of courts "have adopted the 'predominant purpose test' to determine whether or

327. *Id.* at 256.
328. Hudson Energy Services, LLC v. The Great Atlantic & Pacific Tea Company, Inc. (*In re The Great Atlantic & Pacific Tea Company, Inc.*), 538 B.R. 666 (S.D.N.Y. 2015).
329. *Id.*
330. *Id.*
331. *Id.*
332. *In re Circuit City Stores, Inc.*, 416 B.R. 531 (Bankr. E.D. Va. 2009).

not a transaction is in 'goods' and, therefore covered by the Uniform Commercial Code."[333] The predominant purpose test, the court explained, results in "an all or nothing approach"—if the predominant purpose of the items provided is goods, even though some of the items were services, the entire claim is treated as an administrative expense under Section 503(b)(9). Conversely, if the predominant purpose is services, even though some of the items provided were clearly goods, no portion of the claim would be given administrative priority treatment.

In adopting the predominant purpose test, the *Circuit City* Court focused on the second half of Section 503(b)(9) which provides that administrative priority is only for transactions in which "goods have been sold to the debtor in the ordinary course of such debtor's business."[334] According to the *Circuit City* court, this language requires courts to simply determine whether a particular transaction is one for the sale of goods, or not.[335] If the transaction is primarily for the sale of goods, then Section 503(b)(9) is triggered. If not, then a vendor is required to rely on other remedies. The court was persuaded, in part, by the fact that this approach would avoid "fact intensive evidentiary hearings" regarding the allocation between goods and services with respect to a particular invoice.[336]

Contrary to the approach adopted by the court in *In re Circuit City Stores*, the majority of courts have adopted an allocation approach. Under the allocation approach, if goods sold to the debtor can be delineated from the overall transaction, the vendor will be entitled to an administrative expense for the value of those goods only.

The first court to adopt the allocation approach was *In re Plastech Engineered Prods., Inc.*[337] In that case, the court held that de-icing products qualified as Section 503(b)(9) expenses, whereas the costs associated with shoveling snow that were included on the same invoices did not.[338] The *Plastech* court acknowledged that there was a line of nonbankruptcy case law adopting the predominant purpose test to determine whether a contract is for the sale of "goods."[339] Such an approach, the court found, was necessary in those cases so that the court could determine whether the UCC was even applicable to the legal issues before it (i.e., no split could

333. *Id.* (citing BMC Indus., Inc. v. Barth Indus., Inc., 160 F.3d 1322, 1329–30 (11th Cir. 1998)).
334. *Id.* at 537.
335. *Id.*
336. *Id.* at 538.
337. *In re Plastech Engineered Prods., Inc.*, 397 B.R. at 834.
338. *Id.* at 838.
339. *Id.* at 836–37.

be made because either the UCC applied, or it didn't).[340] Conversely, the court reasoned:

> there is nothing in § 503(b)(9) that requires that approach for the purposes of that section of the Code. If a particular transaction provides for *both* a sale of goods and a sale of services, and the value of each can be ascertained, why shouldn't the value of the services be relegated to an unsecured non-priority claim?[341]

Put simply, the court held, nothing in the statute requires an "all or nothing" or "winner take all" approach. Moreover, while the court agreed that it may be more difficult and time-consuming to analyze a contract and to characterize its separate components, the statutory language required that such an analysis be undertaken.[342]

A number of other courts have joined the *Plastech* court in rejecting the predominant purpose test.[343] This would appear to be the proper approach because the application of the predominant purpose test has the potential to create an inequitable result for many vendors. Assume, for example, that a vendor delivers goods valued at $1 million and provides related installation services valued at $1.1 million during the twenty days immediately preceding the petition date. Applying the predominant purpose test would mean that the creditor is not entitled to an administrative expense for the goods provided even though it clearly meets the other statutory requirements of Section 503(b)(9).

D. When Are Goods Received?

Litigation often arises regarding whether goods are "received" by a debtor within the twenty days prior to the petition date. While the term "received" is not defined in either the Bankruptcy Code or the UCC, the term "receipt" is defined in Section 2-103(1)(l) of the UCC as "taking physical possession."[344]

---

340. *Id.* at 837.
341. *Id.*
342. *Id.*
343. *See, e.g., In re Pilgrim's Pride Corp.*, 421 B.R. 231 (Bankr. N.D. Tex. 2009) (the language of Section 503(b)(9) does not support "any basis to exclude from the section's scope goods delivered pursuant to a contract the primary thrust of which is the provision of services"); *In re Grede Foundries, Inc. II*, 440 B.R. at 803 ("[T]he predominant purpose test has no place in § 503(b)(9). Nothing in that statute calls for disqualifying a § 503(b)(9) claim just because the contract under which the eligible goods were sold also provides for the sale of services."); *In re Erving Indus., Inc.*, 432 B.R. at 372; *In re Modern Metal Prods.*, Co., 2009 WL 2969762 at *3 (Bankr. N.D. Ill. Sept. 16, 2009).
344. UCC § 2-103(1)(l).

Several courts have adopted this definition in order to determine whether goods were received within the scope of Section 503(b)(9).[345]

A question that frequently arises is whether goods are "received" for purposes of Section 503(b)(9) when they are delivered to someone other than the debtor. Courts have generally held that the goods themselves must be received *by the debtor* and, thus, goods delivered to common carriers (en route to the debtor) or drop-shipped to the debtor's customers at the request of a debtor do not fall within the scope of the statute.[346] Nevertheless, constructive receipt of goods by a debtor's agent or bailee may constitute receipt.[347] Courts generally agree that passage of legal title and risk of loss is irrelevant to the analysis of whether goods were "received" for purposes of Section 503(b)(9).[348]

1. Delivery to Common Carriers

In *In re World Imports, Ltd.*,[349] the Third Circuit Court of Appeals held that "receipt," for purposes of Section 503(b)(9), requires physical possession of the goods by the debtor or its agent. The creditors in *World Imports* shipped goods via common carrier from China to the debtors in the United States. The parties agreed that the goods were in the physical possession of the common carrier more than twenty days before the bankruptcy filing. The parties also agreed that the debtors took physical possession

345. *See, e.g., In re World Imports, Ltd.*, 862 F.3d 338, 345 (3d Cir. 2017); *In re Momenta Inc.*, 455 B.R. 353, 357 (Bankr. D. N.H. 2011); *In re Pridgen*, 2008 WL 1836950 at *4 (Bankr. E.D.N.C. Apr. 22, 2008); *In re SemCrude, L.P.*, 416 B.R. 399 (Bankr. D. Del. 2009).

346. *See e.g., In re Plastech Engineered Products, Inc.*, 394 B.R. 147 (Bankr. E.D. Mich. 2008); *In re Momenta, Inc.*, 2012 WL 3765171 (D. N.H. Aug. 29, 2012); *In re Circuit City Stores, Inc.*, 432 B.R. 225, 228 (Bankr. E.D. Va. 2010); *In re Pridgen*, 2008 WL 1836950 (Bankr. E.D.N.C. April 22, 2008); *In re World Imports*, 516 B.R. 296 (Bankr. E.D. Pa. 2014).

347. *See e.g., In re ADI Liquidation, Inc.*, 572 B.R. 543, 548 (Bankr. D. Del. 2017) ("Possession may be actual or constructive, and occurs when the seller can no longer stop delivery and is left only with the remedy of reclamation."); *In re World Imports, Ltd.*, 862 F.3d 338, 346 (3d Cir. 2017) ("receipt as used in 11 U.S.C. § 503(b)(9) requires physical possession by the buyer or his agent."); *In re Momenta, Inc.*, 2012 WL 3765171 at *6 (D.N.H. Aug. 29, 2012) ("[T]he phrase 'received by the debtor' as used in Section 503(b)(9) means: possessed by the debtor, either actually or constructively.... [and] under Section 503(b)(9), delivery to, or possession by, a debtor's customer under a drop-shipment arrangement does not constitute constructive possession by the debtor for Section 503(b)(9) purposes.").

348. *See, e.g., In re Pridgen*, 2008 WL 1836950 (Bankr. E.D.N.C. Apr. 22, 2008) (in consignment relationship, possession and control is sufficient, title to the goods need not have transferred); *see also In re SemCrude*, L.P., 416 B.R. 399 (Bankr. D. Del. 2009); *In re Wezbra Dairy, LLC*, 493 B.R. 768 (Bankr. N.D. Ind. 2013).

349. *In re World Imports, Ltd.*, 862 F.3d 338 (3d Cir. 2017).

of the goods from the common carrier within the twenty-day period. The parties disagreed regarding whether "receipt" occurred by the debtors, for purposes of Section 503(b)(9), when the goods were placed on the common carrier's boat (in which case the creditors would not be entitled to an administrative expense) or when the goods were actually delivered to the debtors within the twenty day period (in which case the creditors would be entitled to an administrative expense).

The Third Circuit held that "receipt of the goods by a common carrier is not deemed constructive possession by a buyer, but rather is deemed to be possession by the common carrier."[350] The court rejected the argument that the goods were constructively received by the debtors upon delivery to the common carrier, stating: "While it is true that a buyer may be deemed to have received goods when his agent takes physical possession of them, common carriers are not agents."[351] This was true notwithstanding the fact that legal title and risk of loss with respect to the goods passed upon delivery of the goods from the creditors to the common carrier.[352] Because receipt, for purposes of Section 503(b)(9), requires physical possession by the buyer or his agent, receipt did not occur until the common carrier delivered physical possession of the goods to the debtors. Thus, the creditors were not entitled to an administrative expense.

Similarly, in *In re SRC Liquidation, LLC*,[353] the Bankruptcy Court for the District of Delaware held that goods in the possession of a common carrier on their way to the debtor's customer did not fall within the scope of Section 503(b)(9). The shipments were in the hands of UPS on the petition date. The goods were being delivered to the debtor's customers at the debtor's direction and utilizing the debtor's account with UPS. The vendor sought an administrative expense for the goods shipped. The purchaser of substantially all of the debtor's assets, who was responsible for paying all administrative expenses under the debtor's confirmed plan, objected to the request alleging, among other things, that the drop-shipped goods were not "received" by the debtor during the twenty days prior to the petition date.

The court began its analysis by noting that although the phrase "received by the debtor" is not defined in the Bankruptcy Code, "case law teaches that courts may look to Article 2 of the UCC when analyzing

---

350. *Id.* at 346.
351. *Id.* at 344.
352. *Id.* (citing UCC § 2-103 cmt. 2; *In re Trico Steel Co., LLC*, 282 B.R. 318, 324 (Bankr. D. Del. 2002); Montello Oil Corp v. Marin Motor Oil, Inc. (*In re Marin Motor Oil, Inc.*), 740 F.2d 220, 225 (3d. Cir. 1984)).
353. *In re SRC Liquidation, LLC*, 573 B.R. 537 (Bankr. D. Del. 2017).

section 503(b)(9) claims."[354] The court found that the UCC recognizes "receipt" in both its actual and constructive forms.[355] More specifically, Section 2-705 of the UCC contemplates actual, physical receipt of goods along with three forms of constructive receipt: (i) acknowledgment to the buyer by any bailee of the goods; (ii) acknowledgment to the buyer by an agent; and (iii) negotiation to the buyer of any negotiable document of title covering the goods.[356] The purchaser argued that receipt under Section 503(b)(9) should be restricted to the four situations listed in Section 2-705 of the UCC, none of which existed in the present case.

The court agreed. "Only UPS possessed the goods," the court found, "and as a carrier UPS does not qualify as an agent."[357] Accordingly, the court held that the goods were *never* received by the debtor within the meaning of Section 503(b)(9) and, thus, the vendor's request for an administrative expense was denied.

2. Shipment to a Customer

In *In re Plastech Engineered Prods., Inc.*,[358] a vendor asserted an administrative expense under Section 503(b)(9) for goods that it shipped not to the debtor but, rather, to the debtors' customer. Although the debtors never physically received the goods, the vendor contended that it was entitled to an administrative expense because the debtors had received the "*value* of the goods."[359]

The court ruled, based on the plain language of the statute, that Section 503(b)(9) requires receipt of the "goods" themselves, and not just the "value of the goods."[360] According to the court:

> the word *received* modifies the word *goods* in § 503(b)(9). It is the *goods* and not the *value* that must be received by the debtor to trigger § 503(b)(9). The word *value* in the statute is merely the measure of the amount of the "allowed administrative expense" under § 503(b)(9).

---

354. *Id.* at 540 (citing *In re Momenta, Inc.*, 455 B.R. 353, 358 (Bankr. D. N.H. 2011); *In re Erving Industries, Inc.*, 432 B.R. 354, 364 (Bankr. D. Mass. 2010)).
355. *Id.* at 540–41.
356. *Id.* at 541 n. 2 (citing UCC § 2-705(2)).
357. *Id.* at 542 (citations omitted).
358. *In re Plastech Engineered Prods., Inc.*, 2008 WL 5233014 (Bankr. E.D. Mich. Oct. 7, 2008); *see also* Bimbo Bakeries USA, Inc. v. AW Liquidation, Inc. (*In re ADI Liquidation, Inc.*), 2019 WL 211528 (D. Del. 2019) (holding that goods are not constructively "received" by a debtor for purposes of section 503(b)(9) when they are shipped directly to a debtor's customers).
359. *Id.*
360. *Id.* at *3.

> The statute does not say *value received.* Instead, it says *goods received.*[361]

To rule otherwise, the court held, "strain[s] and ignore[s] the plain meaning of the language used in the statute."[362]

Conversely, in *In re Momenta,*[363] the court held that receipt of goods, for purposes of Section 503(b)(9), can include constructive receipt when such goods are shipped to the debtor's customer.[364] The supplier argued that the phrase "received" should be interpreted broadly enough to include both traditional physical possession and constructive possession.[365] On this point, the court found, the UCC is silent since the term "possession" is not defined. Nevertheless, after reviewing several provisions of the UCC, the court concluded that the term possession is broad enough to include constructive possession in circumstances where the debtor actually obtains legal title to goods delivered to its customer.[366]

3. Consignment Relationships

On a handful of occasions, courts have interpreted the meaning of the term "received" in the context of a consignment relationship. In *In re Pridgen,*[367] the debtors operated a grocery business that included the sale of gasoline. A supplier of gasoline filed an application for allowance of an administrative expense under Section 503(b)(9) for gasoline purchased by the debtors prepetition. The debtors objected to the application because actual delivery of the gasoline had occurred prior to the twenty days preceding the petition date. The supplier argued that, under the consignment relationship, the gasoline was owned by the supplier until it was sold to the retail consumer by the debtors (at which point title to the gasoline passed from the supplier to the debtors). Thus, receipt of the gasoline by the debtors did not actually occur until the final sales by the debtors to their retail customers, which sales occurred within the twenty-day period.[368]

The court disagreed, holding that "receipt" of the goods is what is required by the statute, and "receipt" is defined as "taking physical possession of them."[369] Thus, even if the title to the gasoline did not transfer until it was sold, such transfer was not necessary to trigger a Section

---

361. *Id.* at *2.
362. *Id.*
363. *In re Momenta, Inc.*, 455 B.R. 353 (Bankr. D.N.H. 2011).
364. *Id.* at 356.
365. *Id.* at 359.
366. *Id.* at 360.
367. *In re Pridgen*, 2008 WL 1836950 (Bankr. E.D.N.C. Apr. 22, 2008).
368. *Id.* at *2.
369. *Id.* (citing N.C. Gen. Stat. § 25-2-103(1)(c) (2006)).

503(b)(9) claim.[370] All that was required was possession and control, which occurred prior to the twenty-day period.[371]

Likewise, in *In re Circuit City Stores, Inc.*,[372] the court addressed the meaning of the term "received" in the context of consumer electronic equipment that was sold on a consignment basis. The issue before the court was whether consignment goods are received on the date that such goods were physically delivered or, alternatively, on the date that the goods were sold by the debtors to their customers, thereby resulting in title to the goods passing from the creditor to the debtors under the governing consignment agreement.[373] The court ultimately adopted the UCC's definition of the term "receipt" (i.e., taking physical possession) as a federal definition for the term "received" for purposes of Section 503(b)(9). Thus, the court found, at least in the consignment context, goods are received when the debtor takes physical possession of the goods, regardless of when title is transferred.[374]

E. How Is Value Defined?

The term "value" is also not defined in the Bankruptcy Code. To date, at least two courts have addressed the definition of the term "value" when applying Section 503(b)(9). Both courts held that the contract or invoice price is presumptively the best determinant of value.[375] That said, at least one court has held that this presumption may be rebutted "by evidence indicating that, under the facts and circumstances of a particular transaction, the purchase or invoice price is not an appropriate or relevant indicator of 'value' obtained."[376]

F. Are Administrative Expenses Claims?—Application of Section 502(d) to Administrative Expenses Under Section 503(b)(9)

Section 502(d) of the Bankruptcy Code acts to temporarily disallow claims against the estate held by a transferee of a voidable transfer (often

370. *Id.*
371. *Id.*
372. *In re Circuit City Stores, Inc.*, 432 B.R. 225 (Bankr. E.D. Va. April 8, 2010).
373. *Id* at *2.
374. *Id.* at *3.
375. *In re Pilgrim's Pride Corp.*, 421 B.R. 231 (Bankr. N.D. Tex. 2009); *In re SemCrude*, L.P., 416 B.R. 399 (Bankr. D. Del. 2009).
376. *In re Semcrude,* L.P., 416 B.R. 399, 405 (Bankr. D. Del. 2009).

a preference) if the transferee has not turned over the voidable transfer.[377] More specifically, Section 502(d) of the Bankruptcy Code provides:

> Notwithstanding subsections (a) and (b) of this section, the court shall disallow any claim of any entity from which property is recoverable under section 542, 543, 550 or 553 of this title or that is a transferee of a transfer avoidable under section 522(f), 522(h), 544 545, 547, 548, 549 or 724(a) of this title, unless such entity or transferee has paid the amount, or turned over any such property, for which such entity or transferee is liable....[378]

Section 502(d) clearly disallows all "claims" of a creditor until that creditor returns any avoidable transfers received. For years, however, courts have struggled with the issue of whether, and to what extent, Section 502(d) applies to administrative expenses.[379]

In *In re Ames Department Stores, Inc.*,[380] the Second Circuit Court of Appeals went a long way toward resolving this issue when it held that Section 502(d) of the Bankruptcy Code does not bar allowance of administrative expenses within the scope of Section 503(b) of the Bankruptcy Code because Section 502(d), on its face, applies only to claims. The court reasoned that administrative expenses simply are not claims subject to the provisions of Section 502 but, rather, are asserted and allowed under Section 503.

However, it can be argued that the *Ames* holding should not be extended to prepetition administrative expenses under Section 503(b)(9). First, Section 503(b)(9) was enacted as part of BAPCPA and, thus, was not in effect when Ames filed for bankruptcy protection in August 2001. In fact, the *Ames* court noted in footnote 2 of its opinion that "Neither party has suggested that section 503(b)(9) has any relevance to this appeal, and we do not specifically address its interaction with section 502(d)."[381] Second, the *Ames* court framed the issue on appeal in the first paragraph of its opinion as follows:

---

377. 4 Collier on Bankruptcy, ¶ 502.05[1] (citing H.R. Rep. No. 595 (1977)).

378. 11 U.S.C. 502(d).

379. *Compare* Beasley Forest Products, Inc. Inc. v. Durango Ga. Paper Co. (*In re Durango Ga. Paper Co.*), 297 B.R. 326, 329-31 (Bankr. S.D. Ga. 2003) (holding that section 502(d) does not apply to administrative expenses under section 503); *In re Lids Corp.*, 260 B.R. 680, 683-84 (Bankr. D. Del. 2001) (same) *with* MicroAge, Inc. v. Viewsonic Corp. (*In re MicroAge, Inc.*), 291 B.R. 503 (B.A.P. 9th Cir. 2002) (holding that administrative expenses are claims that fall within the scope of section 502(d)); Movitz v. Baker (*In re Triple Star Welding, Inc.*), 324 B.R. 778, 794 (B.A.P. 9th Cir. 2005) (same).

380. *In re Ames Dep't Stores, Inc.*, 582 F.3d 422 (2d Cir. 2009).

381. *Id.* at 424, n. 2.

> whether section 502(d) of the Bankruptcy Code, which bars allowance of certain claims filed against the debtor's estate by alleged recipients of preferential transfers, also bars allowance to such a claimant of *postpetition* administrative expenses pursuant to section 503(b) of the Bankruptcy Code.[382]

Given that the court's holding was expressly limited to "postpetition" administrative expenses, a debate remains regarding whether Section 502(d) can be utilized to temporarily disallow a prepetition administrative expense under Section 503(b)(9). Although no appellate courts have addressed this specific issue, a few bankruptcy courts have. To date, the majority of these courts have agreed that Section 502(d) does not apply to administrative expenses under Section 503(b)(9).

Courts adopting the so-called "majority approach" note that the allowance of claims and the allowance of administrative expenses are separate and distinct processes.[383] Together, Sections 501 and 502 prescribe procedures for the filing and allowance of claims. These procedures, the courts have found, are separate and distinct from the procedures for the assertion and allowance of administrative expenses set forth in Section 503. As such, it would be inappropriate to apply a provision of Section 502—Section 502(d)—to an administrative expense arising under Section 503.

These courts point to the introductory language of Section 502(d) as further support for their conclusion. As stated by the court in *In re Momenta*:

> The introduction to § 502(d) states "[n]otwithstanding subsections (a) and (b) of this section," which indicates "that the only claims to which subsection (d) applies are those that would otherwise have been allowed pursuant to subsection (a) and (b)" of § 502. Applying § 502(d) to all claims, including administrative expenses [which are not allowed under section 502 at all but, rather, are allowed under section 503], would make the phrase "notwithstanding subsections (a) and (b) of this section" wholly unnecessary. It is a cardinal principle of statutory construction that courts must give effect, if possible, to every clause and word of a statute."[384]

---

382. *In re Ames Dep't Stores, Inc.*, 582 F.3d at 423-24 (emphasis added).
383. *In re Plastech Engineered Products, Inc.*, 397 B.R. 828 (Bankr. E.D. Mich. 2008); *In re TI Acquisition, LLC*, 410 B.R. 742 (Bankr. N.D. Ga. 2009); *In re Momenta, Inc.*, 455 B.R. 353 (Bankr. D. N.H. 2011); *In re Energy Conversion Devices, Inc.*, 486 B.R. 872 (Bankr. E.D. Mich. 2013).
384. *In re Momenta, Inc.*, 455 B.R. at 363 (internal citations omitted).

Finally, the "majority approach" courts note that Section 503(b) cannot be subject to Section 502(d) because both statutory sections are written with mandatory language without a qualifying clause. More specifically, both Section 502(b) (dealing with claims) and Section 503(b) (dealing with administrative expenses) contain mandatory allowance provisions. At the same time, Section 502(d) states that the court "shall disallow" a claim of any entity from which property is recoverable. While the contrasting mandatory language in Sections 502(b) and 502(d) can be squared because of the introductory sentence of Section 502(d), which states "notwithstanding subsections (a) and (b)," no such qualifying language exists with respect to Section 503. Thus, subjecting Section 503(b) to the disallowance provision of Section 502(d) would create an unnecessary conflict between two mandatory statutory provisions, an approach which is contrary to accepted principles of statutory construction.

Conversely, the "minority approach" was articulated by the court in *In re Circuit City Stores.*[385] In that case, the court concluded that administrative expenses under Section 503(b)(9) were both administrative expenses <u>and</u> claims. The court noted that:

> even if the [majority approach courts] are correct that § 502(d) can only be used to disallow claims filed under 501(a) of the Bankruptcy Code, § 503(b)(9) claims, unlike other § 503(b) administrative expenses, *must* be filed under § 501(a) of the Bankruptcy Code.[386]

The court's rationale for the conclusion that Section 503(b)(9) administrative expenses must be filed under Section 501 was that Bankruptcy Rule 3002(a) mandates that a "creditor" file a proof of claim for such claim to be allowed. The term "creditor", the court noted, is defined in Section 101(10)(A) of the Bankruptcy Code as an "entity that has a claim against the debtor that arose at the time of or before" the petition date.[387] Because Section 503(b)(9) claimants are entities whose debts arose prepetition, the court continued, such claimants are creditors within the meaning of the Bankruptcy Code and Bankruptcy Rule 3002 and, therefore, needed to file a proof of claim in order to receive a distribution.[388]

In the *Circuit City* court's view, the language in Section 503(a) that requires an entity to file a "request for payment" of an administrative expense (the very language that the "majority approach" courts found persuasive in reaching their respective conclusions) applies only to the

385. *In re Circuit City Stores, Inc.*, 426 B.R. 560 (Bankr. E.D. Va. 2010).
386. *Id.*
387. *Id.*
388. *Id.*

act of obtaining priority for a preexisting claim of a creditor that was previously allowed under Sections 501 and 502 of the Bankruptcy Code.[389] As such, according to the *Circuit City* court:

> If a "creditor" wishes to be granted an administrative priority under § 503(b)(9), then the creditor must, first, file a proof of claim under § 501, second, have the claim allowed under section 502, and then, third, request administrative expense priority under 503(a).[390]

Because, as creditors, Section 503(b)(9) claimants must file claims, the court held, such claims can be temporarily disallowed under Section 502(d) until the preference litigation is resolved.

G. Can the Holder of an Administrative Expense Under Section 503(b)(9) Use Goods Shipped during the Twenty Days prior to the Petition Date as New Value?

Whether the holder of an administrative expense under Section 503(b)(9) can use goods received by the debtor during the twenty days prior to the petition date as subsequent new value to offset an alleged preferential transfer has troubled practitioners since the enactment of Section 503(b)(9). To understand this issue, it is important to understand how the subsequent new value defense, which is set forth in Section 547(c)(4), works. The subsequent new value defense provides that a preferential transfer to or for the benefit of a creditor may not be avoided:

> [T]o the extent that, after such transfer, such creditor gave new value to or for the benefit of the debtor-
> (A) not secured by an otherwise unavoidable security interest; and
> (B) on account of such new value the debtor did not make an otherwise unavoidable transfer to or for the benefit of such creditor....[391]

Generally speaking, Section 547(c)(4) permits creditors to reduce their preference exposure by subtracting the value of the goods shipped subsequent to receipt of the preferential transfers but prior to the petition date from the aggregate preference demand amount.

---

389. *Id.*
390. *Id.*
391. 11 U.S.C. § 547(c)(4).

Much like Section 503(b)(9), the legislative history to Section 547(c)(4) suggests that the subsequent new value defense was enacted to encourage creditors to continue to sell on credit to companies experiencing financial hardship.[392] For trade vendors, who may ship goods to a debtor on a daily basis, the new value defense (along with the ordinary course of business defense) is perhaps the best protection to a preference.

Despite the clear mandate of Section 547(c)(4), however, the issue of whether the holder of an administrative expense under Section 503(b)(9) can still use the value of goods shipped during the twenty-day period as new value is hotly contested. To be sure, there are compelling statutory and policy arguments in support of both sides of the debate. For example, creditors argue that the twenty-day invoices fall squarely within the definition of new value set forth in the statute (which remained unchanged after the enactment of BAPCPA). Moreover, from a policy standpoint, the fact that Congress elected to give such invoices priority in payment over older invoices does not change the fact that the creditor replenished the estate at a time when the debtor was experiencing financial hardship. On the other end of the spectrum, debtors and trustees argue that permitting a creditor to receive payment on its twenty-day invoices as part of a Section 503(b)(9) administrative expense *and* use those same invoices as new value to offset a preference allows such creditor to "double dip" with respect to the twenty-day invoices, to the detriment of the estate and other creditors.

As is evidenced by the case law discussed below, a related issue is whether a creditor is entitled to use paid invoices as new value to offset a preference. The recent trend in the case law is that a creditor can use invoices that were subsequently paid as new value to offset a preference *only if* the subsequent payment ultimately can be avoided by the estate.[393] Debtors and trustees argue that a creditor should not be entitled to use its twenty-day invoices as new value because the estate cannot avoid any subsequent payment that is made on account of such invoices post petition (because any postpetition payment would have been made pursuant to a court order or by statute upon confirmation of a plan).

Based on the requirement in Section 547(c)(4) and the recent case law that new value either: (i) remain unpaid by the debtor, or (ii) be paid by a transfer that can be avoided, debtors and trustees would argue, twenty-day invoices that are paid pursuant to an allowed Section 503(b)(9) claim

392. Roberds, Inc. v. Broyhill Furniture (*In re Roberds, Inc.*), 315 B.R. 443, 468 (Bankr. S.D. Ohio 2004).

393. *See, e.g.*, Wahoski v. American & Efrid, Inc. (*In re Pillowtex Corp.*), 416 B.R. 123 (Bankr. D. Del.. 2009); *In re Check Reporting Servs., Inc.*, 140 B.R. 425 (Bankr. W.D. Mich. 1992).

simply do not fall within the scope of allowable "paid" new value. As one court noted in a slightly different context:

> An unavoidable post-petition transfer on account of new value extended subsequent to a preference *should* limit the use of § 547(c)(4) by the amount of the unavoidable transfer, as without a reduction in the new value the transferee would be receiving double use of the new value....[394]

On the other hand, creditors cite to the majority view wherein courts have ignored postpetition payments when conducting a new value analysis, holding that the statutory language closes the window for determining whether a transfer is avoidable, and whether subsequent invoices can be used as new value to offset such a transfer, at the petition date. One such court noted: "The plain language of § 547 closes the preference window at the petition, limiting the § 547(c)(4) defense to new value supplied and payments made before the debtor crosses into bankruptcy."[395]

One rationale for this conclusion is that payments on potential new value invoices that are made postpetition are not made by the *debtor* (as required by Section 547(c)(4)) but, rather, involve a transaction with the *debtor in possession*.[396] That being the case, creditors argue, twenty-day invoices that are paid postpetition pursuant to an allowed Section 503(b)(9) claim are actually deemed to remain "unpaid" for purposes of calculating the new value defense. Thus, citing the two-part test for new value set forth above, creditors argue that they are entitled to use twenty-day invoices as new value because such invoices were not actually repaid by the debtor (despite the fact that they may have been subsequently paid by the debtor in possession).

394. *See, e.g.* MMR Holding Corp. v. C & C Consultants (*In re MMR Holding Corp.*), 203 B.R. 605, 609 (Bankr. M.D. La. 1996); Wallach v. Vulcan Steam Forging (*In re DJ Mgmt. Group*), 164 B.R. 831, 836 (Bankr. W.D.N.Y. 1994) ("Had the post-petition payment not occurred, Vulcan would have a § 547(c)(4) 'new value' defense to the present preferences to that dollar amount.").

395. Phoenix Rest. Group, Inc. v. Ajilon Prof'l Staffing LLC (*In re Phoenix Rest. Group, Inc.*), 317 B.R. 491 (Bankr. M.D. Tenn. 2004) (citing Bergquist v. Anderson-Greenwood Aviation Corp. (*In re Bellanca Aircraft Corp.*), 850 F.2d 1275, 1284 (8th Cir. 1988)).

396. Bergquist v. Anderson-Greenwood Aviation Corp. (*In re* Bellanca Aircraft Corp.), 850 F.2d at 1284 (8th Cir. 1988).

The first court to address this issue was *In re Commissary Operations, Inc.*[397] Citing to *In re Phoenix Restaurant Group,*[398] a prior opinion which held that goods provided subject to a reclamation demand could not be used as new value because the vendor could take such goods back if it did not receive payment in full, the debtor in *Commissary Operations* argued that the twenty-day invoices could likewise not be used as new value because creditors would essentially receive double credit for the same invoices.[399]

The court held that twenty-day invoices are not disqualified from constituting new value for purposes of Sections 547(a)(2) and 547(c)(4). The court distinguished the district court's holding in *In re Phoenix Restaurant Group,* noting that with reclamation claims, the debtor is obligated to segregate and return the goods, depriving the debtor of its ability to use or sell the goods in the ordinary course of business.[400] Conversely, even once a Section 503(b)(9) claim is asserted, the holder is still not entitled to a lien on the goods subject to the claim and cannot demand the return of such goods. Rather, the claimant is only entitled to request priority payment for the value of such goods.[401] Because a debtor can freely use goods subject to a Section 503(b)(9) claim after the petition date, the court reasoned, "goods shipped to and received by a debtor in the 20 days prior to bankruptcy are exactly the same money or money's worth as goods shipped free of the seller's strings."[402]

Next, the court explained that Section 503(b)(9) claims are more analogous to prepetition claims which are paid post petition as part of a critical vendor payment than reclamation claims because the vendor does not have a lien.[403] The court noted that a number of courts have held that goods paid for postpetition under a critical vendor order can still be used as new value to offset a preference because "the preference window closes at the petition date."[404] Thus, postpetition occurrences, including payment of the new value invoices pursuant to a critical vendor order, do not impact a creditor's subsequent new value defense. By analogy, the court found, payment postpetition under a Section 503(b)(9) claim should be ignored for purposes of determining a creditor's preference exposure.

---

397. Commissary Operations, Inc. v. Dot Foods, Inc. (*In re Commissary Operations, Inc.*), 421 B.R. 873 (Bankr. M.D. Tenn. 2010).
398. Phoenix Rest. Group, Inc. v. Proficient Food Co. (*In re Phoenix Rest. Group, Inc.*), 373 B.R. 541 (M.D. Tenn. 2007).
399. *Id.* at 876.
400. *Id.* at 878.
401. *Id.* at 877-78.
402. *Id.* (citing Phoenix Rest. Group, Inc. v. Proficient Food Co. (*In re Phoenix Rest. Group, Inc.*), 373 B.R. at 548 (M.D. Tenn. 2007)).
403. *Id.* (citing Phoenix Rest. Group, Inc. v. Ajilon Prof'l Staffing, LLC (*In re Phoenix Rest. Group, Inc.*), 317 B.R. 491, 496 (Bankr. M.D. Tenn. 2004)).
404. *Id.*

Moreover, the court continued, the possibility that the holder of an administrative expense under section 503(b)(9) might subsequently receive payment on such claim postpetition "does not remove those deliveries from the definition of 'new value.'"[405] Subsequent payment for such deliveries "does not negate the value represented by the claim that the creditor provided to the debtor."[406] Regardless of payment, the court found, the deliveries benefitted the bankruptcy estate because the debtor in possession:

> realized the mark-up profit on the re-sale of the goods (or use of the goods incorporated into a finished product for sale, for a manufacturing or distributor debtor) and has the ability to fill an order to its customers' satisfaction. Meeting and fulfilling the expectation of customers achieves the most important goal of a business entity—to maximize its goodwill.[407]

Finally, the court reasoned that the similar congressional policies behind the enactment of Sections 503(b)(9) and 547(c)(4) supported its conclusion, whereas forcing a creditor to choose between asserting an administrative expense under Section 503(b)(9) and preserving its right to assert a subsequent new value defense that includes the twenty-day invoices "would work a disservice on Congress' inherent policy goals" when enacting the respective statutes.[408] Requiring creditors to make such a choice "would chill their willingness to do business with troubled entities" and "deprives sellers of goods of the benefits Congress conferred upon them" when it enacted the statute.[409] This was particularly true, the court found, because Congress did not amend the subsequent new value defense to provide for a reduction of new value by the amount of any Section 503(b)(9) claims when it enacted BAPCPA.

Two other courts that have addressed this issue have held that a preference defendant cannot use its twenty-day invoices as new value to offset a preference, at least where funds are set aside to pay the Section 503(b)(9) administrative expenses in the bankruptcy case.

First, in *In re TI Acquisition, LLC,*[410] the funds to pay the preference defendants' allowed Section 503(b)(9) claims were held in reserve pending resolution of the preference. The court distinguished *Commissary Operations,* noting that no payment of Section 503(b)(9) claims, or

405. *Id.*
406. *Id.*
407. *Id.* at 878–79.
408. *Id.* at 879.
409. *Id.*
410. TI Acquisition, LLC v. Southern Polymer, Inc. (*In re TI Acquisition, LLC*), 429 B.R. 377 (Bankr. N.D. Ga. 2010).

reservation for payment, appeared to have been made in that case. As in *Commissary Operations*, the court began its analysis of the interplay between Sections 547(c)(4) and 503(b)(9) by comparing Section 503(b)(9) claims to: (i) reclamation claims, and (ii) claims paid postpetition pursuant to a critical vendor order. Unlike *Commissary Operations,* the court found that the administrative priority given under Section 503(b)(9) of the Bankruptcy Code is more analogous to a creditor's right to recover goods subject to a reclamation demand.[411]

The court noted that the *Commissary Operations* court had sought to distinguish Section 503(b)(9) administrative expenses from reclamation claims by focusing "on the liens reclamation creditors have on the goods delivered" instead of the enhanced priority afforded to holders of both types of claims.[412] The court disagreed with the *Commissary Operations* court's approach, concluding that although Section 503(b)(9) claims may be distinguishable from reclamation claims on the basis that 503(b)(9) claimants face the risk that an estate may be administratively insolvent (a risk that reclamation creditors do not have because they can simply take back their goods), the 503(b)(9) claims in the present case were fully funded through reserves and, thus, were "not any more vulnerable than a reclamation creditor's [claims]."[413]

As additional support for its conclusion that Section 503(b)(9) claims are more analogous to reclamation claims than they are to critical vendor claims, the *TI Acquisition* court raised the paid vs. unpaid new value issue. The court noted that there are two prevailing approaches with respect to the new value defense, the "remains unpaid" approach (wherein a creditor can only use unpaid new value) and the "subsequent advance" approach (allowing both paid and unpaid new value so long as the payment on the new value itself was an avoidable transfer).[414] The court determined that, based on the nature of the 503(b)(9) claims and the reserve account intended to fund such claims, either approach would lead to a reduction in the creditor's new value. Under the remains unpaid approach, the court stated, "postpetition payment of [the creditor's] § 503(b)(9) claim would deplete [the creditor's] new value defense" because the invoices were paid.[415] Likewise, the creditor's new value defense would be reduced under the subsequent advance approach because fully funded Section 503(b)(9) administrative expenses, like reclamation claims, do not replenish the estate since the debtor is denied the uninhibited use of the new value.

411. *Id.* at 381.
412. *Id.*
413. *Id.*
414. *Id.*
415. *Id.*

Thus, the court held, a creditor that delivered goods to the debtor prepetition is not entitled to the new value defense when that creditor has been paid (or will be paid) in full by a Section 503(b)(9) claim. However, the court stated: "If the estate were administratively insolvent, there may be no basis to hold that the claim was paid and the decision of the Court might be different."[416]

In *In re Circuit City Stores, Inc.*,[417] the court likewise held that a preference defendant could not use its twenty-day invoices as new value to offset a preference because the creation of a reserve to pay the defendant's Section 503(b)(9) claim was an "otherwise unavoidable transfer" within the scope of Section 547(c)(4)(b) of the Bankruptcy Code.

The court began its analysis by discussing the subsequent new value defense.[418] The court found that the establishment of the reserve by the debtor constituted a transfer on account of the new value provided within the twenty days before the petition date, stating:

> The Debtors did make a "transfer to or for the benefit of [the] creditor" on account of the subsequent new value the Debtors received from [the creditor]. [The Creditor's] argument to the contrary that no such transfer has occurred because it has not yet received payment of its 503(b)(9) Claim is without moment. The statute does not by its terms require repayment of the new value but only a transfer on account thereof. [The] 503(b)(9) Claim was not denied. Allowance of the claim was merely deferred in order to enable this Court to consider the "double payment" concerns raised by the Debtors in the context of this preference litigation. The establishment of the reserve fund is absolute. The Debtors have parted with their interest in the monies that have been set aside in the reserve fund for the exclusive "benefit of" [the creditor].... The creation of the reserve fund constitutes a "transfer" "for the benefit of" [the creditor] within the meaning of § 547(c)(4)(B) of the Bankruptcy Code.[419]

---

416. *Id.*

417. Circuit City Stores, Inc. v. Mitsubishi Digital Elec. Am. Inc. (*In re Circuit City Stores, Inc.*), 2010 WL 4956022 (Bankr. E.D. Va. Dec. 1, 2010).

418. *Id.* at *5.

419. *Id.* (noting that the term transfer is broadly defined in section 101(54) of the Bankruptcy Code as "each mode, direct or indirect, absolute or conditional, voluntary or involuntary, of disposing of or parting with an interest in property.").

The court then adopted the modern approach regarding paid new value and stated: "whenever a subsequent advance is made by a debtor to pay for new value extended after receipt of a preferential transfer, the new value defense is only available if the new value was repaid with a subsequent transfer that is itself avoidable."[420] Having concluded that the establishment of the reserve on account of the creditor's Section 503(b)(9) claim was a transfer, the only remaining issue was whether such transfer was "otherwise unavoidable." The court noted that such determination "turns on the provisions of the Bankruptcy Code governing the avoidance powers of a trustee" (*i.e.* Sections 544, 545, 547, 548, 549, 553(b) and 724(a)).[421] After considering each of these avoidance powers in order, the court concluded that the establishment of the reserve fund was not avoidable under any of the above-referenced statutory provisions.[422]

Accordingly, based on the paid new value requirement that the payment itself be avoidable, the court found that the creditor could only get credit for the twenty-day goods once. "As a matter of law," the court reasoned, "the Transfer for the Benefit of [the creditor] on account of its 503(b)(9) Claim precludes [the creditor] from utilizing the value of the same goods that comprise the 503(b)(9) Claim a second time as the basis for asserting a new value defense under § 547(c)(4) of the Bankruptcy Code."[423]

A shift in this debate occurred in late 2013 when the Third Circuit Court of Appeals issued an opinion in *In re Friedman's Inc.*[424] In that case, the new value at issue was not paid pursuant to Section 503(b)(9) of the Bankruptcy Code but, rather, was paid under a postpetition critical vendor/wages order. Nevertheless, it is generally acknowledged that the rationale of the Third Circuit in *Friedman's* would be equally applicable in the Section 503(b)(9) context.

In *Friedman's*, the Third Circuit Court of Appeals held that a postpetition payment made to a preference defendant on account of prepetition invoices did not affect the ability of the preference defendant to use such prepetition invoices as new value to reduce its preference exposure. Designating the issue as one of first impression, the court specifically found that "where

---

420. *Id.* at *7 (citing Wahoski v. American & Efrid, Inc. (*In re Pillowtex Corp.*), 416 B.R. 123 (Bankr. Del. 2009); Hall v. Chrysler Credit Corp. (*In re JKJ Chevrolet, Inc.*), 412 F.3d 545 (4th Cir. 2005)).
421. *Id.*
422. *Id.* at *8.
423. *Id.* (citing Hall v. Chrysler Credit Corp. (*In re JKJ Chevrolet, Inc.*), 412 F.3d 545 (4th Cir. 2005); Moglia v. Am. Psych. Ass'n (*In re Login Bros. Book Co.*), 294 B.R. 297, 300 (Bankr. N.D. Ill. 2003)).
424. Friedman's Liquidating Trust v. Roth Staffing Companies, LP (*In re Friedman's Inc.*), 738 F.3d 547 (3d. Cir. 2013).

'an otherwise unavoidable transfer' is made after the filing of a bankruptcy petition, it does not affect the new value defense."[425]

The debtor in *In re Friedman's* filed a Chapter 11 and continued to operate for a period of time. In the ninety days prior to the petition date, the debtor made payments to the defendant, an employee staffing company, totaling $81,997.57. After receipt of the transfers, but prior to the petition date, the defendant provided staffing services valued at $100,660.88 to the debtor, and invoiced the debtor for such services. Such invoices remained unpaid as of the petition date.

Postpetition, the debtor filed a motion seeking authority to pay its employees and independent contractors, including the defendant, prepetition wages, compensation, and related benefits. The bankruptcy court granted the motion and the debtor paid the defendant $72,412.71 pursuant to the order postpetition on account of its prepetition staffing services.

Over a year later, a liquidating trustee commenced a preference action seeking to recover the payments made to the defendant during the ninety days prior to the petition date. Among other defenses, the defendant argued that the transfers were not avoidable because it had provided new value subsequent to their receipt, which new value exceeded the amount of the transfers. The trustee argued that the defendant's new value had to be reduced by the postpetition payment of $72,412.71 that the debtor had paid to the defendant pursuant to the wage order.[426]

The Third Circuit began its analysis by explaining that the language of the subsequent new value defense is silent as to when a payment must be made by a debtor to defeat a creditor's new value defense. The court noted that district and bankruptcy courts are nearly equally divided on this issue.[427] Nevertheless, as the court noted, the fact that courts are divided in their interpretations of the subsequent new value defense does not mean that the provision is ambiguous.[428] Indeed, the plain meaning of the statutory language could be determined by considering the statutory context and the underlying policy goals.

Starting with the statutory context, the court pointed to numerous contextual indicators in the Bankruptcy Code that point to the petition date as the cutoff for analysis of the new value defense.[429] First, the court relied on Section 547, which is titled "Preferences," and which suggests that it concerns transactions "occurring during the preference period, which is by definition pre-petition."[430] Second, the court noted that the hypothetical

---

425. *Id.* at 549.
426. *Id.* at 551.
427. *Id.* (citing cases).
428. *Id.* at 554.
429. *Id.* at 555.
430. *Id.*

liquidation test contained in Section 547(b)(5) must be performed as the petition date supports using that date as the cutoff for determining new value.[431] Third, the court pointed out that the preference cause of action accrues as of the petition date, as evidenced by the fact that the statute of limitations for filing a preference action in a voluntary case begins to run on that date.[432] "The fact that the statute of limitations for a preference avoidance action under § 547 generally begins on the petition date suggests that the calculation of preference liability should remain constant post petition."[433] Fourth, extending the preference analysis past the petition date would be inconsistent with the "improvement-in-position" defense articulated in Section 547(c)(5) for creditors with a floating lien on a debtor's inventory and receivables. That provision, the court explained, requires an analysis of a creditor's collateral position "as of the date of the filing of the petition."[434] Lastly, the court reasoned that if it allowed postpetition payments to affect the preference analysis, it would seem logical also to consider postpetition extensions of new value to be available as a defense, an approach that has been almost universally rejected by bankruptcy courts.

Turning to the policy goals underlying the preference provision and the new value defense, the court rejected the plaintiff's argument that such policy should compel it to conclude that postpetition payments defeat a new value defense. The court noted that both the Supreme Court and Congressional records articulate two primary policies underlying Section 547, specifically: (i) discouraging creditors from racing to the courthouse to dismember the debtor during its slide into bankruptcy, and (ii) facilitating the prime policy of equality of distribution among creditors of the debtor.[435] otably, the court stated, these purposes focus on the prepetition period.[436] Thus, the court reasoned, "it makes sense that the equality should be measured, and inequalities rectified, as of the petition date."[437]

The court next focused on the policies behind the subsequent new value defense, identifying two primary purposes of the defense: (i) encouraging trade creditors to continue dealing with troubled businesses, and (ii) treating fairly a creditor who has replenished the estate after having received a preference.[438] The court emphasized the importance of treating a creditor

---

431. *Id.* at 555-56.
432. *Id.* at 556.
433. *Id.*
434. *Id.* (discussing 11 U.S.C. § 547(c)(5)).
435. *Id.* at 557–58 (citing Union Bank v. Wolas, 502 U.S. 151, 161, 112 S. Ct. 527 (1991) and H.R. Rep. No. 95-595, at 177–78, U.S. Code Cong. & Admin. News 1978, pp. 6137–38).
436. *Id.* at 558.
437. *Id.*
438. *Id.* (citing *In re New York City Shoes,* 880 F.2d 679, 680–81 (3d. Cir. 1989)).

who provides new value to a distressed debtor fairly.[439] The court noted that it is clear that even if a creditor is paid post petition for new value it provided prepetition, the creditor still replenished the debtor's estate during the preference period, and therefore aided the debtor in avoiding bankruptcy to whatever extent possible. The fact that the defendant happens to get paid for such new value post petition as a result of a court order or some other provision of the Bankruptcy Code does not negate this fact.

Accordingly, the court held that the defendant's receipt of the postpetition payments pursuant to the wage order did not affect the calculation of its preference liability. The preference analysis closes at the petition date. Given the number of bankruptcy cases that are filed in the District of Delaware, where opinions by the Third Circuit are binding precedent, the significance of *Friedman's* cannot be overstated. And although *Friedman's* did not specifically address section 503(b)(9), the analysis suggests that a preference defendant would be permitted to use twenty-day invoices in its subsequent new value defense even if such invoices are paid post petition under section 503(b)(9).

439. *Id.* at 559.

8

Rejection Damages Claims

A. Overview

Section 365 authorizes a bankruptcy trustee (or debtor-in-possession), upon court approval, to reject any executory contract or unexpired lease.[440] Executory contracts are those in which neither party to the contract has fully performed its obligations.[441] The Bankruptcy Code does not provide

440. 11 U.S.C. § 365(a); Milstead v. Tele Media Broadcasting, Inc. (*In re Milstead*), 197 B.R. 33, 35 (Bankr. E.D. Va. 1996).

441. While the term "executory contract" is not defined in the Bankruptcy Code, the classic definition is that of Professor Vern Countryman:

> a contract under which the obligation of both the bankrupt and the other party to the contract are so far unperformed that the failure of either to complete performance would constitute a material breach excusing the performance of the other.

See Vern Countryman, *Executory Contracts in Bankruptcy* (Part I), 57 Minn. L. Rev. 439, 460 (1973).

a definition for "executory contracts." "Executory contracts have been characterized as those with 'reciprocal remaining obligations.'"[442]

Types of contracts that have been held to be executory include insurance contracts, partnership agreements, franchise agreements, repurchase options, trademark licensing agreements, software licenses, collective bargaining agreements, joint venture agreements, and settlement agreements. The application of section 365 is limited to true leases and not a disguised financing transaction.[443] Assumption of an executory contract or unexpired lease essentially continues performance under such contract or lease.[444] If the debtor assumes a contract or lease and later breaches it, the resulting claim is an administrative expense of the bankruptcy estate.[445] Likewise, if a debtor enters into a new postpetition contract or lease that has been approved by a court, and the debtor later breaches, the resulting claim is also entitled to administrative priority.[446] Unpaid rent owed under a lease of real estate pending assumption or rejection is generally entitled to administrative priority.[447]

Rejection pursuant to section 365 generally constitutes a prepetition breach of the executory contract or lease under section 365(g)[448] and

---

442. Gibson v. Resolution Trust Corp., 51 F.3d 1016, 1023 (11th Cir. 1995); *see also In re Martin Brothers Toolmaker, Inc.*, 796 F.2d 1435, 1439 (11th Cir. 1986) ("The determination in bankruptcy, however, of whether a particular agreement is in fact a lease or a security agreement for purposes of § 365 often depends on which characterization will best serve the interests of the estate. Section 365 enables the bankruptcy trustee to affirm or reject leases and executory contracts and is based on the trustee's long-standing power to abandon obligations burdensome to the estate.").
443. Section 365(m) of the Bankruptcy Code provides that "[f]or purposes of this Section 365 ... leases of real property shall include any rental agreement to use real property." 11 U.S.C. § 365(m); *see also* United Airlines, Inc. v. HSBC Bank USA, N.A., 416 F.3d 609 (7th Cir. 2005), cert. denied, 547 U.S. 1003, 126 S. Ct. 1465 (2006).
444. If an executory contract or unexpired lease is to be assumed by a debtor, the debtor must "cure" all the outstanding defaults. 11 U.S.C. § 365(b)(1). In case there is a dispute between the debtor and the creditor regarding what is required to cure the defaults, the parties have an opportunity to present the matter to the bankruptcy court for determination.
445. *In re* Klein Sleep Products, Inc. 78 F.3d 18, 30 (2d Cir. 1996); *see also* NLRB v. Bildisco & Bildisco, 465 U.S. 513, 631-36 (1984).
446. *See In re Merry-Go-Round Enterprises, Inc.*, 180 F.3d 149, 156–162 (4th Cir. 1999).
447. *In re Cukierman*, 265 F. 3d 846, 850 (9th Cir. 2001); *In re New Valley Corp.*, 2000 WL 1251858 (D. N.J. 2000).
448. 11 U.S.C § 365(g) provides, in pertinent part—

    (g) Except as provided in subsections (h)(2) and (i)(2) of this section, the rejection of an executory contract or unexpired lease of the debtor constitutes a breach of such contract or lease—(1) if such contract or lease has not been assumed under this section or under a plan confirmed under chapter 9, 11, 12, or 13 of this title, immediately before the date of the filing of the petition.

entitles the non-debtor party to a rejection damages claim pursuant to section 502(g).[449]

In *Thompkins v. Lil' Joe Records,* the United States Court of Appeals for the Eleventh Circuit (the "Eleventh Circuit"), discussing the effect of rejection explained:

> "[R]ejection 'does not embody the contract-vaporizing properties so commonly ascribed to it . . . Rejection merely frees the estate from the obligation to perform; it does not make the contract disappear.' *In re Drexel Burnham Lambert Group, Inc.,* 138 B.R. at 703. More specifically, '[r]ejection has absolutely no effect upon the contract's continued existence; the contract is not cancelled, repudiated, rescinded or in any other fashion terminated."[450]

An executory contract or unexpired lease that goes unassumed as of the applicable deadline is deemed rejected. With the exception of Chapter 7 bankruptcy proceedings, the trustee or debtor-in-possession may assume or reject an executory contract any time before plan confirmation. Section 365(d)(1), which governs the effect of rejection in Chapter 7 cases, provides that "if the trustee does not assume or reject an executory contract or unexpired lease of residential real property or of personal property of the debtor within 60 days after the order for relief, or within such additional time as the court, for cause, within such 60-day period, fixes, then such contract or lease is deemed rejected."[451]

B. Rejection of Real Property Leases

In cases where the debtor is the lessor (or landlord) of real property the effect of the rejection is governed by section 365(h) and the non-debtor lessee's election pursuant thereto. "Once a debtor lessor rejects a lease, the lessee may either treat the lease as terminated and vacate or may remain in possession of the leasehold for the balance of the lease."[452] Section 365(h) provides, in pertinent part –

---

449. Mission Product Holdings, Inc. v. Tempnology, LLC, 139 S. Ct. 1652 (2019).

450. Thompkins v. Lil's Joe Records, Inc., 476 F.3d 1294, 1306–07 (11th Cir. 2007) (internal citations omitted).

451. 11. U.S.C. § 365(d)(1); *see also In re Ideal Mortg. Bankers, Ltd.,* 539 B.R. 409 (Bankr. E.D.N.Y. 2015); *In re Annabel,* 263 B.R. 19, 22 (Bankr. N.D.N.Y. 2001) ("The term 'deemed rejected' in § 365 has been interpreted as providing for a self-executing statute of limitations on the trustee's time to act in assuming an executory contract.").

452. *In re Milstead,* 197 B.R. at 35.

> (h)(1)(A) If the trustee rejects an unexpired lease of real property under which the debtor is the lessor and—
> (i) if the rejection by the trustee amounts to such a breach as would entitle the less to treat such lease as terminated by virtue of its terms, applicable nonbankruptcy law, or any agreement made by the lessee, then the lessee may treat such lease as terminated by the rejection; or
> (ii) if the term of such lease has commenced, the lessee may retain its rights under such lease (including rights such as those relating to the amount and timing of payment of rent and other amounts payable by the lessee and any right of use, possession, quiet enjoyment, subletting, assignment, or hypothecation) that are in or appurtenant to the real property for the balance of the term of such lease and for any renewal or extension of such rights to the extent that such rights are enforceable under applicable nonbankruptcy law.[453]

The non-debtor lessee who elects to treat the lease as terminated by the rejection is entitled to a prepetition unsecured claim for damages that resulted from the rejection of the lease.[454]

By contrast, a non-debtor lessee who elects to retain possession is not entitled to assert a rejection damage claim against the estate.[455] Instead, such a lessee who elects to remain in possession of the property despite the debtor's rejection of the lease is entitled to offset against the rent the value of any damage caused by the nonperformance after the date of rejection.

---

453. 11 U.S.C. § 365(h).

454. *See* 11 U.S.C. § 502(g); *In re Legg*,51 B.R. at 447 ("Here, the Defendant-Lessee elected to vacate and terminated the lease . . . Having done so, the Lessee is a general unsecured creditor to the extent of such claims as may be filed and allowed or determined under 11 U.S.C. § 502(g)."); *In re Milstead*,197 B.R. at 36 (relocation costs of lessee who vacated premises as a result of rejection constituted a general unsecured claim against the estate. *In re Carter*,2004 WL 212991 (Bankr. M.D.N.C. January 21, 2004) (finding lessees who elected to vacate premises were entitled to unsecured claim for moving expenses as damages resulting from the rejection).

455. McDonalds Corp. v. Stratosphere Corp.(*In re Stratosphere Corp.*),23 Fed. Appx. 749, 2001 WL 1519412 (9th Cir. 2001) (claim for rejection damages barred by 11 U.S.C. § 365(h), because lessee remained in possession of the leased premises); *In re Samaritan Alliance*, No. 07-50735, 2007 WL 4162918 *5 (Bankr. E.D. Ky. November 21, 2007) (remedies of lessee that retained possession despite rejection were limited to offsetting rent against its damages and lessee had no additional rights to assert a rejection damages claim).

The relevant subsection is Section 365(h)(1)(B), formerly Section 365(h)(2),[456] which provides:

> (B) If the lessee retains its rights under subparagraph (A)(ii), the lessee may offset against the rent reserved under such lease for the balance of the term after the date of the rejection of such lease and for the term of any renewal or extension of such lease, the value of any damage caused by the nonperformance after the date of such rejection, of any obligation of the debtor under such lease, but the lessee shall not have any other right against the estate or the debtor on account of any damage occurring after such date caused by such nonperformance.[457]

In re Chestnut Ridge Plaza Assocs., the court explained:

> One option given to a tenant by § 365(h)(1) is to treat the lease as terminated, quit the premises and state its claim against the estate as an unsecured claim. It does not give the tenant who elects to stay in possession the choice of treating the lease as terminated, retaining possession and limiting its damage claim to an offset of rents. Rather, the tenant who stays in possession does *not* treat the lease as terminated . . . Therefore, when a lessee elects to remain in possession when a debtor-lessor rejects a lease, the only logical interpretation of [§ 365(h)(1)(B)] is that the terms of the lease remain operative between the parties to the lease but that damages against the debtor for nonperformance are limited to an offset against rents.[458]

C. Bar Date for Rejection Damages Claims

Similar to administrative expenses, rejection damages claims are generally not subject to the ordinary bar date imposed on prepetition creditors unless the debtor requests that the general bar date specifically include such claims.

---

456. Section 365(h) was amended as part of the Bankruptcy Reform Act of 1994 such that former subsection 365(h)(2) is now subsection 365(h)(1)(B). It appears however that the drafters neglected to amend the corresponding section 365(g) referenced supra in note 1. *See In re Chestnut Ridge Plaza Assocs.*, 156 B.R. at 482 ("Furthermore, where the tenant remains in possession, the lease the lease is not breached by virtue of the rejection because of § 365(g).").

457. 11 U.S.C. § 365(h)(1)(B).

458. *In re Chestnut Ridge Plaza Assocs.,* 156 B.R. at 482 (emphasis in original).

The Bankruptcy Rules do not set an automatic bar date for filing rejection damage claims. Bankruptcy Rule 3002(c)(4) provides that claims arising from the rejection of executory contracts or unexpired leases may be filed in such time as the court may direct. However, many courts have adopted local rules establishing the deadline or authorizing the establishment of a deadline for filing rejection damage claims.[459]

Since rejection of an executory contract or unexpired lease requires court approval, courts will often set or authorize a bar date for filing a rejection damage claim as part of, among other orders: (i) an order authorizing or approving rejection of such claim, (ii) an order approving a sale of the debtor's assets, or (iii) an order confirming a plan of reorganization.

D. Rejection Damages Cap

In the case where a debtor-tenant rejects an unexpired lease of real property, it is important to note that the Bankruptcy Code caps a creditor-landlord's allowed claim for future damages against the debtor-tenant. Once the rejection damage claim is properly filed with the court, the claim is deemed allowed unless the debtor-tenant or another interested party files an objection to the claim.[460]

If an objection is raised, Section 502(b)(6) of the Bankruptcy Code limits the amount of a landlord's claim for damages resulting from the rejection of a nonresidential real property lease to the amount of the rent reserved by such lease, without acceleration, for the greater of (a) one year, or (b) fifteen percent, not to exceed three years, of the remaining term of the lease, following the earlier of (i) the filing of the bankruptcy petition, and (ii) the date on which the lessor repossessed, or the debtor surrendered, the leased premises.[461]

While there is a split in the case law, most courts have found that such cap only limits a landlord's claims for future damages due to unpaid rent after the rejection of the contract. Other claims, including claims arising due to the debtor's failure to maintain and repair the premises, are generally

---

459. *See* D. N.J. Local Bankr. R. 3003-1(b) where "A proof of claim arising from rejection of executory contracts or unexpired leases shall be filed within the later of: (1) 30 days after the date of rejection; or (2) 90 days after the first date set for the meeting of creditors called pursuant to § 341(a)." *See also* S.D.N.Y. Local Bankr. Rule 3003-1 ("A request for an order establishing a deadline for filing proofs of claim in a Chapter 11 case shall conform to procedural guidelines for requests for bar orders contained in any applicable standing order issued by the Court.").

460. 11 U.S.C. § 502(a).

461. 11 U.S.C. § 502(b)(6).

not capped.[462] The premise behind this cap is to provide a landlord actual compensation from the rejection of its lease, but also place some sort of limitation on a landlord's claim to the extent there is a large damage claim from the rejection of a long-term lease that could potentially displace the other creditors in the case.[463]

There is no such cap for a landlord's claim for unpaid prepetition rent from the debtor-tenant that is due at the time of the filing. The landlord is entitled to include all amounts that constitute "rent" under the lease, which may include taxes, utilities, common area maintenance charges, insurance, and attorneys' fees depending on the terms of the lease.

462. *See, e.g., In re Energy Conversion Devices, Inc.*, 483 B.R. 119 (Bankr. E.D. Mich. 2012) (holding that the statutory cap on a landlord's claim for damages resulting from termination of a real property lease set forth in § 502(b)(6) of the Bankruptcy Code does not preclude a landlord's separate claim for additional damages resulting from a debtor's breach of its obligation to maintain and repair the premises).

463. *See In re PPI Enterprises (U.S.), Inc.*, 324 F.3d 197, 207 (3d Cir. 2003) (The cap on a landlord's rejection damage claim is "to compensate the landlord for his loss while not permitting a claim so large as to prevent other general unsecured creditors from recovering a dividend from the estate.").

9

Class Proofs of Claim

A. Overview

Class actions and bankruptcy cases have similar underpinnings—both are proceedings that can resolve multiple claims in a single judicial proceeding. Despite this systemic similarity, or perhaps because of it, the Bankruptcy Code and the Bankruptcy Rules do not specifically provide any guidance regarding the propriety or procedure for filing a proof of claim for an entire class. There is no express authority for filing a class claim, although the Bankruptcy Rules do provide that "a creditor or its authorized agent" can file a claim.[464]

Historically, bankruptcy courts were reticent to accept class claims.[465] In fact, the Bankruptcy Act of 1898 precluded consideration of class claims all together. Under today's Bankruptcy Code and applicable rules, a majority of courts recognize that a proof of claim may be filed by a representative on behalf of an entire class of creditors regardless of whether that class had been certified pursuant to Bankruptcy Rule 7023 prior to the bankruptcy filing.[466] However, after the claim is filed, a court has wide discretion on

---

464. Fed. R. Bankr. P. 3001(b).

465. *In re Standard Metals Corporation,* 817 F.2d 625 (10th Cir. 1987).

466. *See, e.g.*, Gentry v. Siegel (*In re Circuit City*), 668 F.3d 83 (4th Cir. 2012); Birthing Fisheries Inc. v. Lane (*In re Birthing Fisheries*), 92 F.3d 939 (9th Cir. 1996); *In re Charter Co.*, 876 F.2d 866 (11th Cir. 1989); Reid v. White Motor Corp., 886 F.2d 1462 (6th Cir. 1989); *In re American Reserve Corp*, 840 F.2d 487 (7th Cir. 1988). *Compare, Kahler v. FirstPlus Fin., Inc. (In re FirstPlus Fin., Inc.),* 248 B.R. 60, 68 (Bankr. N.D. Tex. 2000).

how to treat the claim, including refusing to certify the class or refusing to allow the parties asserting the class claim to proceed to adjudication.[467]

B. Procedure

A putative representative may initiate the class process by filing a proof of claim on behalf of a class. Bankruptcy Rule 7023 provides that Rule 23 of the Federal Rules of Civil Procedure, which governs the process and requirements for a class action proceeding generally, can be applied in a bankruptcy case. However, in order to make Bankruptcy Rule 7023 applicable, the claimant must first file a motion under Bankruptcy Rule 9014 asking the court to apply Bankruptcy Rule 7023. The motion can be filed in response to an objection to claim, or prior to any objection. Absent an objection to the claim being filed, there is no express deadline for the motion. If the claim itself is filed timely, it generally does not matter that the motion was filed after a court-ordered bar date for filing claims.[468]

A claimant has two separate hurdles at this stage. First, the court must determine whether it is appropriate to use the class action provisions of Bankruptcy Rule 7023 or, alternatively, whether it is in the best interests of the estate to simply use the bankruptcy claim resolution process to resolve the individual claims at issue. In connection with this first hurdle, courts typically apply three factors: (1) whether the class was certified prepetition, (2) whether members of the putative class received notice of the claims bar date; and (3) whether class certification will adversely affect administration of the estate.[469] If the court makes the determination that treating claimants as a class is appropriate, it must then apply the factors of Bankruptcy Rule 7023 to determine whether the class should be certified. If the class was certified prepetition in another forum, the court may deem that certification to be dispositive on the issue. If the class is certified, the claims can then be resolved through one trial in the bankruptcy case.

C. Class Membership

After class claim allowance is established, it is important to consider class membership. Some courts considering this issue have resolved to limit

467. *In re CommonPoint Mortg. Co.,* 283 B.R 469 (Bankr. W.D. Mich. 2002); Gray v. Shapiro *(In re Dehon, Inc.),* 298 B.R. 206 (Bankr. D. Mass. 2003); *In re Craft,* 321 B.R. 189, 195 (Bankr. N.D. Tex. 2005).

468. *Id.*

469. *In re Musicland Holding Corp.*, 362 B.R. 644, 651 (Bankr. S.D.N.Y. 2007); *In re PG&E Corporation*, No. 19-30088 (Bankr. N.D. Cal. Feb. 24, 2020).

composition to those individuals to satisfy the claims bar date.[470] However, at least one court has determined that "if the class claim is certified, then the claims of all the members of the class are incorporated in the proof of claim that was timely filed."[471]

470. Scoggin v. In re Adam Aircraft Indus. *(In re Adam Aircraft Indus.),* Adv. Case No. 08-1366 MER2009, Bankr. LEXIS 4589 (Bankr. D. Colo. Mar. 19, 2009); Burgio v. Protected Vehicles, Inc. *(In re Protected Vehicles, Inc.),* 397 B.R. 339, 346 (Bankr. D.S.C. 2008) (finding claims bar date is essential to providing case finality and holding limiting class to members who timely filed proofs of claim is consistent with the equitable principles of section 105).

471. *In re Kaiser Grp. Int'l,* 278 B.R. 58, 63–64 (Bankr. D. Del. 2002).

10

Reclamation

A. Overview

Outside of bankruptcy, a vendor's limited ability to reclaim goods from a purchaser is governed by Article 2 of the UCC, as adopted under applicable state law.[472] Once a purchaser of goods files a bankruptcy petition, however, a vendor's right to reclamation is set forth in Section 546(c) of the Bankruptcy Code, which permits a trade vendor to demand from the debtor the return of certain delivered goods. The language of the statute establishes this right by making a trustee's (or debtor in possession's) powers under Sections 544(a), 545, 547, and 549 subject to a seller's right to reclaim goods.[473] Importantly, this reclamation right is subject to the

---

472. UCC § 2-702 authorizes a seller to reclaim goods delivered to an insolvent buyer on credit, if a demand is made within ten days after the buyer received the goods.
473. 11 U.S.C. § 546(c):

> (1) Except as provided in subsection (d) of this section and in Section 507(c), and subject to the prior rights of a holder of a security interest in such goods or the proceeds thereof, the rights and powers of the trustee under Sections 544(a), 545, 547, and 549 are subject to the right of a seller of goods that has sold goods to the debtor, in the ordinary course of such seller's business, to reclaim such goods if the debtor has received such goods while insolvent, within 45 days before the date of the commencement of a case under this title, but such seller may not reclaim such goods unless such seller demands in writing reclamation of such goods—
>
> (A) not later than 45 days after the date of receipt of such goods by the debtor; or
>
> (B) not later than 20 days after the date of commencement of the case, if the 45-day period expires after the commencement of the case.
>
> (2) If a seller of goods fails to provide notice in the manner described in paragraph (1), the seller still may assert the rights contained in Section 503(b)(9).

rights of a secured creditor that holds a lien on the goods or proceeds of the goods sought to be reclaimed.[474]

B. Requirements for Reclamation

To successfully assert a reclamation claim against a debtor, a vendor must comply with the requirements of Section 546(c)(1) of the Bankruptcy Code, namely: (i) the goods must have been sold in the ordinary course of the seller's business, (ii) the debtor must have been insolvent at the time it received the goods, (iii) the debtor must have received the goods in the forty-five days prior to the commencement of the debtor's bankruptcy case, (iv) the demand must be made in writing,[475] (v) the demand must be made no later than forty-five-days after the debtor received the goods or, if the forty-five-day period expires after commencement of the case, then not later than twenty days after the commencement of the case, and (vi) the goods must be in the debtor's possession and identifiable The elements to establish a reclamation claim pursuant to Section 546(c), which a creditor needs to establish by a preponderance of the evidence,[476] are different from the elements to establish a reclamation right under state law.

1. Ordinary Course of Business Requirement

Regarding the first element, that goods must be sold in the ordinary course of business, notwithstanding the language in section 546(c) that the goods involved must be sold "in the ordinary course of such seller's business," courts have interpreted this language to require that the goods sold must

---

474. *See, e.g.*, Simon & Schuster, Inc. v. Advanced Mktg. Servs., Inc. (*In re Advanced Mktg. Servs., Inc.*), 360 B.R. 421, 426 (Bankr. D. Del. 2007) ("11 U.S.C. § 546(c)(1) ... explicitly provides that the rights of a seller of goods are 'subject to the prior rights of a holder of a security interest in such goods or the proceeds thereof.'").

475. Case law also suggests that equitable principals cannot excuse the written demand requirement; the demand must be made by the seller, and must be clear that the seller is seeking to reclaim goods. *See* 5 Collier on Bankruptcy, ¶ 546.04 ("This demand is mandatory and may not be altered under equitable principals. Demand must be made by the seller, as opposed to third parties, such as a warehouseman or bailee of the seller, and must be clear on its face that the seller is seeking to reclaim goods.") (citing *In re Lockwood Enters., Inc.*, 54 B.R. 829 (Bankr. S.D.N.Y. 1985); Oakland Gin Co. v. Marlow (*In re Julien Co.*), 44 F.3d 426, 432 n.4 (6th Cir. 1995); Montello Oil Corp. v. Marin Motor Oil, Inc. (*In re Marin Motor Oil, Inc.*), 740 F.2d 220 (3d Cir. 1984)).

476. *See, e.g., In re Adventist Living Ctrs., Inc.*, 171 B.R. 310 (N.D. Ill. 1994), aff'd, 52 F.3d 159 (7th Cir. 1995); Toshiba America, Inc. v. Video King of Illinois, Inc. (*In re Video King of Illinois, Inc.*), 100 B.R. 1008, 1013 (Bankr. N.D. Ill. 1989); see also Flav-O-Rich, Inc. v. Rawson Food Serv., Inc. (*In re Rawson Food Serv., Inc.*), 846 F.2d 1343 (11th Cir. 1988).

also be purchased as part of the ordinary course of business of the debtor.[477] While the bankruptcy code does not define "ordinary course of business," the term not only appears in section 546(c) but also in Sections 363(b)(1), 547(c)(2(A), and 502(f) of the Bankruptcy Code. Case law considering the meaning of "ordinary course of business" has developed two tests for determining what amounts to an ordinary course of business transaction: the horizontal test and the vertical test.[478] Under the horizontal test, courts ask "whether, from an industry-wide perspective, the transaction is of the sort commonly undertaken by companies in that industry."[479] The vertical test views the disputed transaction "from the vantage point of a hypothetical creditor and inquires whether the transaction subjects a creditor to economic risks of a nature different from those he accepted when he decided to extend credit."[480] Generally courts require that both tests be met for a transaction fall under the "ordinary course of business" umbrella.[481]

2. Insolvency

As to the second element, that the debtor was insolvent at the time of the transfer, there is a difference as to what amounts to insolvency under the UCC in comparison to the Bankruptcy Code. Pursuant to UCC § 1-201, the definition of "insolvent," in addition to including the definition of "insolvent" in the Bankruptcy Code, also includes the following two definitions: "having generally ceased to pay debts in the ordinary course of business other than as a result of bona fide dispute" and "being unable to pay debts as they become due." While asserting a reclamation claim in bankruptcy, notwithstanding that it is at its core a state law claim, a creditor must establish insolvency through the Code definition which is as follows: a "financial condition such that the sum of such entity's debts is greater than all of such entity's property, at a fair valuation...."[482]

---

477. *In re Adventist Living Ctrs.*, 52 F.3d 159, 162 (7th Cir. 1995); *In re Pester Refining Co.*, 964 F.2d 842, 845 (8th Cir. 1992); and Toshiba America, Inc. v. Video King of Illinois, Inc. (*In re Video King of Illinois, Inc.*), 100 B.R. 1008, 1013 (Bankr. N.D. Ill. 1989).

478. Healthtrio, Inc. v. Scruggs, 599 B.R. 119, 127 (D. Colo. 2019) (discussing both tests); *In re Lappin*, 2002 Bankr. LEXIS 2114, 2002 WL 34720012, at *3 (considering the term in 11 U.S.C. §§ 363(b–c)(1), 364(a)).

479. *In re Roth Am., Inc.*, 975 F.2d 949, 953 (3d Cir. 1992).

480. *In re Dant & Russell, Inc.*, 853 F.2d 700, 705 (9th Cir. 1988).

481. *In re Media Cent., Inc.*, 115 B.R. 119, 124 (Bankr. E.D. Tenn. 1990) ("If either test or dimension is not satisfied, most likely the disputed transaction is not in the ordinary course of business.").

482. 11 U.S.C. §101(32).

Proof of insolvency pursuant to the non-Bankruptcy Code definitions in the UCC is not enough.[483]

3. Receipt of Goods

Consideration of the third element, receipt of goods within 45 days of the petition date, often results in litigation over what amounts to a "good "(as opposed to a service) and what actual receipt means. As to what amounts to a "good," courts generally use the UCC definition.[484] Substances such as water and gas,[485] typically transmitted through utilities, are generally considered "goods."[486] However, while technically qualifying as goods, water and gas, once received cannot be returned. As a result, reclamation of such substances is not truly feasible. Thus, utility claimants are more appropriately allowed to pursue priority in payment pursuant to Section 503(b)(9).

4. Written Demand

The fourth element, requiring a written demand to be served upon the debtor, is not in and of itself sufficient to preserve the reclamation rights in bankruptcy. Indeed, courts have also required a showing of a diligent

483. *See In re World Imps., Ltd.*, 862 F.3d 338, 345 (3d Cir. 2017) (In the context of Section 546(c) holding that "[w]hile actual possession by an agent on behalf of a buyer constitutes constructive receipt, our caselaw is clear that common carriers do not qualify as agents.); Seiler v. Hadley (*In re GIC Gov. Sec.*), 64 B.R. 161 (Bankr. M.D. Fla. 1986) (applying the UCC, as adopted in Florida, definition of "goods" to determine that investment securities could not be reclaimed under Section 546(c)(1) of the Bankruptcy Code); Montello Oil Corp. Cities Service Co. v. Marin Motor Oil, Inc. (*In re* Marin Motor Oil, Inc.), 740 F.2d 220, 224–26 (3d Cir. 1984) (applying the UCC definition of "receipt of goods" and holding debtor received gas at the time it was pumped from the common carrier's barge into the storage terminal of the buyer's bailee, not at the time the seller pumped the gas into the common carrier's barge); Haywin Textile Prods., Inc.v. Bill's Dollar Stores, Inc. (*In re Bill's Dollar Stores*, Inc.) 164 B.R. 471, 474–75 (Bankr. D. Del. 1994) (applying the UCC definition of "receipt of goods" and holding goods were received by debtor at the time they arrived at the debtor's yard, not when they were unpacked).
484. Section 2-105(1) states that "[g]oods means all things (including specially manufactured goods) which are movable at the time of identification to the contract for sale other than the money in which the price is to be paid, investment securities (Article 8) and things in action. 'Goods' also includes the unborn young of animals and growing crops and other identified things attached to realty as described in the section on goods to be severed from realty (Section 2-107)."
485. The UCC specifically includes "natural gas" as a "good" in § 2-107(1).
486. Compare *In re Pilgrim's Pride Corp.*, 421 B.R. 231, 240 (Bankr. N.D. Tex. 2009) (holding that water and gas are "goods" but electricity is not) with *In re Erving Indus., Inc.*, 432 B.R. 354, 356 (Bankr. D. Mass. 2010) (Holding electricity to be "goods").

pursuit such as a motion asserting reclamation rights and seeking relief or the initiation of an adversary proceeding to enforce the demand.[487]

5. Timing of Written Demand

Considering the fifth element, requiring that any written demand be made within 45 days from the receipt of the goods or 20 days after the petition date if the deadline expires postpetition, disputes generally arise as to how the deadline is calculated and when goods are received. In calculating the deadline, courts look to Bankruptcy Rule 9006(a), which has been used to extend the reclamation demand deadline.[488] As to the receipt of the goods, courts look to bankruptcy jurisprudence and Section 2-103 of the Uniform Commercial Code which defines "receipt" of goods as "taking physical possession of them" to resolve the complicated issue.[489] Receipt of the goods from the seller to a common carrier may not be enough.[490] Actual possession by the debtor has required by some courts examining the issue.[491]

6. Goods in Possession of Debtor Must be Identifiable

The final element, that the goods in the possession of the debtor be identifiable, turns on whether the goods at issue have been subsumed either into a larger mass of fungible product or incorporated into a manufactured

487. *See e.g., In re Circuit City Stores, Inc.*, 441 B.R. 496, 508 (Bankr. E.D. Va. 2010) *citing to In re McLouth Steel Prods. Corp.*, 213 B.R. 978, 987 (Bankr. E.D. Mich. 1997) ("[T]he burden is on the reclamation claimant to further diligently pursue its claim by, for example, filing a motion or complaint for reclamation in bankruptcy court for the goods, or commencing an adversary proceeding"); Tate Cheese Co. v. Crofton & Sons, Inc., 139 B.R. 567, 569 (Bankr. M.D. Fla. 1992) (holding that a creditor's failure to diligently pursue its reclamation demand through appropriate judicial channels defeated its right to reclaim goods); and Islat Klondike Co. v. Sunstate Dairy & Food Prods. Co., 145 B.R. 341, 344 (Bankr. M.D. Fla. 1992) (holding that to demonstrate a right of reclamation, a creditor must show "diligent assertion of the right of reclamation").

488. *In re Meyer-Midway, Inc.*, 68 B.R. 181, 182 (N.D. Ill. 1986) ("Rule 9006(a) is not limited by its terms to only those time limits which involve filing a document with a court. Rather, Rule 9006(a) is quite broad and applies to 'any' applicable statute.").

489. *In re O.W. Bunker Holding N. Am. Inc.,* 607 B.R. 32, 37 (Bankr. D. Conn. 2019) (noting "[a] review of the existing case law, …demonstrates that determining whether [the goods were] 'received by the debtor' is complicated).

490. *In re Momenta, Inc.*, 455 B.R. 353, 359 (Bankr. D. N.H. 2011).

491. Montello Oil Corp. v. Marin Motor Oil, Inc. *(In re Marin Motor Oil, Inc.),* 740 F.2d 220, 223-26 (3d Cir. 1984); *see also,* Haining Washeng Sofa Co., Ltd, Fujian Zhangtzhou Foreign Trade Co., Ltd v. World Imports, Ltd *(In re World Imports, Ltd., et al.),* 862 F.3d 338 (3d Cir. 2017).

product.[492] Generally, the seller must trace the goods from its possession to the debtor's and carry the burden of establishing such tracing.[493]

C. Reclamation Is Subject to Prior Perfected Secured Creditor

Perhaps the biggest difficulty that a reclamation vendor faces is the problem that a validly perfected lien of a secured creditor comes ahead of a vendor's right of reclamation. The existence of a lender with a floating lien on inventory, along with the cost of litigation over the issues, frequently makes any reclamation right illusory.

For many years, courts have debated the enforceability of reclamation rights with respect to goods subject to blanket security interests. At the heart of the dispute was whether a creditor asserting a blanket lien qualifies as a "good-faith purchaser" under applicable bankruptcy law, even though the UCC incorporates a creditor holding a security interest or lien within the definition of "good-faith purchaser." Some courts had taken the position that reclamation rights are effectively extinguished by the superior interest of a secured creditor in the goods.[494] According to this view, if the superior rights of a secured creditor supersede a seller's reclamation right under applicable nonbankruptcy law, the seller has no rights under Section 546(c) of the Bankruptcy Code and holds merely an unsecured claim for the value of the goods. This approach was referred to as the "prior lien defense." Other courts, representing the minority view, took the position that such rights survive regardless of a secured creditor's superior right, and the seller should be compensated in the form

492. *Compare* Bethlehem Steel Corp. v. Wheeling-Pittsburgh Steel Corp. (*In re Wheeling-Pittsburgh Steel Corp.*), 74 B.R. 656 (Bankr. W.D. Pa. 1987 (majority of coal delivered to steel plant had been used to produce manufactured goods and could not be reclaimed) *with In re Charter Co.*, 54 B.R. 91 (Bankr. M.D. Fla. 1985) (holding that crude oil commingled with other oil in a pipeline was still identifiable for purposes of Section 546(c)).

493. Flav-O-Rich, Inc. v. Rawson Food Serv., Inc. (*In re Rawson Food Serv., Inc.*), 846 F.2d 1343, 1348 (11th Cir. 1988).

494. *See, e.g., In re Circuit City Stores, Inc.*, 441 B.R. 496, 509 (Bankr. E.D. Va. 2010) ("[T]he Reclamation Goods sold by the Respondents to the Debtors became part of the Pre-petition Lenders' collateral and were not reclaimable…."); *In re Reliable Drug Stores, Inc.*, 70 F.3d 948 (7th Cir. 1995) (holding administrative expense or lien granted under § 546(c) is valueless if the inventory lien exceeds the value of the debtor's inventory); *In re Pittsburgh-Canfield Corp.*, 305 B.R. 688 (Bankr. N.D. Ohio 2003) (holding that under Section 546 and UCC § 2-702, if specific goods that were subject of reclamation demands were used to repay secured creditors, then reclamation demands were nullified, regardless of whether secured creditors were over-secured).

of an administrative expense in the amount of the value of the goods or a lien on other assets of the bankruptcy estate.[495]

Section 546(c)(1), as enacted by BAPCPA, codifies the majority view of pre-BAPCPA case law that subjected reclamation rights to the rights of a prior secured creditor with a floating security interest in the debtor's inventory. As a result, trade creditors continue to face the same hurdles to relief on their reclamation claims that they had faced in pre-BAPCPA cases. A few cases have addressed the reclaiming seller's rights under BAPCPA where there exists a blanket lien on such assets.

First, in *In re Advanced Marketing Services, Inc.,*[496] the court dealt with this issue in the context of a reclamation creditor's motion for a temporary restraining order to prevent the debtor from disposing of the vendor's reclamation goods. The court denied injunctive relief, holding that the vendor could not demonstrate a probability of success on the merits of its reclamation claim because the vendor's reclamation rights were likely valueless in the face of the secured lenders' floating security interest in all of the debtor's inventory.[497]

Similarly, the court in *In re Dana Corp.*[498] held as follows:

> [T]he limitation that the reclamation claimant's right is "subject to the prior rights of a holder of a security interest in such goods or the proceeds thereof" does not deal with the rights of other "purchasers" or "buyers" of goods whereas the UCC specifically makes a seller's reclamation right "subject to the rights of a buyer in ordinary course or other good faith purchaser." If amended 546(c) created an independent

495. *See, e.g.*, Phar-Mor, Inc. v. McKesson Corp., 534 F.3d 502 (6th Cir. 2008), which applied the pre-BAPCPA version of Section 546(c). In *Phar-Mor*, the Sixth Circuit Court of Appeals held that the reclamation creditor's administrative expense priority claim was not extinguished when the goods subject to reclamation were sold and the proceeds used to satisfy a secured creditor's superior claim. The court's holding was premised on the ground that a secured creditor is not the type of good faith purchaser addressed in UCC § 2-207(3) and, therefore, the disposition of the goods to satisfy the secured creditor's claims did not extinguish the reclamation creditor's valid reclamation right. Citing to prior precedent, the court noted that "[a] priority in bankruptcy should not depend for its existence upon the contingency of whether specific assets are within the bankrupt's estate" and that "[i]t would certainly be unjust to subject to the payment of the debts of their fraudulent vendee, goods [the vendee] had improperly obtained from [the aggrieved vendors], and which in equity, [the vendors] were entitled to reclaim." *Id.* at 507 (citing *In re Mel Golde Shoes*, 403 F.2d 658, 660 (6th Cir. 1968)).

496. *In re Advanced Marketing Servs., Inc.*, 360 B.R. 421 (Bankr. D. Del. 2007).

497. *Id.* at 429.

498. *In re Dana Corp.*, 367 B.R. 409 (Bankr. S.D.N.Y. 2007).

federal reclamation right that replaced state law, then in bankruptcy a reclaiming seller would conceivably have broad rights superior to those of buyers in the ordinary course of business, lien creditors or good faith purchasers other than a holder of a prior security interest. Clearly, Congress could not have intended to permit reclamation of goods that have been sold to consumers or other good faith purchasers.[499]

499. *Id.* at 417 (footnote omitted).

11

Equitable Subordination and Debt Recharacterization

A. Equitable Subordination

The principle of equitable subordination gives the court the power to reprioritize claims of creditors during bankruptcy and is largely unique to the federal bankruptcy process. The Bankruptcy Code specifically provides for equitable subordination under Section 510(c).[500] The need for equitable subordination arises when a debt or equity holder gains priority in bankruptcy over similar creditors due to some form of inequitable conduct. The doctrine of equitable subordination is "remedial, not penal, and should be applied only to the extent necessary to offset the specific harm that the creditors suffered on account of the inequitable conduct."[501]

Equitable subordination is an affirmative move that generally must be brought by a party in interest. Indeed, absent a bankruptcy plan provision that expressly provides for subordination of a particular claim, a party must undertake an adversary proceeding in order to subordinate any claims.[502] It is widely accepted that trustees and creditors have the power to commence

---

500. 11 U.S.C. § 510(c).
501. Fabricators, Inc. v. Technical Fabricators, Inc. (*In re Fabricators, Inc.*), 926 F.2d 1458, 1466–67 (5th Cir. 1991).
502. *See* Fed. R. Bankr. P. 7001(8).

an equitable subordination action,[503] but courts are split on whether the debtor itself is allowed to seek action to subordinate claims.[504]

Further, some courts have ruled that an equitable subordination action may not be pursued by parties who purchased their claims against the debtor after the alleged misconduct occurred.[505] Most importantly, the court cannot use equitable subordination to disrupt the statutory distribution scheme in the Bankruptcy Code in order to reach a result it finds more equitable. Instead, it may only look at inequities that relate to a particular claim.[506]

Virtually all courts apply the following three-pronged test for equitable subordination: (i) the claimant must have engaged in some type of inequitable conduct;[507] (ii) the misconduct must have resulted in injury to the creditors of the debtor or conferred an unfair advantage on the claimant; and (iii) equitable subordination of the claim must not be inconsistent with the provisions of the Bankruptcy Code.[508] The burden of proving these elements is on the party moving for the subordination of the claim.[509]

Under the first prong, inequitable conduct is typically found in three different situations: (i) when a fiduciary of the debtor misuses the fiduciary's position to the detriment of other creditors; (ii) when a third party dominates or controls the debtor to the detriment of other creditors; or (iii) when a third party defrauds other creditors. The most common application of the doctrine occurs when an insider—a director, officer, or a person in control of the debtor[510]—engages in deceptive conduct that results in injury to *other* creditors rather than injury to the debtor itself. While these transactions between a debtor and an insider are highly scrutinized,

---

503. *See In re Vitreous Steel Prods. Co.*, 911 F.2d 1223 (7th Cir. 1990).

504. *Compare, e.g.*, Reagor Auto Mall, Ltd. v. Firstcapital Bank of Tex., N.A. (*In re Reagor-Dykes Motors, LP*), No. 18-50214-RLJ-11, 2020 WL 4939180, at *11–12 (N.D. Tex. Aug. 24, 2020); Audre Recognition Sys. Inc. v. Casey (*In re Audre, Inc.*), 210 B.R. 360, 363–64 (Bankr. S.D. Cal. 1997); Bunker Exploration Co. v. Clarke (*In re Bunker Exploration Co.*), 42 B.R. 297, 301–02 (Bankr. W.D. Okla. 1984) *with* Weeks v. Kinslow (*In re Weeks*), 28 B.R. 958, 960 (W.D. Okla. 1983).

505. *E.g.*, Consolidated Pet Foods, Inc. v. Millard Refrigeration Svcs. (*In re S & D Foods, Inc.*), 110 B.R. 34, 37 (Bankr. D. Colo. 1990); *In re W. T. Grant Co.*, 4 B.R. 53, 78 (Bankr. S.D.N.Y. 1980).

506. *In re Perry*, 425 B.R. 323, 377–80 (Bankr. S.D. Tex. 2010).

507. The Supreme Court has not yet decided "whether a bankruptcy court must always find creditor misconduct before a claim may be equitably subordinated," United States v. Noland, 517 U.S. 535, 543 (1996), but the lower courts generally require such a showing.

508. *See, e.g.*, Life Partners Holdings, Inc. v. Cowley (*In re Life Partners Holdings, Inc.*), 926 F.3d 103, 122 (5th Cir. 2019); Benjamin v. Diamond (*In re Mobile Steel Co.*), 563 F.2d 692, 699–700 (5th Cir. 1977).

509. Chorches v. Ogden (*In re Bolin & Co., LLC*), 437 B.R. 731, 760 (D. Conn. 2010).

510. 11 U.S.C. § 101(31).

courts have also applied the doctrine to noninsiders.[511] In order for the action to be sustained against noninsiders, the misconduct must be gross or egregious.[512]

Addressing the second prong, the existence of injury to other creditors is vital for the subordination of a claim. The mere existence of inequitable conduct is not enough to subordinate a claim.[513] There must be an actual injury to other creditors; if no such injury exists, equitable subordination cannot be applied, because there is nothing to remedy.[514] The third prong of the equitable subordination test "recognizes that the doctrine is not a mechanism to be used by courts to alter the statutory scheme in an effort to reach a result the court considers more equitable than the distribution scheme provided for in the Bankruptcy Code."[515]

Once the party seeking subordination of a claim establishes a prima facie case by proving the three elements, the burden shifts to the nonmovant to prove that it conducted itself with good faith and fairness.[516]

There are, however, limitations to equitable subordination. The claim at issue must be an allowed claim in order for it to be subordinated, though Section 510(c) gives the court the power to functionally disallow claims entirely.[517] Additionally, courts may not subordinate a creditor's claim to equity interests, but it may subordinate an equity interest behind other equity interests.[518] Of course, for any subordination to occur, the estate must have assets that can be distributed to debt and equity holders.[519] Equitable subordination would effectively be useless in an administratively insolvent case.

More importantly, it is imperative that the bankruptcy court make specific findings as to the inequitable conduct. As one court noted, Section 510(c) houses the court's ability to apply equitable subordination to the

511. *E.g.*, Schubert v. Lucent Techs. Inc. (*In re Winstar Commc'ns, Inc.*), 554 F.3d 382, 411–15 (3d Cir. 2009); Capitol Bank & Trust Co. v. 604 Columbus Ave. Realty Trust (*In re 604 Columbus Ave. Realty Trust*), 968 F.2d 1332, 1360 (1st Cir. 1992).

512. *In re 604 Columbus Ave. Realty Trust*, 968 F.2d at 1360.

513. *See* Grede v. Bank of New York Mellon Corp. (*In re Sentinel Mgmt. Grp., Inc.*), 809 F.3d 958, 965 (7th Cir. 2016); 201 Forest St. LLC v. LBM Fin. LLC (*In re* 201 Forest St., LLC), 409 B.R. 543, 572 (Bankr. D. Mass. 2009).

514. *Id.*

515. Off. Comm. of Unsecured Creditors of Sunbeam Corp. v. Morgan Stanley & Co. (*In re Sunbeam Corp.*), 285 B.R. 355, 364 (Bankr. S.D.N.Y. 2002).

516. Olympia & York Fla. Equity Corp. v. Bank of New York (*In re Holywell Corp.*), 913 F.2d 873, 880–81 (11th Cir. 1990); Rodolakis v. Chertoff (*In re 1236 Dev. Corp.*), 188 B.R. 75, 82 (Bankr. D. Mass. 1995).

517. *See* Lehman Commercial Paper, Inc. v. Palmdale Hills Prop., LLC (*In re Palmdale Hills Prop., LLC*), 423 B.R. 655, 666 (B.A.P. 9th Cir. 2009).

518. *See* Rich Capitol, LLC v. Wachovia Bank, N.A. (*In re Rich Capitol, LLC*), 436 B.R. 224, 235 (Bankr. S.D. Fla. 2010); *In re Perry*, 425 B.R. at 380.

519. Floret, LLC v. Sendecky (*In re Sendecky*), 315 F.3d 904, 906 (8th Cir. 2003).

claim, but it "does not otherwise set forth the circumstances under which equitable subordination is appropriate."[520] The *Wooley I* court also emphasized the added requirement that "a claim should be subordinated only to the extent necessary to offset the harm which the debtor or its creditors have suffered as a result of the inequitable conduct."[521] The court noted that the bankruptcy court failed to make any findings of inequitable conduct with regard to a specific transaction. In fact, the absence of any finding by the bankruptcy court that either the debtor or unsecured creditors were harmed by the transaction rendered the equitable subordination claim meritless.[522]

Consequently, a court is still bound by the Bankruptcy Code and the distribution scheme in the statutes.[523] The court is not given unlimited discretion to subordinate claims but instead is given the limited power to prevent injury to creditors as a result of inequitable conduct.

B. Debt Recharacterization

Similar to equitable subordination, debt recharacterization allows the court to reclassify a claim as equity rather than as debt.[524] Unlike equitable subordination, however, recharacterization is not specifically provided for in the Bankruptcy Code. The circuits are split as to whether the authority to recharacterize purported "debt" as equity comes from Section 502 of the Bankruptcy Code and applicable state law or, alternatively, from the court's inherent powers contained in Bankruptcy Code Section 105(a).[525] Recharacterization is generally used to remedy situations where an insider or capital contributor attempts to decrease the investment's risk by labeling the transaction as debt, because debt receives statutory priority in bankruptcy. A party, however, may request the court to disregard form over substance and "recharacterize" certain transactions in order to achieve a more equitable treatment of claims and creditors.

The most significant difference between subordination and recharacterization is the conduct in question. Debt recharacterization questions the substance of a transaction to determine if it meets the Bankruptcy Code's definition of a claim, while equitable subordination

520. Wooley v. Faulkner (*In re SI Restructuring, Inc.*), 532 F.3d 355, 360 (5th Cir. 2008) ["*Wooley I*"].
521. *Id.* at 360–361.
522. *Id.* at 361–362.
523. *In re Perry,* 425 B.R. at 379–80.
524. FCC v. Airadigm Commc'ns (*In re Airadigm Commc'ns, Inc.*), 616 F.3d 642, 658 (7th Cir. 2010).
525. *See* Off. Comm. of Unsecured Creditors v. Hancock Park Capital II, L.P. (*In re Fitness Holdings Int'l, Inc.*), 714 F.3d 1141, 1148–9 (9th Cir. 2013); *see also* Redmond v. Jenkins (*In re Alternate Fuels, Inc.*), 789 F.3d 1139, 1146–49 (10th Cir. 2015).

is concerned with the existence of misconduct by a creditor.[526] Because in bankruptcy, equity holders only receive distributions after creditors have been paid in full, the resulting effects of both recharacterization and equitable subordination are very similar.[527]

Still, while the effect may be the same, the cause is not. Recharacterization is generally pled when the form of money from an insider given to an undercapitalized company in the form of a loan is, in substance, a capital contribution. In an effort to protect noninsider creditors, a court may recharacterize the loan from debt to equity. In short, recharacterization cases turn on whether a debt actually exists, not on whether the claim should be equitably subordinated. "[I]f the court determines that the advance of money is equity and not debt, the claim is recharacterized and the effect is subordination of the claim…."[528]

The roots of recharacterization owe their history to cases involving the sale and lease-back transactions of personal property, such as equipment.[529] History, however, does not dictate acceptance, and the law on recharacterization is neither uniform nor predictable. Most notably, the more recent decisions stemming from the United Airlines bankruptcy illuminate that. Those rulings on recharacterization reached opposite results—despite the fact that it was the same circuit, the same panel, and the same debtor.[530]

Recharacterization is extremely fact-intensive. Two main issues arise when determining whether to recharacterize debt: (i) whether the transaction in question appears to be at arm's length and (ii) the type of transaction the parties intended to create.[531] Whereas several courts apply different multifactor tests, the most common test, adopted in *In re AutoStyle Plastics, Inc.*,[532] includes the following factors:

(1) the names given to the instruments, if any, evidencing the indebtedness;

---

526. *In re Airadigm Commc'ns, Inc.*, 616 F.3d at 658.

527. *In re Alternate Fuels, Inc.*, 789 F.3d 1139, 1147 (10th Cir. 2015); Drake v. Franklin Equip. Co. (*In re Franklin Equip. Co.*), 416 B.R. 483, 508 (Bankr. E.D. Va. 2009).

528. Bayer Corp. v. MascoTech, Inc. (*In re AutoStyle Plastics, Inc.*), 269 F.3d 726, 749 (6th Cir. 2001) (emphasis omitted).

529. *See, e.g., In re Velasco*, 13 B.R. 872 (Bankr. W.D. Ky. 1981); Ryen v. Cottrone Dev. Co. (*In re G.A. Giancaterin & Assoc.*), 9 B.R. 26 (Bankr. W.D.N.Y. 1981).

530. *See* United Air Lines Inc. v. HSBC Bank USA N.A., (*UAL San Francisco*), 416 F.3d 609, 610 (7th Cir. 2005); United Air Lines Inc. v U.S. Bank Nat'l Assoc. Inc. (*UAL Los Angeles*), 447 F.3d 504 (7th Cir. 2006); and United Air Lines Inc. v. HSBC Bank USA (*UAL Denver*), 453 F.3d 463 (7th Cir. 2006).

531. Fairchild Dornier GmbH v. Off. Comm. of Unsecured Creditors (*In re Dornier Aviation (N. Am.), Inc.*), 453 F.3d 225, 234–35 (4th Cir. 2006).

532. *In re* AutoStyle Plastics, Inc., 269 F.3d at 749–50.

(2) the presence or absence of a fixed maturity date and schedule of payments;
(3) the presence or absence of a fixed rate of interest and interest payments;
(4) the source of repayments;
(5) the adequacy or inadequacy of capitalization;
(6) the identity of interest between the creditor and the stockholder;
(7) the security, if any, for the advances;
(8) the corporation's ability to obtain financing from outside lending institutions;
(9) the extent to which the advances were subordinated to the claims of outside creditors;
(10) the extent to which the advances were used to acquire capital assets; and
(11) the presence or absence of a sinking fund to provide repayments.[533]

No one factor is dispositive, since the court is concerned with finding the true intent behind the transaction.

As with equitable subordination, insiders are more likely to be subject to a recharacterization action. Recharacterization prevents capital contributions and other transactions from being classified as debt merely because the contributor was savvy enough to label it a "loan." Instead, the transaction in question must possess the characteristics of debt in order not to be recharacterized.

The greatest limitation on debt recharacterization is the lack of universal adoption across the circuit courts. Only six circuits (Third, Fourth, Fifth, Sixth, Ninth, and Tenth) have expressly adopted the recharacterization doctrine—but they take different approaches in identifying the legal framework for this doctrine.[534] The Seventh Circuit, while not expressly adopting the doctrine, acknowledges its wide acceptance in other circuits and in bankruptcy courts.[535]

As discussed previously, the *United Airlines* recharacterization cases exemplify the inconsistencies related to recharacterization. To give the decisions some context, United Airlines entered into several transactions in the 1990s that were designed to build or improve the facilities at airports in San Francisco, Los Angeles, and Denver. At a basic level, these deals provided United with funds from the proceeds of state-issued bonds. For its part, United agreed to retire the bonds and cover certain transaction

533. *See also In re Dornier Aviation* (N. Am.), Inc., 453 F.3d at 233.
534. *See In re Fitness Holdings Int'l, Inc.*, 714 F.3d at 1148–49.
535. *In re Airadigm Commc'ns, Inc.*, 616 F.3d at 657–58.

overhead costs. At the airports, United leased its facilities from the bond issuers who could, in turn, evict United if it defaulted. When United filed for bankruptcy in 2002, it argued that each of the transactions constituted a secured loan rather than a lease (which would require certain actions if United sought to assume under 11 U.S.C. Section 365).

It was a strategic maneuver that would allow United to continue operating in those airports without having to cure its default on the payments owed under the agreements. The bond issuers objected, and ultimately the recharacterization contests wound their way to the Seventh Circuit. The Seventh Circuit accepted United's argument as to the premises in San Francisco and Los Angeles, and deemed the transactions to be secured loans. As to the Denver transaction, however, the court held that the transaction was, in fact, a true lease.[536]

The Seventh Circuit launched its recurring framework for the recharacterization analysis in all three cases. Beginning with the San Francisco case, after a lengthy discussion of leases and Section 365, the court set out a two-pronged prelude to recharacterization: (i) case law requires a court to look at the substance of a transaction over its form, and (ii) the substance of the transaction is determined by state law (the caveat being that if state law allowed form to prevail over substance, then state law must be rejected).[537] The court then reviewed the characteristics of each transaction and compared them to leases and loans to arrive at its decision.

As the above shows, recharacterization can be a tricky argument to prevail on. Nonetheless, while the *United Airlines* and other cases demonstrate the many factors weighed when a court considers the question of recharacterization, there are consistent markers: substance will prevail over form, state law will control, and the individual facts of a case are critical.

---

536. *See UAL San Francisco*, 416 F.3d at 618; *UAL Los Angeles*, 447 F.3d at 510; *UAL Denver*, 453 F.3d at 472.

537. *UAL San Francisco*, 416 F.3d at 612, 615.

12

Critical Vendor Claims

A. Overview

After a Chapter 11 case is commenced, a debtor may find it difficult to convince creditors to continue supplying it with goods and services. Already feeling burned by the prospect of not receiving payment in full on prepetition debt, creditors are often reluctant to continue providing credit to a struggling debtor as it attempts to reorganize. Unless the creditor is a party to an executory contract, the Bankruptcy Code does not provide a mechanism for a debtor to compel a creditor to continue to provide goods or services.

However, debtors may be permitted to pay an unsecured creditor's prepetition claim if the creditor is deemed a "critical" or "essential" vendor. Debtors ask the bankruptcy court for orders authorizing them to pay those vendors deemed "critical" or "essential," early on in the case, typically through a "first-day" motion. Courts have approved payments to vendors who are found to be "critical" or "essential" based on the debtor's proof that such payments are necessary for the success of the debtor's reorganization efforts. However, because paying prepetition debt before a plan is approved, and before creditors with higher priority are paid, is contrary to the Bankruptcy Code's distribution scheme, a request to pay critical vendors is subject to significant scrutiny.

B. Authority for Critical Vendor Payments

There is no express provision in the Bankruptcy Code that allows debtors to pay prepetition claims prior to a plan of reorganization being approved. Courts that have authorized payments to critical vendors have relied on

Sections 105(a), 363(b), 1107(a), and 1108 of the Bankruptcy Code, as well as the "doctrine of necessity."[538]

1. Section 363

Section 363(b)(1) provides that, after notice and a hearing, a debtor in possession "may use, sell, or lease ... property of the estate."[539] Absent authorization under Section 363(b)(1), debtors are not permitted to use their cash to pay critical vendors or otherwise use their property for transactions outside the ordinary course of business. Courts typically apply a "sound business purpose" standard when deciding whether to approve payments made outside the ordinary course of business.[540] In extending this standard, some courts have authorized debtors to pay pre-petition amounts owed to critical vendors where the debtor is able to "articulate some business justification, other than the mere appeasement of major creditors."[541]

2. Section 105(a)

Section 105(a) of the Bankruptcy Code empowers courts in equity to "issue any order, process, or judgment that is necessary or appropriate to carry out the provisions of [the Bankruptcy Code]."[542] In some cases, courts have held that the equitable powers granted under Section 105(a) permit them to authorize a debtor to pay prepetition obligations owed by the debtor to critical vendors.[543] However, most courts agree that Section 105(a) does not provide authority to override the Bankruptcy Code's priority scheme; rather, Section 105 can only be used to implement provisions within the Bankruptcy Code.[544] Because of the lack of a statutory provision authorizing critical vendor payments, and in light of the fundamental bankruptcy

538. *In re Pioneer Health Serv., Inc.*, 570 B.R. 228, 232–34 (Bankr. S.D. Miss. 2017).

539. 11 U.S.C. § 363(b)(1).

540. Stephens Indus., Inc. v. McClung, 789 F.2d 386, 389–90 (6th Cir. 1986) (citing Comm. of Equity Sec. Holders v. Lionel Corp. (*In re Lionel Corp.*), 722 F.2d 1063, 1070 (2d Cir. 1983)).

541. *See, e.g., In re Ionosphere Clubs, Inc.*, 98 B.R. 174, 175 (Bankr. S.D.N.Y. 1989) (finding that a sound business justification existed to pay prepetition wages).

542. 11 U.S.C. § 105(a).

543. *See, e.g., In re Just for Feet, Inc.*, 242 B.R. 821, 824-45 (Bankr. D. Del. 1999) (noting that, in the Third Circuit, debtors may pay prepetition claims that are essential to the continued operation of the debtor's business); *In re Ionosphere Clubs, Inc.*, 98 B.R. at 175 (granting the debtor the authority to pay prepetition wages); Armstrong World Indus., Inc. v. James A. Phillips, Inc., (*In re James A. Phillips, Inc.*), 29 B.R. 391, 397 (Bankr. S.D.N.Y. 1983). (relying on Section 363 to allow a contractor to pay the prepetition claims of suppliers who were potential lien claimants).

544. *See, e.g.*, Norwest Bank Worthington v. Ahlers, 485 U.S. 197, 206–07 (1988); *In re Kmart Corp.*, 359 F.3d 866, 871 (7th Cir. 2004); *In* re *Combustion Engineering*, 391 F.3d 190, 236 (3d Cir. 2004).

tenet that similarly situated creditors should be treated equally, a number of courts have questioned whether Section 105(a) provides any authority whatsoever for a court to approve payments to critical vendors.[545]

3. *Sections 1107 and 1108*

Sections 1107(a) and 1108 of the Bankruptcy Code have also been cited as a "bridge" between Section 105(a) and the doctrine of necessity to support requests to pay critical vendors. These sections provide that a debtor in possession is a fiduciary charged with "holding the bankruptcy estate and operating the business for the benefit of its creditors and (if the value justifies) equity owners."[546] Section 1107(a) compels a Chapter 11 debtor in possession to perform all of the "functions and *duties*" of a trustee.[547] Section 1108 of the Bankruptcy Code authorizes and directs a debtor in possession to "operate the debtor's business."[548] Debtors have argued that Sections 1107(a) and 1108, when read together, provide authorization for paying critical vendors. The argument is that a debtor in possession's fiduciary duties includes an obligation to protect and preserve the bankruptcy estate, including the business's going-concern value; further, the going-concern value can only be preserved by paying certain prepetition claims prior to the confirmation of a plan.[549] For example, in *In re CoServ, LLC*, the Bankruptcy Court reasoned that it had authority under Section 105(a) to implement a valid exercise of the debtor's fiduciary duties, which could include satisfaction of prepetition claims prior to a plan, when the payment "is the only means to effect a substantial enhancement of the estate."[550]

4. *The Doctrine of Necessity or Necessity of Payment*

Finally, courts have also relied on the "doctrine of necessity" or the "necessity of payment" rule to approve requests to pay critical vendors. The doctrine of necessity originated in an 1882 opinion by the U.S. Supreme Court in *Miltenberger v. Logansport, C. & S.W.R. Co.*, which dealt with

545. *See In re GVM, Inc.*, 606 B.R. 220, 228 (Bankr. M.D. Pa. 2019) (denying request to pay critical vendors and stating that, "While [Section 105(a)] may be used to fashion orders as necessary to further substantive provisions of the Code, it may not be used to create substantive rights that are otherwise unavailable under the Code as is the case here."); *In re Pioneer Health Services, Inc.*, 570 B.R. at 233–34 (noting criticism by various courts that Section 105(a) cannot be used to override the priorities established under the Bankruptcy Code).
546. *In re CoServ, LLC*, 273 B.R. 487, 497 (Bankr. N.D. Tex. 2002).
547. 11 U.S.C. § 1107(a) (emphasis added).
548. 11 U.S.C. § 1108.
549. *In re CoServ, LLC*, 273 B.R. at 497.
550. *Id.*

a railroad receivership.[551] In that case, the Court acknowledged the basic duty of an equity receiver to "protect and preserve the trust funds in its hands" for the benefit of all creditors.[552] Expanding on this duty, the Court held that, "Many circumstances may exist which may make it necessary and indispensable to the business ... and the preservation of the property, for the receiver to pay pre-existing debts ... out of the earnings of the [debtor] ... under the order of the court."[553]

Since *Miltenberger*, a number of courts have expanded the application of the doctrine of necessity beyond railroad reorganizations to cover other types of proceedings, including reorganizations under Chapter 11 of the Bankruptcy Code.[554]

C. Limiting Payments to Critical Vendors – Kmart Decision

Based on Sections 105(a), 363(b), 1107, 1108 of the Bankruptcy Code, and the doctrine of necessity, courts approved critical vendor payments when the debtor established that: (i) the critical vendors provide vital goods and/or services to the debtor, (ii) payment is essential to a debtor's reorganization efforts, and (iii) the critical vendors will refuse to provide

551. Miltenberger v. Logansport, C. & S.W.R Co., 106 U.S. 286 (1882).
552. *Id.* at 310.
553. *Id.* at 311.
554. Dudley v. Mealey, 147 F.2d 268, 271 (2d Cir. 1945) (holding that, in a hotel reorganization, the court was not "helpless" to apply the doctrine of necessity to supply creditors where the alternative was the cessation of operations); *In re Lehigh & New England Ry. Co.*, 657 F.2d 570, 581 (3d Cir. 1981) (stating that a court may authorize payment of prepetition claims when there "is the possibility that the creditor will employ an immediate economic sanction, failing such payment"); *In re Penn. Cent. Transp. Co.*, 467 F.2d 100, 102 n.1 (3d Cir. 1972) (noting that the necessity of payment doctrine permits "immediate payment of claims of creditors where those creditors will not supply services or material essential to the conduct of the business until their pre-reorganization claims have been paid"); *In re Just for Feet, Inc.*, 242 B.R. at 824–25 (noting that debtors may pay prepetition claims that are essential to continued operation of the business); *In re Columbia Gas Sys., Inc.*, 171 B.R. 189, 191–92 (Bankr. D. Del. 1994) (same); *In re Tropical Sportswear Int'l Corp.*, 320 B.R. 15, 17 (Bankr. M.D. Fla. 2005) (same).

such goods and/or services absent payment on their prepetition claims.[555] Courts have conditioned payment to critical vendors on the creditor's agreement to continue extending credit to the debtor during or after the Chapter 11 case.[556]

For example, in *In re CoServ, LLC*, the court conditioned payments to critical vendors on the debtor's proof that: (i) the vendor was indispensable to the debtor's profitable operations because the vendor was a major customer of the debtor or the sole supplier of a particular product the debtor needed, (ii) the payment of the vendor's prepetition claim would result in a meaningful economic gain or the avoidance of serious economic harm to the debtor that materially exceeded the amount of the payment, and (iii) there was no practical or legal alternative to dealing with the vendor, except by paying its prepetition unsecured claim.[557]

In 2004, the Seventh Circuit Court of Appeals issued the *Kmart* opinion, affirming a district court's reversal of a bankruptcy court order that authorized payments to critical vendors.[558] Early in its Chapter 11 cases, Kmart sought authorization to pay prepetition claims of roughly 54% of its trade creditors that it asserted were "critical vendors." The Bankruptcy Court authorized the proposed payments, concluding that the equitable provisions of Section 105(a) of the Bankruptcy Code and the doctrine of necessity authorized it to approve such payments, which were conditioned on the designated vendors agreeing to provide goods to Kmart for two years on customary trade terms.[559] Certain objecting creditors who were not designated as critical vendors appealed.[560]

On appeal, the Seventh Circuit held that a critical vendor order cannot be upheld if it is based solely on Section 105(a) of the Bankruptcy Code.[561] The Seventh Circuit held that Section 105(a) "does not create discretion

---

555. *See, e.g.*, *In re Ionosphere Clubs, Inc.*, 98 B.R. at 176. *See also*, *In re Just For Feet*, 242 B.R. at 826 (reasoning that certain trade vendors provided vital merchandise to debtor and that payment of trade vendors' prepetition claims was "essential to the survival of the debtor during the Chapter 11 reorganization."). *In re Eagle-Picher Indus.*, Inc., 124 B.R. 1021, 1023 (Bankr. S.D. Ohio 1991) (approving payment of prepetition unsecured claims of tool makers as "necessary to avert a serious threat to the Chapter 11 process"); Burchinal v. Cent. Wash. Bank (*In re Adams Apple, Inc.*), 829 F.2d 1484, 1490 (9th Cir. 1987) (noting that courts have provided for the "unequal treatment of pre-petition debts when [such treatment is] necessary for rehabilitation."); 1 Collier on Bankruptcy, ¶ 105.02(4)(a) (discussing cases in which courts have relied on the "doctrine of necessity" or the "necessity of payment" rule to pay prepetition claims immediately).

556. *In re Just for Feet*, 242 B.R. at 827.

557. *In re CoServ, LLC*, 273 B.R. at 498–99.

558. *In re Kmart Corp.*, 359 F.3d 866.

559. *Id.* at 869.

560. *Id.*

561. *Id.* at 871–72.

to set aside the Code's rules about priority and distribution; the power conferred by § 105(a) is one to implement rather than override."[562] The Seventh Circuit described the "'doctrine of necessity' [as] just a fancy name for a power to depart from the Code," that was used to justify reordering priorities and paying particular creditors prior to codification of the current Bankruptcy Code.[563]

The Seventh Circuit then suggested, in *dicta*, that a debtor might be able to justify critical vendor payments through the use of Section 363(b) of the Bankruptcy Code.[564] However, because critical vendor payments do damage to the priority scheme established by other parts of the Bankruptcy Code, the court set forth a challenging test that must be satisfied before such payments can be authorized under Section 363(b). First, a debtor must establish that the creditor would not (or could not) do business with the debtor on *any* terms postpetition (including cash in advance) without receiving payment in full on its prepetition claim.[565] The Seventh Circuit felt that most trade creditors at the very least would be willing to do business with debtors postpetition if they were paid cash in advance. Second, a debtor must establish that the disfavored creditors will be as well off in the reorganization (with the critical vendor payments being made) as they would be in a liquidation where such payments would not be made.[566] The Seventh Circuit acknowledged that this requirement is similar to the requirement set forth in Section 1129(b) for "cramdown" of a Chapter 11 plan.[567]

D. Critical Vendors Post-*Kmart*

The Seventh Circuit's *dicta* have been widely adopted as the test to determine whether critical vendor payments should be authorized.[568] While the Seventh Circuit's two-part test is stringent,[569] many courts authorize payments to critical vendors after applying a variation of the two-part test.[570]

562. *Id.* at 871.
563. *Id.*
564. *Id.* at 872–73.
565. *Id.* at 873.
566. *Id.*
567. *Id.* at 872–73.
568. *See In re Murray Metallurgical Coal Holdings*, LLC, 613 B.R. 442, 451 (Bankr. S.D. Ohio 2020) (utilizing the Seventh Circuit's reasoning to determine whether a "sound business purpose exist[ed] in the critical vendor context."); *In re News Pub. Co.*, 488 B.R. 241, 244 (Bankr. N.D. Ga. 2013); *In re Pioneer Health Services, Inc.*, 570 B.R. at 234–35.
569. *In re TI Acquisition, LLC*, 429 B.R. 377, 382 (Bankr. N.D. Ga. 2010).
570. *See e.g., In re Jeans.com, Inc.*, 502 B.R. 250, 255–56 (Bankr. D.P.R. 2013) (recognizing the two-prong test in *Kmart* and ultimately authorizing critical vendor payments by applying reasoning in *In re Tropical Sportswear Int'l Corp.*, 330 B.R. at 19–20).

For example, bankruptcy courts in the District of Delaware,[571] the Southern District of New York,[572] and the Middle District of Florida[573] have approved critical vendor requests in cases – albeit, with increased scrutiny post-*Kmart*.[574] Consistent with the Seventh Circuit's analysis, particular attention now seems to be paid to the financial health of a proposed critical vendor (i.e., whether it can continue to provide the debtor with goods or

---

571. *See, e.g., In re OTC Holdings Corp.*, Case No. 10-12636 (Bankr. D. Del. Sept. 17, 2010) (authorizing payment of up to $15 million in prepetition critical vendor claims, approximately 50 percent of the debtors' total trade debt); *In re Am. Safety Razor Co.*, LLC, Case No. 10-12351 (Bankr. D. Del. Aug. 23, 2010) (authorizing payment of up to $7 million in prepetition critical vendor claims, approximately 45% of the debtors' total trade debt); *In re NEC Holdings Corp.*, Case No. 10-11890 (Bankr. D. Del. July 13, 2010) (authorizing payment of up to $7.5 million in prepetition critical vendor claims); *In re Orleans Homebuilders, Inc.*, Case No. 10-10684 (Bankr. D. Del. Apr. 6, 2010) (authorizing payment of up to $10 million in prepetition critical vendor claims); *In re Neenah Enters., Inc.*, Case. No. 10-10360 (Bankr. D. Del. Mar. 8, 2010) (authorizing payment of up to $9 million in prepetition critical vendor claims); *In re Atrium Corp.*, Case No. 10-10150 (Bankr. D. Del. Feb. 22, 2010) (authorizing payment of up to $7.5 million in prepetition critical vendor claims); *In re Visteon Corp.*, Case No. 09-11786 (Bankr. D. Del. June 19, 2009) (authorizing payment of up to $5.1 million in prepetition foreign critical vendor claims); *In re Motor Coach Indus. Int'l, Inc.*, Case No. 08-12136 (Bankr. D. Del. Oct. 7, 2008) (authorizing payment of up to $22.6 million in prepetition critical vendor claims, approximately 81 percent of the debtors' total trade debt); *In re Leiner Health Prods. Inc.*, No. 08-10446 (Bankr. D. Del. Apr. 8, 2008) (authorizing payment of up to $25.5 million in prepetition critical vendor claims, approximately 35 percent of the debtors' total trade debt); *In re Trade Secret, Inc.*, No. 10-12153 (Bankr. D. Del. July 7, 2010) (authorizing payment of up to $14 million in prepetition critical vendor claims, approximately 50% of the debtors' total trade debt).
572. *See, e.g., In re Chrysler, LLC*, No. 09-50002 (AJG) (Bankr. S.D.N.Y. May 20, 2009) (authorizing debtors to make substantial essential supplier payments on prepetition unsecured claims subject to various restrictions); *In re Gen. Motors Corp.*, No. 09-50026 (REG) (Bankr. S.D.N.Y. June 25, 2009) (same); *In re Dana Corp.*, No. 06-10354 (BRL) (Bankr. S.D.N.Y. Mar. 3, 2006 and Mar. 29, 2006) (orders authorizing the debtors to pay the prepetition claims of certain essential suppliers up to $52.1 million); *In re Delphi Corp.*, No. 05-44481 (RDD) (Bankr. S.D.N.Y. Oct. 13, 2005) (order authorizing the debtors to continue vendor rescue program and payment of $90 million in prepetition claims of financially distressed sole source suppliers and vendors); *In re Tower Auto., Inc.*, No. 05-10578 (ALG) (Bankr. S.D.N.Y. Mar. 14, 2005) (order authorizing the debtors to pay $40 million in prepetition claims of essential suppliers); *see also, In re* Windstream Holdings Inc., 614 B.R. 441 (S.D.N.Y. 2020), appeal dismissed as moot *sub nom. In re:Windstream Holdings, Inc.* GLM DFW, Inc., Creditor-Appellant, v. Windstream Holdings, Inc., Debtor-Appellee., No. 20-1275-BK, 2021 WL 627502 (2d Cir. Feb. 18, 2021) (dismissing appeal as equitably moot and determining that it would be inequitable to unwind payments over a year later).
573. *In re Tropical Sportswear Int'l Corp.*, 330 B.R. at 21–22.
574. The cases cited are a sampling of cases; the authors acknowledge there are many other courts and districts that have analyzed the issue.

services absent payment on its prepetition claims) and whether the product or service provided by the vendor can be obtained from another source.[575]

575. *See, e.g.*, *In re Kmart Corp.*, 359 F.3d 866 (7th Cir. 2004); *In re CoServ, LLC*, 273 B.R. 487 (Bankr. N.D. Tex. 2002); *In re United Am., Inc.*, 327 B.R. 776 (Bankr. E.D. Va. 2005); *In re Mirant Corp.*, 296 B.R. 427 (Bankr. N.D. Tex. 2003); *In re Goodrich Quality Theaters, Inc.*, 616 B.R. 514, 518 (Bankr. W.D. Mich. 2020) (reasoning that popcorn and drinks, and candy "are critical to the success of a modern movie chain, but this means only that the products are critical, not the vendors who supply them"), supplemented, No. DG 20-00759, 2020 WL 1180534 (Bankr. W.D. Mich. Mar. 9, 2020).

13

D&O Policies and Advancement of Legal Fees

A. Overview[576]

To encourage persons to serve as directors and officers of corporations and other entities—and, in that capacity, to make difficult decisions and take worthwhile risks—companies promise to indemnify their directors and officers against liability for actions taken in their corporate capacities and to advance or reimburse costs they incur for defending against lawsuits asserting such liability.[577]

Directors and officers liability insurance policies ("D&O Insurance" or "D&O Policies") provide funds ("D&O Proceeds") to back up those promises.[578] For directors and officers of a solvent company, access to, and the appropriate use of, D&O Proceeds may never become issues.

576. An in-depth examination of the duties of directors and officers, the law on indemnification, the many possible configurations of critical defined terms (such as "claim," "loss," and "wrongful act"), offered and excluded coverage, policy limits and sublimits, and the myriad other matters that can affect coverage is beyond the scope of this chapter. Useful resources include James A. Fanto et al., *Directors' and Officers' Liability* (2d ed. 2011); Richard L. Epling et al., *Intersections of Bankruptcy Law and Insurance Coverage Litigation*, 21 Norton J. Bankr. L. & Prac. 103 (2012); Elina Chechelnitsky, *D&O Insurance in Bankruptcy: Just Another Business Contract*, 14 Fordham J. Corp. & Fin. L. 825 (2009).

577. *See, e.g., In re La. World Exposition, Inc.*, 832 F.2d 1391, 1398 (5th Cir. 1987) (directors' and officers' liability insurance functions as inducement to directors and officers); *In re First Cent. Fin. Corp.*, 238 B.R. 9, 13 (Bankr. E.D.N.Y. 1999) (indemnification is incentive for persons to accept employment as director or officer).

578. *See, e.g., In re Christian Life Ctr.*, 821 F.2d 1370, 1374 (9th Cir. 1987) (corporation's duty to indemnify its officer, whether contractual or statutory, is a form of compensation); *First Central*, 238 B.R. at 13 (D&O Policy is part of executive benefits package offered as incentive for employment).

In bankruptcy, however, D&O Policies and D&O Proceeds become uniquely coveted assets that give rise to a complex array of issues. Directors and officers will see them as their sole protection against calamitous litigation costs;[579] creditors and shareholders will see them as a source of funds to mitigate potentially hundreds of millions of dollars of losses; trustees will see them as a source of cash that will maximize both the bankruptcy estate and their trustee fees.[580] Among the matters these parties may dispute are: (i) whether the debtor's D&O Policy and/or the D&O Proceeds are assets of the bankruptcy estate, (ii) whether the automatic stay imposed by the Bankruptcy Code[581] bars advancing defense costs to directors and officers and, if it does, whether it should be lifted in a given circumstance to permit such payments, (iii) whether an insurer under a D&O Policy must pay damages sought by a trustee or debtor in possession in a suit against the debtor's own directors and officers, and (iv) whether a court should authorize the "buy-back" of a D&O policy by an insurer in settlement of the insurer's liability.

D&O Policies are complex, negotiated contracts that can vary significantly by carrier. The resolutions of the issues described above depend heavily on the specific language of the relevant D&O Policy and the factual circumstances of the case. The discussion below describes the principal characteristics of D&O Insurance and summarizes how courts approach issues at the intersection of D&O Insurance and bankruptcy law. Evaluating any specific matter requires close analysis of the D&O Policy at issue and examination of the case law in the controlling jurisdiction.[582]

579. *See, e.g., In re MF Global Holdings Ltd.*, 469 B.R. 177 (Bankr. S.D.N.Y. 2012) (lifting automatic stay to permit insurers to advance funds to pay legal fees of directors and officers which, in five months since date of filing, had reached $8.3 million); *In re Lehman Bros. Holdings, Inc.*, No. 08-13555 (JMP) (Bankr. S.D.N.Y. July 27, 2010) (motion to lift stay to permit insurers to advance defense costs; motion indicated that cumulative D&O Policy limit of $45 million would be fully expended on such costs within two years after case was filed).

580. Statutory compensation for the services of a Chapter 7 or Chapter 11 trustee is calculated on a sliding scale as a percentage of funds disbursed or money turned over to parties in interest, including creditors. 11 U.S.C. § 326(a).

581. 11 U.S.C. § 362(a).

582. *See, e.g., In re Downey Fin. Corp.*, 428 B.R. 595, 603 & n.31 (Bankr. D. Del. 2010); *In re* Allied Digital Techs. Corp., 306 B.R. 505, 509 (Bankr. D. Del. 2004) ("the cases are controlled by the language and scope of the policy at issue[,] not by broad, general statements"); *In re CyberMedica, Inc.*, 280 B.R. 12, 14–16 (Bankr. D. Mass. 2002) (whether D&O Proceeds are estate property "must be analyzed in light of the facts of each case").

B. Relevant Characteristics of D&O Policies

1. Types of D&O Insurance Coverage

While individual D&O Policies can vary substantially, they will generally incorporate the following concepts, often using the following terms: coverage under D&O Policies is typically for *losses* resulting from *claims* that arise from *wrongful acts*. "Losses" include defense costs, judgments, and settlements. "Claims" include (i) direct claims by third parties for violations of federal or state securities laws, (ii) derivative claims brought by shareholders on behalf of the corporation, and (iii) under some D&O Policies, violations of certain employment laws. "Wrongful acts" range over acts or omissions, including breaches of duty, committed by a director or officer in his or her capacity as such, but they generally exclude fraud and criminal acts.

The D&O Policy may provide for payment commencing with the first dollar of allowable claims for losses, or it might include a provision for a self-insured retention (*SIR*)—an amount, similar to a deductible, that the company must pay out of its own funds before the insurer will pay for covered losses.

Modern D&O Policies offer three types of coverage (although a company need not purchase all three):

a. Side A or Coverage A—Direct Payment to Individual Directors and Officers for Nonindemnified Losses

Side A covers losses of the directors and officers to the extent that the company has not indemnified the directors and officers. Some D&O Policies merely require that no indemnification payments have been made, while others cover losses when the company "cannot or will not provide" indemnification. The directors and officers are often the named insureds under Side A coverage and are its direct beneficiaries. The company is not itself a beneficiary of Side A coverage and has no claim to D&O Proceeds paid on account of Side A coverage.

Side A coverage is particularly salient in a corporate bankruptcy. The filing of the bankruptcy case itself may prompt the filing of actions against the directors and officers, who will quickly begin to incur defense costs. Those defense costs (as well as the amounts of any eventual judgments assessed against the directors and officers) constitute claims of the directors and officers against the debtor's bankruptcy estate. Claims that arise from prepetition indemnification agreements (e.g., the company's bylaws, an employment agreement, or a separate indemnification agreement) are treated as general, unsecured prepetition claims, which have the lowest priority for distribution in a bankruptcy case, ahead only of the interests held by a debtor's equity holders (and of any claims subordinated contractually or by court order).[583] For this reason, directors and officers of a debtor company should file proofs of claim in the bankruptcy case based on their indemnification rights, even if they have incurred no indemnifiable losses as of the petition date.[584]

The automatic stay prevents the directors and officers from pursuing the debtor or its property for immediate payment of claims.[585] Moreover, even if the debtor had cash to pay indemnification claims, it may not voluntarily do so in preference to all other claims of similar priority without a court order.[586] Therefore, those claims of the directors and officers are literally ones for which the debtor "cannot provide indemnification," thereby implicating Side A coverage.[587] If directors and officers cannot obtain access to D&O Proceeds under Side A to cover their attorneys' fees and costs, they may have no practical way to defend themselves in complex and expensive litigation.

When a company enters bankruptcy, its D&O insurer may seek to void or rescind the D&O Policy on the ground that the company committed fraud in applying for the D&O Policy. In particular, the D&O Insurance provider might comb the company's insurance application for information regarding its financial condition at the time of the application that the provider can then argue was materially misstated. If the provider is permitted to rescind the D&O Policy on that basis, the directors and officers will lose coverage. To protect directors and officers from rescission, some D&O Insurance providers offer *nonrescindable Side A coverage*. Such coverage costs more than ordinary Side A coverage, but it provides payment to directors and

583. *See, e.g.*, Olin Corp. v. Riverwood Int'l (*In re Manville Forest Prods. Corp.*), 209 F.3d 125, 129 (2d Cir. 2000) (contingent indemnification claim arises when indemnification agreement is executed); *In re Hemingway Transp., Inc.*, 954 F.2d 1, 8–9 (1st Cir. 1992) (Bankruptcy Code's definition of "claim" includes unliquidated, contingent right to payment under prepetition indemnification agreement, even if triggering contingency occurs postpetition); *In re Farmland Indus., Inc.*, 318 B.R. 159, 165 (Bankr. W.D. Mo. 2004) (same); *In re Christian Life Center*, 821 F.2d 1370, 1374 (9th Cir. 1987) (corporation's duty to indemnify its officer, whether contractual or statutory, is a form of compensation; duty to indemnify arising from officer's prepetition services gives rise to prepetition, not administrative, claim); Stratton v. Mariner Health Care, Inc. (*In re Mariner Post-Acute Network, Inc.*), 303 B.R. 42, 45 (Bankr. D. Del. 2003) (breach of a prepetition indemnification agreement gives rise to a prepetition claim).

584. *See, e.g., In re Huffy Corp.*, 424 B.R. 295, 305–06 (Bankr. S.D. Ohio 2010) (because claim under prepetition contract for indemnification is prepetition claim, failure of indemnified party to file proof of claim by bar date prevented distributions to party and resulted in discharge of claim); *In re Downey Fin. Corp.*, 428 B.R. at 607 (Bankr. D. Del. 2010) (indicating that failure of directors or officers to file indemnification claims against debtor would bar payment of such claims from property of estate).

585. 11 U.S.C. §§ 362(a)(1), (3).

586. *See, e.g., In re Kmart Corp.*, 359 F.3d 866 (7th Cir. 2004).

587. *See, e.g., In re Downey Fin. Corp.*, 428 B.R. at 601 & n.16 (Bankr. D. Del. 2010).

officers for nonindemnified losses even in situations where the provider might arguably have issued the D&O Policy in reliance on fraudulent misstatements in the D&O Policy application.

b. Side B or Coverage B—Reimbursement of Company to Extent of Indemnification Provided to Individual Directors and Officers

Side B covers the company's own expenditures for losses incurred by its directors and officers where the company has provided indemnification. Although Side B recoveries are paid to the company, Side B coverage can be characterized as the inverse of Side A: while Side A provides coverage directly to the directors and officers, Side B does so indirectly. However, Side B is no less for the benefit of the directors and officers, because the company receives coverage for its out-of-pocket reimbursement of losses suffered by its directors and officers rather than for its own direct liability.

c. Side C or Coverage C—Direct Payment to Company Itself for Its Own Defense Costs and Liability

Side C coverage pays the company for its own defense costs and liability incurred as a result of an action brought against it, such as a third-party securities law claim or a shareholder derivative action.

2. *Coverage Limits*

While some D&O Policies provide separate dollar coverage limits for Sides A, B, and C, the majority of D&O Policies dealt with in case law are "wasting" policies: the D&O Policy provides that the insurer will pay a single aggregate maximum dollar amount under the D&O Policy, regardless of whether the payments are for Side A, B, or C coverage. Therefore, every dollar paid for one purpose (e.g., the fees of a director's defense attorney under Side A) is a dollar that is not available to be paid for another purpose (e.g., satisfying a judgment against the company under Side C). Companies may purchase excess D&O Policies, which pay only after the limits of liability on specified prior D&O Policies are first exhausted.

3. *"Priority of Payment" Provisions*

While some D&O Policies do not distinguish among payments made for different types of coverage, current D&O Policies often provide for the order in which coverage may be accessed. These D&O Policies prioritize Side A coverage—D&O Proceeds paid directly to directors and officers on account of losses for which the company does not indemnify them—over coverage under Sides B and C. The effect of such provisions is to require the payment of the defense costs of directors and officers under Side A before any payment may be made to the company for its own expenses or liability under Side B or C.[588]

4. *Waiver by Company of Benefit of Automatic Stay*

As additional assurance that D&O Proceeds will be accessible to the directors and officers in a company bankruptcy, the D&O Policy may contain a waiver by the company of the protections of the automatic stay and an agreement not to contest a request to lift the stay made by the insurer or an insured director or officer. While some courts will not enforce such prepetition waivers (on the ground that the automatic stay is for the protection of all creditors, not solely the party for whose benefit the waiver was made), other courts may do so. In any event, the waiver makes clearer the intent of the parties that D&O Proceeds should be made available immediately to directors and officers of a company in bankruptcy.[589]

5. *"Claims Made" Policies*

D&O Policies are typically "claims made" policies: they cover claims asserted against an insured person during a specific period of time (the "Policy Period"). "Assertion" of a claim encompasses a wider range of actions than just the formal filing of a lawsuit and can include the receipt of a demand letter, the commencement of an investigation by a federal or state law enforcement authority (even if no charges have been brought), a request for information by a government agency, or the reporting by the insured itself of circumstances that might give rise to a claim in the future. Insurers may permit policy holders to "lock in" coverage for claims that may be asserted after the Policy Period on account of circumstances that arose during the Policy Period by requiring that the policyholder report such circumstances to the insurer during the Policy Period.

6. *"Insured vs. Insured" Exclusion*

Like all liability insurance, D&O Policies typically include provisions that exclude or bar coverage for losses that, absent the exclusion, would give rise to covered claims. The most commonly litigated exclusion in the

---

588. *See, e.g.*, *In re MF Global Holdings Ltd.*, 469 B.R. at 193–94 (Bankr. S.D.N.Y. 2012); Adelphia Commc'ns Corp. v. Associated Elec. & Gas Ins. Servs. (*In re Adelphia Commc'ns Corp.*), 285 B.R. 580, 586–87 (Bankr. S.D.N.Y. 2002), *vacated on other grounds*, 298 B.R. 49 (S.D.N.Y. 2003) (no priority of payment provision); *In re Downey Fin. Corp.*, 428 B.R. at 599–600 (Bankr. D. Del. 2010) (describing effect of "Order of Payment" provisions).

589. *See, e.g.*, *In re Downey Fin. Corp.*, 428 B.R. at 600 (Bankr. D. Del. 2010) (explaining meaning of company's waiver of protections of automatic stay).

bankruptcy context is the "Insured vs. Insured Exclusion." The Insured vs. Insured Exclusion bars coverage for any claims asserted under a D&O Policy by one insured person against another insured person. It is intended to prevent collusive lawsuits. For example, suppose a company's directors take actions that result in the company bearing a financial loss. The company's directors might cause the company to sue those same directors for their money-losing decision. If the plaintiff company were to win a judgment against the defendant directors and officers, the insurer would have to pay the judgment to the company on behalf of the losing defendants (while also paying those defendants' defense costs), thereby making the insurer a guarantor of the competence of the company's management. If the company were to lose the suit, the defendant directors and officers would still be paid for their defense costs. In this example, the Insured vs. Insured Exclusion would protect the insurer from paying any amounts, because the plaintiff and defendants were both insured parties under the D&O Policy.

As discussed below, the analysis of the Insured vs. Insured Exclusion becomes more complicated when the plaintiff is a bankruptcy trustee or the postpetition company acting as a debtor in possession in Chapter 11.

C. Frequent Issues Concerning the Treatment of D&O Insurance in Bankruptcy

Fallout from filing a bankruptcy case can include the commencement of multiple lawsuits against the directors and officers of the insolvent company. Directors and officers will seek current payment of their claims for defense costs from the D&O Proceeds, which they view as a pot of funds created specifically for their benefit, to protect them in cases where the company has failed and shareholders are looking to shift their investment risk to managers who exercised reasonable business judgments that nonetheless led to an undesirable outcome. Standing in their way may be shareholders, injured creditors, or the bankruptcy estate (in the person of the trustee or debtor in possession), all of whom see the same D&O Proceeds as a pot of money for recouping their losses—a shrinking pot reduced by every dollar paid to directors and officers to assist them in avoiding responsibility for the debtor's financial calamity.

As described above, claims of directors and officers for defense costs usually constitute general prepetition claims against the debtor, which may not be paid out of, or enforced against, estate property without the court's permission.[590] Courts must therefore answer two principal questions in deciding whether to authorize D&O Proceeds to be used currently to

590. 11 U.S.C. §§ 362(a)(1), (3).

pay the defense costs of directors and officers: (i) are the D&O Proceeds property of the debtor's bankruptcy estate, and (ii) if so, may the court permit payment of the D&O Proceeds to the directors and officers notwithstanding the automatic stay?

1. D&O Policies as Property of the Company's Bankruptcy Estate

Perhaps the least controversial issue at the intersection of D&O Insurance and bankruptcy law is the status of the D&O Policy itself (as distinguished from D&O Proceeds). Courts have consistently held that the D&O Policy itself is property of the company's bankruptcy estate.[591] Because a D&O Policy is property of the debtor's bankruptcy estate, the insurer may not unilaterally cancel it without violating the automatic stay.[592]

2. D&O Proceeds as Property of the Company's Bankruptcy Estate

Courts have struggled for years with whether or not D&O Proceeds constitute property of the bankruptcy estate under various available coverages and policy provisions.[593] If the D&O Proceeds are *not* property of the estate, then they are not protected by the automatic stay and may be paid to the directors and officers as required or permitted by the D&O Policy. If the

---

591. *See, e.g.*, *In re Adelphia Commc'ns Corp.*, 298 B.R. at 52–53 (Bankr. S.D.N.Y. 2003); *In re MF Global Holdings Ltd.*, 469 B.R. at 190 (Bankr. S.D.N.Y. 2012) (describing issue as "well-settled"); *In re Downey Fin. Corp.*, 428 B.R. at 603 & n.29 (Bankr. D. Del. 2010) (collecting cases); *In re Allied Digital Tech. Corp.*, 306 B.R. 505, 509 (Bankr. D. Del. 2004); Ochs v. Lipson (*In re First Cent. Fin. Corp.*), 238 B.R. 9, 15–16 (Bankr. E.D.N.Y. 1999); *but see* Homsy v. Floyd (*In re Vitek*), 51 F.3d 530, 533–35 (5th Cir. 1995) (questioning the relevance of the distinction between "policies" and "proceeds").

592. *See In re Minoco Group of Cos., Ltd*, 799 F.2d 517, 519 (9th Cir. 1986); *First Central*, 238 B.R. at 16–17. The bankruptcy court also has jurisdiction to authorize the sale of the D&O Policy, which may occur as part of a "buy-back" settlement between the debtor and insurer, subject to the requirements of the Bankruptcy Code. *See generally* 11 U.S.C. § 363(b) (governing use, sale, or lease of estate property outside ordinary course of business).

593. *See In re La. World Exposition, Inc.*, 832 F.2d at 1399–1400 (5th Cir. 1987) (noting that the court could find no cases to date addressing issue with regard to D&O Proceeds, as opposed to D&O Policies). Sources that provide an overview of the case law in this area include Richard L. Epling et al., *Intersections of Bankruptcy Law and Insurance Coverage Litigation*, 21 Norton J. Bankr. L. & Prac. 103 (2012); Elina Chechelnitsky, *D&O Insurance in Bankruptcy: Just Another Business Contract*, 14 Fordham J. Corp. & Fin. L. 825 (2009); *see also In re Downey Fin. Corp.*, 428 B.R. 595 (Bankr. D. Del. 2010); *In re Allied Digital Tech. Corp.*, 306 B.R. 505 (Bankr. D. Del. 2004).

D&O Proceeds *are* property of the estate, however, the payments may not be made to the directors and officers absent an order of the court lifting the stay.

An insolvent company's directors or officers are the most likely parties to initiate a court proceeding to require payment of D&O Proceeds to cover their current defense costs; however, it is not unusual for debtors and insurers to make such motions. Corporate officials may submit to the insurer under a D&O Policy direct claims for defense costs, and a prudent insurer will often seek a protective order from the bankruptcy court before paying on those claims. A trustee or debtor in possession may similarly seek to pay those costs, on the ground that leaving the directors or officers unable to defend themselves would increase the likelihood of a judgment entered against the directors and officers that would bind the debtor in future litigation under a collateral estoppel theory.[594]

Conversely, a trustee, as a representative of the bankruptcy estate, may commence a lawsuit against the directors and officers with an eye to obtaining the D&O Proceeds for the estate as a whole in order to benefit all creditors. Because most D&O Policies are "wasting policies," under which one aggregate liability limit applies to all losses and all coverages, the trustee may seek to prevent current payment of defense costs, because each dollar paid to a director is a dollar less of potential recovery for the estate.[595]

Recent case law has begun to synthesize an approach from precedents out of multiple jurisdictions whose outcomes have depended upon, among other things, (i) the scope of the D&O Policy coverage; the intended recipients of D&O Proceeds (as provided by, or inferred from, the D&O

594. The debtors made this argument in *In re Lehman Bros. Holdings, Inc.*, No. 08-13555 (JMP) (Bankr. S.D.N.Y. July 27, 2010). The court granted the motion to allow D&O Proceeds to pay defense costs, which exceeded $35 million as of the date of the motion. *Id.* at Docket No. 10963. *See also* SN Liquidation, Inc. v. Icon Int'l, Inc. (*In re SN Liquidation, Inc.*), 388 B.R. 579, 584–85 (Bankr. D. Del. 2008) (finding automatic stay applies to third-party suit against nondebtor officers, because judgment could have collateral estoppel effect in other litigation, to detriment of estate); Goldin v. Primavera Familienstiftung Tag Assocs. (*In re Granite Partners, LP*), 194 B.R. 318, 337–38 (Bankr. S.D.N.Y. 1996) (indicating that potential for collateral estoppel against debtor is appropriate consideration in determining whether suit against directors and officers should be stayed).

595. *See, e.g., In re Allied Digital Techs. Corp.*, 306 B.R. at 513 (Bankr. D. Del. 2004) ("The bottom line is that the Trustee seeks to protect the amount he may receive in his suit against the directors and officers while limiting coverage for the defense costs of the directors and officers."); *In re CyberMedica, Inc.*, 280 B.R. at 14–15 (Bankr. D. Mass. 2002); *In re First Cent. Fin. Corp.*, 238 B.R. at 15 (Bankr. E.D.N.Y. 1999) (trustee sought to enjoin payment of defense costs to directors and officers in order to preserve D&O Proceeds for payment to estate in satisfaction of anticipated judgment in trustee's action against debtor's directors and officers).

Policy); (ii) the likelihood of covered claims being asserted against the debtor directly; and, relatedly, (iii) the actual need for the D&O Policy to protect against diminution of the debtor's estate.[596] The spectrum of results on the issue of whether D&O Proceeds are property of a debtor's bankruptcy estate can be summarized as follows.

If the D&O Policy provides only direct liability coverage to directors and officers (Side A), then the D&O Proceeds are *not* property of the debtor's estate, and the insurer may pay the defense cost claims of the directors and officers (without a court order, although a prudent insurer will seek such an order).[597] If the D&O Policy provides only direct liability coverage to the debtor company (Side C), then the D&O Proceeds *are* property of the debtor's bankruptcy estate.[598]

If the D&O Policy provides both Side A coverage directly to directors and officers as well as coverage to the debtor company under Side B and/or Side C, the analyses diverge among the courts. Some courts hold that all of the D&O Proceeds of a D&O Policy are property of the estate if the estate has *any* interest in *any* of the D&O Proceeds, regardless of whether Side A coverage is also provided directly to directors and officers.[599] Alternatively, some courts hold that, in the same situation as just described, D&O Proceeds are *not* property of the estate, largely on the ground that "D&O Policies are obtained for the protection of individual directors and officers. Indemnification coverage [Side B] does not change this fundamental purpose... In essence and at its core, a D&O policy remains a safeguard of officer and director interests and not a vehicle for corporate protection."[600]

596. *See, e.g., In re Downey Fin. Corp*, 428 B.R. at 603–08 (Bankr. D. Del. 2010); *Allied Digital*, 306 B.R. at 510–13 (cited extensively in *Downey Financial*).

597. *See, e.g., In re La. World Exposition Inc.*, 832 F.2d at 1399 (5th Cir. 1987) (considering only the status of D&O Proceeds under D&O Policy's direct liability coverage for directors and officers, although D&O Policy also included Side B indemnification coverage to debtor); *In re SN Liquidation, Inc.*, 388 B.R. at 584 (Bankr. D. Del. 2008); *Allied Digital*, 306 B.R. at 512 (if "the liability insurance policy only provides direct coverage to the directors and officers the proceeds are not property of the estate").

598. *See Downey Financial*, 428 B.R. at 603; *SN Liquidation*, 388 B.R. at 584; *Allied Digital*, 306 B.R. at 511–12.

599. *See, e.g., In re The Leslie Fay Cos., Inc.*, 207 B.R. 764 (Bankr. S.D.N.Y. 1997); *In re Sacred Heart Hosp. of Norristown*, 182 B.R. 413 (Bankr. E.D. Pa. 1995); *In re Circle K Corp.*, 121 B.R. 257 (Bankr. D. Ariz. 1990).

600. *First Central*, 238 B.R. at 16 (D&O Policy covered reimbursement of indemnification costs (i.e., Side B), with a rider that provided entity coverage (i.e., Side C)). *See also* Youngstown Osteopathic Hosp. Ass'n v. Ventresco (*In re Youngstown Osteopathic Hosp. Ass'n*), 271 B.R. 544, 550–51 (Bankr. N.D. Ohio 2002) (citing *First Central*; D&O Policy had Side A and Side B coverage only); *In re Daisy Sys. Sec. Litig.*, 132 B.R. 752, 755 (N.D. Cal. 1991) (D&O Proceeds "are not simply assets of [the debtor's] bankruptcy estate to be divided among creditors according to bankruptcy law").

A third set of courts applies a more nuanced analysis, holding that the D&O Proceeds of policies that provide coverage both to directors and officers and to the debtor company "will be property of the estate if depletion of the proceeds would have an adverse effect on the estate to the extent the policy *actually* protects the estate's other assets from diminution."[601]

Critical to this third line of cases is that the D&O Proceeds at issue protect against "actual" threats to estate assets. Even if the D&O Policy provides for reimbursement to the debtor company of amounts paid to indemnify directors and officers (i.e., Side B coverage) and/or direct coverage for the debtor's own entity liability for claims made against it (i.e., Side C coverage), D&O Proceeds would nonetheless *not* be property of the debtor's bankruptcy estate, if the likelihood is small, hypothetical, or merely speculative that (i) any claims subject to its Side C coverage will actually be made against the debtor or (ii) the debtor will ever pay any defense or liability costs for its directors and officers for which the debtor could seek reimbursement under its Side B coverage.[602]

---

601. *Allied Digital*, 306 B.R. at 512 (emphasis added). *See also Downey Fin.*, 428 B.R. at 604 (following *Allied Digital*); *SN Liquidation*, 388 B.R. at 584 (adopting *Allied Digital* analysis).

602. *See, e.g., Downey Fin.*, 428 B.R. at 604–07 (debtor had no interest in D&O Proceeds as to *Side C* coverage, because the only pending securities action against debtor had been dismissed with prejudice and the remaining shareholder derivative action had been stayed and did not seek relief against debtor itself; debtor had no interest in D&O Proceeds as to *Side B* coverage, because (a) it had not paid defense costs of its directors and officers prepetition in excess of its self-insured retention amount; (b) directors and officers had made no postpetition claims for indemnification from the debtor, and (c) the trustee was not offering to pay any such defense costs out of estate assets; therefore, debtor's ability to access Side B coverage was "hypothetical or speculative"); *Allied Digital*, 306 B.R. at 512–13 (if "indemnification [by debtor of directors and officers] either has not occurred, is hypothetical, or speculative, the proceeds are not property of the bankruptcy estate"; trustee's concern is that proceeds be available to him as *plaintiff* in action against directors and officers, but, because no plaintiff outside bankruptcy would be permitted to limit the right of directors and officers to obtain payment of their defense costs from D&O Proceeds, the trustee may not do so either); *In re Adelphia Commc'ns Corp.*, 298 B.R. at 53 (S.D.N.Y. 2003) (debtor had neither made nor committed to make any payments to directors or officers on account of defense costs, so had no interest in Side B reimbursement proceeds, any more than "a car owner with collision coverage [may claim] he has the right to proceeds from his policy simply because there is a . . . possibility that his car will collide with another"); *First Central*, 238 B.R. at 17–18 (if coverage "is hypothetical and fails to provide some palpable benefit to the estate, it cannot be used by a trustee to lever himself into a position of first entitlement to policy proceeds"). *Cf. SN Liquidation*, 388 B.R. at 584 (D&O Proceeds *are* property of estate in case where "indemnification is not merely speculative [as in *Allied Digital*; rather, in this case,] the defendants have made a formal request for indemnification"; court concluded a risk existed that "indemnity payments to directors and officers will result in insufficient coverage available to the debtor").

Among the facts that may be relevant in determining whether a D&O Policy protects against an "actual" or "hypothetical" threat to estate assets are: (i) existence and status (including expiration of any statute of limitations under nonbankruptcy law) of lawsuits against the debtor that might implicate Side C coverage; (ii) existence and status of lawsuits (including expiration of any statute of limitations under nonbankruptcy law) against directors and officers that might implicate Side B coverage; (iii) whether the debtor had exhausted its self-insured retention amount under Side B or Side C (typically, no SIR applies to Side A coverage); (iv) whether the bar date had passed for the filing of indemnification claims by directors and officers against the debtor company; (v) the dollar limit of the insurer's liability compared to accrued and expected defense costs, and (vi) priority-of-payment provisions that require application of any D&O Proceeds directly to the defense costs of directors and officers under Side A before any funds are available to the debtor.

3. *Relief from the Automatic Stay; Section 105(a) Injunctions*

If D&O Proceeds are determined to be property of a debtor's estate, the automatic stay protects them. Directors and officers seeking to obtain coverage for defense costs must obtain a court order modifying the automatic stay. The analysis is fact-specific, and relief is at the discretion of the court. However, courts will normally consider whether the harm to the directors and officers from maintaining the stay in place—thereby denying them access to D&O Proceeds for their ongoing defense costs—outweighs the potential harm to the estate of lifting the stay. Using that analysis, some courts, while holding that D&O Proceeds are estate property protected by the stay, have nonetheless been willing to lift or modify the stay where present harm to the directors and officers outweighed potential or speculative harm to the estate.[603]

In the alternative, some courts have either extended the automatic stay to protect individual directors and officers (who, as nondebtors, would not otherwise be protected against lawsuits by the stay) or used their equitable powers under Section 105(a) to enjoin suits that imposed defense costs on the directors and officers.[604]

4. Suits by Estate Representatives and the "Insured vs. Insured" Exclusion

When a company becomes a debtor in a bankruptcy case, a trustee or a Chapter 11 debtor in possession[605] may sue the directors and officers of the debtor on account of their prepetition actions in managing (or mismanaging) the debtor's affairs. In some instances, the power to sue on behalf of the debtor and its estate may be granted to an official committee of creditors or equity security holders appointed in the case or to a representative appointed under a plan of reorganization or of liquidation. The prize in such litigation is the D&O Proceeds: if the directors and officers are

603. *See, e.g., In re Downey Fin. Corp.*, 428 B.R. at 608–11 (Bankr. D. Del. 2010) (even if D&O Proceeds were property of estate, application of three-factor test for lifting stay, including balance-of-harms test, weighed in favor of directors and officers); *In re Allied Digital Techs. Corp.*, 306 B.R. at 513–14 (Bankr. D. Del. 2004) (even if D&O Proceeds were property of estate, court would lift stay to permit payment of directors' and officers' defense costs; without access to D&O Proceeds, directors and officers "will be prevented from conducting a meaningful defense to the Trustee's claims and may suffer substantial and irreparable harm"; conversely, trustee had no right to D&O Proceeds as plaintiff, harm to estate was hypothetical only, and payment of defense costs directly from D&O Proceeds would reduce indemnification claims of directors and officers against estate assets); *In re CyberMedica, Inc.*, 280 B.R. at 14–15 (Bankr. D. Mass. 2002) (D&O Proceeds were property of estate, but court lifted stay to permit directors to access them for defense costs, finding that their need was immediate, while any harm to estate was speculative).

604. *See, e.g., In re SN Liquidation, Inc.*, 388 B.R. at 584–85 (Bankr. D. Del. 2008) (enjoining suit against nondebtor officers of debtor, because suit threatened D&O Proceeds, which were property of estate that should be available to all litigation claimants equally); *In re Circle K Corp.*, 121 B.R. at 261–62 (Bankr. D. Ariz. 1990) (district court securities litigation threatened D&O Proceeds, which were property of debtor's estate; court therefore had authority to enjoin suit, whether under Section 105(a) or Section 362(a)). *See also In re Zenith Labs., Inc.*, 104 B.R. 659 (D.N.J. 1989) (staying class action against present and former employees of debtor).

605. Typically, a trustee is not appointed in a Chapter 11 case. Instead, the debtor's management continues to operate the debtor's business, manage its financial affairs, and administer its property as a "debtor in possession." In that capacity, the debtor has most of the same powers, rights, and duties as a trustee. *See* 11 U.S.C. §§ 1101(1), 1107.

found liable, they will, in turn, seek indemnification for any monetary judgment from the insurer, and the insurer would be required to pay the D&O Proceeds into the estate, to be distributed to the debtor's creditors.

The insurer may defend against such a claim by asserting the Insured vs. Insured Exclusion. As described above, the Insured vs. Insured Exclusion is intended to discourage the insured company—which, of course, acts only through its directors and officers—from suing its own directors and officers for "wrongful acts" under a D&O Policy, and from obtaining insurance proceeds to cover losses every time the company loses money for whatever reason. The issue in a bankruptcy case becomes whether the Insured vs. Insured Exclusion bars recovery of damages by the trustee or debtor in possession on the ground that each stands in the place of the prepetition company, thereby making the lawsuit as a matter of one insured suing another as it would have been outside of bankruptcy.

D&O Policies may address this issue with respect to suits brought by trustees, receivers, and other independent, third-party fiduciaries by carving such suits out of the Insured vs. Insured Exclusion, thereby providing coverage for judgments resulting from such suits. Case law is divided on the issue of whether the Insured vs. Insured Exclusion should apply to suits brought by a debtor in possession, a creditors' committee, or a plan-appointed creditor representative, if those entities are not specifically included in a carve-out.[606]

5. "Buy-Back" Settlements of D&O Insurance Policies

Because D&O Policies are property of the debtor's bankruptcy estate, the bankruptcy court has jurisdiction to authorize the sale of such policies back to the insurer in exchange for a lump-sum payment.[607] Such a sale is often part of a global settlement of coverage disputes and can bring

606. *Contrast* Biltmore Assocs., LLC v. Twin City Fire Ins. Co., 572 F.3d 663, 670 & n.15, 671 & nn.16–17 (9th Cir. 2009) (debtor in possession initiated lawsuit against directors and officers, consented to judgment against itself, and assigned that judgment to a plan-created creditors' trust; court barred recovery under D&O Policy by trustee of the creditors' trust, finding that, "for purposes of the insured versus insured exclusion, the prefiling company and the company as debtor in possession in Chapter 11 are the same entity") (collecting cases) *with* HA 2003, Inc. v. Fed Ins. Co. (*In re HA 2003, Inc.*), 310 B.R. 710, 717–20 (Bankr. N.D. Ill. 2004) (carve-out from Insured vs. Insured Exclusion for "person . . . authorized under applicable law to act on behalf of a debtor" was broad enough to include suits brought by debtor in possession against former director-CEO; insurer must cover officer). *See also, e.g.,*Yessenow v. Exec. Risk Indemnity, Inc., 953 N.E.2d 433, 443–44 (Ill. App. 2011) (distinguishing *Biltmore* on ground that suit brought by bankruptcy trustee did not implicate insured vs. insured exclusion; insurer must defend defendant directors in underlying suit).

607. 11 U.S.C. § 363(b).

significant cash into the estate. However, it is subject to the same standards for approval as is any sale of estate property, including the requirement that the sale represent an exercise of the sound business judgment of the trustee or debtor in possession.[608]

That determination usually involves four factors: (i) whether a sound business reason exists for the proposed transaction; (ii) whether fair and reasonable consideration is provided; (iii) whether a transaction has been proposed and negotiated in good faith; and (iv) whether adequate and reasonable notice is provided.[609] Insurers who repurchase D&O Policies expect, in exchange, to be protected from lawsuits by releases and injunctions. Debtors should consider how to provide appropriate notice to all affected parties (which may include individual potential claimants) and whether to effect such a sale through a plan of reorganization, as courts may not be authorized to issue such injunctions through an order authorizing a sale of assets.[610]

608. *See, e.g., In re Lionel Corp.*, 722 F.2d 1063, 1071 (2d Cir. 1983).

609. *Id.; see also In re Congoleum Corp.*, 2007 WL 1428477 (Bankr. D.N.J. May 11, 2007) (denying approval of insurance buy-back settlement for failure to meet requirements of Code Section 363(b)).

610. For a more thorough discussion of buy-back settlements and third-party releases, see Richard L. Epling et al., *Intersections of Bankruptcy Law and Insurance Coverage Litigation*, 21 Norton J. Bankr. L. & Prac. 103, 112–15 (2012).

14

Objections to Claims

A. Overview

Sections 501 and 502 of the Bankruptcy Code and Bankruptcy Rules 3001, 3007, and 3008 govern the claims allowance process. Under this framework, "[t]he burden of proof for claims brought in the bankruptcy court under Section 502(a)[of the Bankruptcy Code] rests on different parties at different times"[611]. A proof of claim properly filed in accordance with the applicable Bankruptcy Rules "shall constitute prima facie evidence of the validity and amount of the claim."[612] If the proof of claim is left unchallenged, the claimant will be entitled to a distribution from the estate.[613] Accordingly, a properly filed claim is deemed allowed, unless a party in interest objects on one or more of various grounds.[614]

611. *In re NVF Co.*, 394 B.R. 33, 36 (Bankr. D. Del. 2008).

612. *See* 11 U.S.C. § 502(a) ("A claim or interest, proof of which is filed under Section 501 of this title, is deemed allowed, unless a party in interest … objects."); FED. R. BANKR. P. 3001(f); *See Allegheny*, 954 F.2d at 173 ("[A] claim that alleges facts sufficient to support a legal liability to the claimant satisfies the claimant's initial obligation to go forward."); *In re Carlson*, 126 F.3d 915, 921–22 (7th Cir. 1997) (where the claimant alleges sufficient facts to support its claim, its claim is afforded prima facie validity).

613. *See* 11 U.S.C. § 507 (allowed claims receive distribution in order of priority).

614. *In re Nortel Networks, Inc.*, 469 B.R. 478, 498, fn. 12 (Bankr. D. Del. 2012). In Chapter 11 cases, a creditor may hold an allowed claim absent filing a proof of claim. Under Section 1111(a) of the Bankruptcy Code, claims are deemed filed under Section 501. These claims therefore are deemed allowed under Section 502, unless a party objects.. *In re Trinity Precision Flow Control, LLC*, 10-80341-TRC, 2010 WL 1849412, at *3 (Bankr. E.D. Okla. May 6, 2010).

The ultimate burden of persuasion is always on the claimant to establish entitlement to the claim.[615] Even if a claim is timely filed, creditors must continue to monitor the case. Debtors, creditors' committees, trustees, or other parties in interest may object to the claim or seek to limit a creditor's rights with respect to the claim. After the general bar date has passed, the debtor customarily undertakes a review and analysis of the filed proofs of claim and attempts to reconcile the claims with its books and records to determine which claims, if any, will be the subject of an objection.

As discussed below, since Bankruptcy Rule 3007 does not set a *per se* bar date for filing claims objections, a debtor may strategically object to a large claim or groups of claims just before its plan of reorganization is filed.

B. Burden of Proof

The claims allowance process starts upon a party's objection. Once a party in interest objects to the claim, the objection becomes a "contested matter" requiring judicial resolution pursuant to Bankruptcy Rule 9014.[616] And if the objecting party includes a demand for relief under Bankruptcy Rule 7001, then the matter becomes an adversary proceeding pursuant

615. *In re Plastech Engineered Products, Inc.*, 399 B.R. 1, 10 (Bankr. E.D. Mich. 2008).
616. In the context of a no-asset Chapter 7, the initial objection may also serve as the endpoint because the debtor lacks a pecuniary interest to possess standing. *In re I & F Corp.*, 219 B.R. 483 (Bankr. S.D. Ohio 1998) (a Chapter 7 debtor with an insolvent estate has no standing to object to proofs of claim, as only the trustee or a party with a pecuniary interest may object to proofs of claim); *In re Partners Group Financial, LLC*, 394 B.R. 68, 74 n.2 (Bankr. E.D. Pa. 2008) (a Chapter 7 debtor has a sufficient pecuniary interest in the outcome of a claims objection to have standing to object if the estate is solvent).

to Bankruptcy Rule 3007(d).[617] In addition, because Bankruptcy Rule 9014 incorporates, among other provisions, Bankruptcy Rule 7004, some courts have held that a claim objection must be served in accordance with Bankruptcy Rule 7004.[618]

Objections to claims must be in writing, filed with the court, and served with at least thirty days' notice of the hearing on the objection.[619]

The objecting party has the burden of producing evidence to negate the prima facie validity of the filed claim.[620] In support of its objection to the validity of the claim, the party objecting to the claim must "produce sufficient evidence that would discredit at least one of the allegations essential to the claim's legal sufficiency.[621] Once the objector offers evidence refuting the allegations in the proof of claim and the presumption is overcome, the burden to demonstrate an entitlement to payment on the claim shifts back to the claimant.[622] The claimant must then produce additional evidence to prove the validity of the claim by a preponderance of the evidence.[623]

Because the ultimate burden of providing the validity of a claimant always rests on the claimant, in defending a claim objection, the best preparation is to pay careful attention to the proper filing of the claim

---

617. Fed. R. Bankr.P. 3007(d) ("If an objection to a claim is joined with a demand for relief of the kind specified in Rule 7001, it becomes an adversary proceeding"). This includes (1) a proceeding to recover money or property, other than a proceeding to compel the debtor to deliver property to the trustee, or a proceeding under § 554(b) or § 725 of the Code, Rule 2017, or Rule 6002; (2) a proceeding to determine the validity, priority, or extent of a lien or other interest in property, other than under Rule 3012 or Rule 4003(d); (3) a proceeding to obtain approval under § 363(h) for the sale of both the interest of the estate and of a co-owner in property; (4) a proceeding to object to or revoke a discharge, other than an objection to discharge under §§ 727(a)(8), (a)(9), or 1328(f); (5) a proceeding to revoke an order of confirmation of a Chapter 11, Chapter 12, or Chapter 13 plan; (6) a proceeding to determine the dischargeability of a debt; (7) a proceeding to obtain an injunction or other equitable relief, except when a Chapter 9, Chapter 11, Chapter 12, or Chapter 13 plan provides for the relief; (8) a proceeding to subordinate any allowed claim or interest, except when a Chapter 9, Chapter 11, Chapter 12, or Chapter 13 plan provides for subordination; (9) a proceeding to obtain a declaratory judgment relating to any of the foregoing; or (10) a proceeding to determine a claim or cause of action removed under 28 U.S.C. § 1452. Fed. R. Bankr. P. 7001.
618. *In re Rushton*, 285 B.R. 76 (Bankr. S.D. Ga. 2002); *In re Sunde*, 2007 WL 3275128 (Bankr. W.D. Wis. 2007) (overturning default judgment against creditor because debtor's objection had not been served in accordance with Bankruptcy Rule 7004).
619. Fed. R. Bankr. P. 3007(a).
620. *In re Allegheny Int'l, Inc.*, 954 F.2d at 173.
621. *In re Smurfit-Stone Container Corp.*, 444 B.R. 111, 117 (Bankr. D. Del. 2011) (*citing In re Allegheny Int'l, Inc.*, 954 F.2d at 173).
622. *Id.*
623. *Id.; see also In re South Motor Co. of Dade County*, 161 B.R. 532, 547 (Bankr. S.D. Fla. 1993).

in the first instance, including the timely filing of the claim, correctly completing the claim form, and attaching the necessary documentation and recognizing the legal effect of filing such claim.[624]

C. General Grounds of Disallowance

Section 502 of the Bankruptcy Code governs allowance and disallowance of claims. If a proof of claim or interest is properly filed, it will be "deemed allowed, unless a party in interest...objects."[625] Section 502(b) codifies the bases under which a party may seek to disallow claims. If an objection to a claim is made, "the court, after notice and a hearing, shall determine the amount of such claim ... as of the date of the filing of the petition, and shall allow such claim in such amount" except to the extent that it meets certain conditions.[626] These conditions include:

(1) The claim is unenforceable against the debtor and its property for reasons other than being contingent or unmatured;[627]
(2) The claim is for unmatured interest;[628]
(3) The claim is a property tax that exceeds the estate's interest in the property;[629]
(4) The claim is for services of an insider or attorney of the debtor and exceeds the reasonable value of the services;[630]
(5) The claim is for a date that was unmatured as of the date of the filing and is a domestic support obligation that is excepted from discharge;[631]

624. *In re Plastech Engineered Products, Inc.*, 399 B.R. 1, 10 (Bankr. E.D. Mich. 2008) ("Although the burden of going forward shifts during the claims objection process, the ultimate burden of persuasion is always on the claimant to establish entitlement to the claim."); *see In re Armstrong*, 320 B.R. 97, 104 (Bankr. N.D. Tex. 2005) (A properly filed proof of claim consists of "(1) a creditor's name and address, (2) basis for claim, (3) date debt incurred, (4) amount of claim, (5) classification of claim, and (6) supporting documents.").

625. 11 U.S.C. § 502(a).

626. 11 U.S.C. § 502(b).

627. 11 U.S.C. § 502(b)(1).

628. 11 U.S.C. § 502(b)(2).

629. 11 U.S.C. § 502(b)(3).

630. 11 U.S.C. § 502(b)(4).

631. 11 U.S.C. § 502(b)(5).

(6) The claim is a lessor's claim for damages resulting from termination of a real property lease and exceeds certain amounts;[632]

(7) The claim is an employee's claim for damages resulting from termination of an employment contract and exceeds certain amounts;[633]

(8) The claim results from reduction of a credit given to the debtor in connection with employment taxes, due to late payment;[634]

(9) The proof of claim was not timely filed, unless it was either (i) filed in a Chapter 7 case or (ii) was filed by governmental units within certain time periods (normally 180 days after the order for relief).[635]

Courts are split on whether Section 502(b) sets forth the exclusive basis to disallow a claim.[636]

---

632. 11 U.S.C. § 502(b)(6). Such a claim is limited to the rent reserved by the lease, without acceleration, for the greater of one year, or 15%, not to exceed three years, of the remaining term of the lease, following the earlier of the petition date and the date the landlord repossessed or the debtor surrendered the leased property. The landlord's claim may also include any unpaid rent due under the lease, without acceleration, as of the earlier of such dates *Id.*

633. 11 U.S.C. § 502(b)(7). Such a claim is limited to the compensation provided by the contract, without acceleration, for one year following the earlier of the petition date or the date the employer directed the employee to terminate, or the employee terminated, performance under the contract. The employee›s claim may also include any unpaid compensation due under the contract, without acceleration, as of the earlier of such dates. *Id.*

634. 11 U.S.C. § 502(b)(8).

635. 11 U.S.C. § 502(b)(9).

636. *Compare In re Papercraft Corp.*, 187 B.R. 486, (Bankr. W.D. Pa. 1995), *rev'd on other grounds*, 211 B.R. 813 (W.D. Pa. 1997), *aff'd and remanded*, 160 F.3d 982, 33 (3d Cir. 1998) (insider corporation, holding equity position in parent of debtor and having the ability to control seats on debtor's board of directors, that purchased claims in debtor's case without proper disclosure had such claims disallowed to extent the claims exceeded the purchase price of such claims); *with In re Kirkland*, 379 B.R. 341, 59 Collier Bankr. Cas. 2d (MB) 1991 (B.A.P. 10th Cir. 2007), *rev'd on other grounds*, 572 F.3d 838 (10th Cir. 2009) (overturning bankruptcy court's disallowance of a claim based on its nonconformity with the official claim form and adopting the "Exclusivity Rule" that holds that § 502(b) states the exclusive bases for disallowing a claim); *In re SNTL Corp.*, 571 F.3d 826, 838–839 (9th Cir. 2009) ("As we stated in a recent decision, we 'must find a basis in section 502 to disallow a claim, and absent such basis, we must allow it.'").

Certain claims, though occurring after the date of the petition's filing, will be treated as if they arose before the filing date.[637] Because a claim that is allowed or disallowed may be reconsidered, the court's determination on an objection is not necessarily final.

D. Estimation

Section 502(c) authorizes codifies the right to estimate a claim in two scenarios.[638] Upon a request by a party in interest, the court can estimate a claim for purposes of allowance in certain limited circumstances. Section 502(c) of the Bankruptcy Code grants bankruptcy courts the power to estimate claims for purposes of allowance as long as the claim: (i) is "contingent or unliquidated" and the actual determination of the claim "would unduly delay the administration of the case" or (ii) is a "right to payment arising from a right to an equitable remedy for breach of performance."[639]

The object of such a proceeding is to establish the estimated value of a creditor's claim for purposes of formulating a reorganization plan.[640] Claims estimation under Section 502(c)(1) provides a centralized forum to facilitate the claims allowance process. This accomplishes two goals:(1) streamlines the claims allowance process; and (2) ensures fair distributions through an accurate assessment of uncertain claims.[641] Bankruptcy courts can exercise discretion to determine whether and to what extent claims should be allowed in accordance with the principles of equity.[642] Estimation "avoid[s] the need to await the resolution of outside lawsuits to determine issues of liability or amount owed by means of anticipating and estimating the likely outcome of these actions."[643] Not only does estimation allow the debtor to

637. *See* 11 U.S.C. §§ 502(e)(2) (certain claims for reimbursement or contribution of entities liable with the debtor on or who have secured the claim of a creditor), 502(g) (claims arising from rejection of executory contracts and unexpired leases), 502(h) (claims arising from the recovery of exempt property, avoided transfers, or creditor's right to setoff), and 502(i) (claims arising from certain taxes entitled to priority).

638. 11 U.S.C. § 502(c).

639. 11 U.S.C. § 502(c).

640. *See* Kool, Mann, Coffee & Co. v. Coffey, 300 F.3d 340, 347 (3d Cir. 2002).

641. *In re Ford*, 967 F.2d 1047 (5th Cir.1992).

642. *See In re Corey*, 892 F.2d 829 (9th Cir.1989) (holding that, given highly speculative nature of claims and undue delay that would result in confirmation of proposed plan, court could estimate claims of creditors who voted against proposed reorganization plan), *cert. denied sub nom.*, Kulalani Ltd. v. Corey, 498 U.S. 815 (1990); *In re Continental Airlines Corp.*, 64 B.R. 865 (Bankr. S.D. Tex. 1986) (discussing broad discretion of bankruptcy court regarding estimation and liquidation pursuant to Section 502 of Title 11).

643. *In re Ford*, 967 F.2d 1047, 1053 (5th Cir. 1992).

more rapidly determine the payout to creditors but it also promotes a fair distribution to creditors through a realistic assessment of uncertain claims.[644] The Bankruptcy Code and Rules are silent, however, as to the manner in which contingent or unliquidated claims are to be estimated. Courts have held that when estimating claims in a bankruptcy case, the court should use whatever method is best suited to the circumstances.

E. Temporary Allowance of Claims

Bankruptcy courts also have the power to estimate claims of creditors under Bankruptcy Rule 3018 temporarily allow such claims subject to an objection for the limited purpose of voting on a plan of reorganization.[645] Since Bankruptcy Rule 3007 does not set a per se bar date for filing claims objections, objections may be filed prior to or after confirmation of a plan. Some courts have placed the burden of proof on the claimant while other courts have placed it on the objector.[646]

The policy behind temporarily allowing claims is to prevent possible abuse by plan proponents who might ensure acceptance of a plan by filing last-minute objections to the claims of dissenting creditors.[647] Temporary allowance of a claim under Bankruptcy Rule 3018(a) is not dispositive as to the amount of the claim and provides only voting authority to a creditor.[648]

In a Chapter 11 case, if an objection is filed prior to a plan's confirmation, then unless otherwise subject to an agreement or court order,

---

644. *In re Cont'l Airlines*, 981 F.2d 1450, 1461 (5th Cir. 1993).

645. FED. R. BANKR. P. 3018(a) ("Notwithstanding objection to a claim of interest, the court after notice and a hearing may temporarily allow the claim or interest in an amount which the court deems proper for the purpose of accepting or rejecting a plan."); *In re Experient Corp.,* 535 B.R. 386, 405 (Bankr.D.Colo.2015) ("The Bankruptcy Code and Rules do not provide the courts with any guidance about how and when to temporarily allow a claim.") (citation omitted); *In re Pac. Sunwear of Cal., Inc.,* 2016 WL 4250681, *3 (Bankr. D. Del. Aug. 8, 2016) (acknowledging that "there is no guidance in the Bankruptcy Code on how to determine the proper amount of the claim" under Bankruptcy Rule 3018(a)). The Court, therefore, has discretion to determine the amount of a claim for the limited purpose of voting. *See Armstrong*, 294 B.R. at 354 (temporary allowance of a claim under Bankruptcy Rule 3018(a) "is left to a court's discretion.") (citations omitted).

646. *See, e.g., In re Zolner*, 173 B.R. 629, 633 (Bankr. N.D. Ill. 1994*), aff'd*, 249 B.R. 287 (N.D. Ill. 2000) (burden of proof is on the claimant); *In re Stone Hedge Properties*, 191 B.R. 59, 64 (Bankr. M.D. Pa. 1995) (questioning whether burden of proof in a summary proceeding should be on the objector); *In re Pac. Sunwear of California, Inc.*, 2016 WL 4250681, at *5 (Bankr. D. Del. Aug. 8, 2016) ("Because a Rule 3018 proceeding is meant to enfranchise claimants, there is an inconsistency in using the burden of proof les that apply to objections to claims.")

647. *Id.*

648. *Id.*

a creditor whose claim is subject to an objection may be barred from voting its claim or having its vote count. Section 1126(a) of the Bankruptcy Code provides that the holder of an allowed claim (under Section 502) may accept or reject a plan.[649] Section 502(a) of the Bankruptcy Code states that a claim is deemed allowed unless a party in interest objects.[650] Thus, if the debtor has filed an objection to the claim, the creditor may be effectively disenfranchised if the claim objection is not adjudicated before confirmation.

To prevent possible abuse by plan proponents who might seek to gain acceptance of the plan by filing last-minute objections to claims of adverse creditors, temporary allowance of the claims for voting purposes is prescribed by Bankruptcy Rule 3018(a).[651] A creditor may request the temporary allowance of a claim under one of the following nonexclusive circumstances: (i) when an objection to the claim has been filed and the objection was filed too late to be heard prior to the confirmation hearing, (ii) when fully hearing the objection would delay administration of the case, or (iii) when the objection is frivolous or of questionable merit.[652]

F. Temporary Disallowance of Claims

Section 502(d) of the Bankruptcy Code acts to temporarily disallow certain claims against the estate of a transferee of a voidable transfer (often a preferential or fraudulent transfer) if the transferee has not turned over the property received as required under the applicable section under which the transferee's liability arises.[653]

Section 502(d) applies to disallow all "claims" of a creditor until that creditor returns any avoidable transfers received. When an objection to a claim is based upon Section 502(d), the claim should not be allowed or disallowed until the validity of the transfer is adjudicated. Once adjudicated, the entire claim may be disallowed until the transfer is surrendered. Upon

---

649. 11 U.S.C. § 1126(a).

650. 11 U.S.C. § 502(a).

651. *See In re Armstrong*, 294 B.R. 344, 354 (BAP 10th Cir. 2003).

652. *Id.* (citing 9 Collier on Bankruptcy, ¶ 3018.01[5] (footnotes omitted); *In re Zolner*, 173 B.R. 629, 633 (Bankr. N.D. Ill. 1994), *aff'd.*, 249 B.R. 287 (N.D. Ill. 2000)).

653. Section 502(d) of the Bankruptcy Code provides, in pertinent part:

> Notwithstanding subsections (a) and (b) of this section, the court shall disallow any claim of any entity from which property is recoverable under Sections 542, 543, 550 or 553 of this title or that is a transferee of a transfer avoidable under Sections 522(f), 522(h), 544, 545, 547, 548, 549 or 724(a) of this title, unless such entity or transferee has paid the amount, or turned over any such property, for which such entity or transferee is liable…

11 U.S.C. § 502(d).

timely surrender, the order of disallowance may be vacated and the claim allowed.[654] In short, if a creditor has been sued by the estate for recovery of an alleged preference, it will not receive a distribution from the estate on its claim until the preference action is resolved.

Some courts have held that a judgment must be obtained on the avoidance or turnover action in order to invoke the protections of Section 502(d)[655] Practitioners should thus be aware that to the extent they wish to raise Section 502(d) as the basis to disallow a claim, the rule of law in their jurisdiction may prohibit it unless a prior action on the avoidance or turnover action has been commenced, and perhaps concluded.

As discussed in Chapter 7 of this manual, the courts have disagreed as to whether administrative expenses can be disallowed under Section 502(d).

G. Objecting to Multiple Claims

Normally, "objections to more than one claim shall not be joined in a single objection" unless "otherwise ordered by the court" or permitted by rules governing omnibus objections in Bankruptcy Rule 3007(d).[656] Subject to the below requirements, "objections to more than one claim may be joined in an omnibus objection if all the claims were filed by the same entity, or the objections are based solely on the grounds that the claims should be disallowed, in whole or in part."[657]

H. Omnibus Objections

In cases in which a large number of proofs of claim are filed, it is common for the debtor, trustee, or other objecting party to file omnibus objections to multiple claims and attempt to disallow and expunge hundreds of claims

---

654. In *re Independent Clearing House Co.*, 41 B.R. 985 (Bankr. D. Utah 1984), *decision aff'd in part, rev'd in part on other grounds*, 62 B.R. 118 (D. Utah 1986).

655. *In re Lids Corp.*, 260 B.R. 680, 684 (Bankr. D. Del. 2001); *Creditors of Melon Produce, Inc. v. Braunstein,* 112 F.3d 1232, 1237 (1st Cir.1997) ("the key phrase in this inquiry is 'the amount ... for which such entity or transferee is liable' "); Campbell v. United States (*In re Davis*), 889 F.2d 658, 662 (5th Cir.1989) (section 502(d) "is designed to be triggered after a creditor has been afforded reasonable time in which to turn over amounts adjudicated to belong to the bankruptcy estate"); *In re Mountaineer Coal Co., Inc.,* 247 B.R. 633, 641 (Bankr.W.D.Va.2000) (section 502(d) "would not appear applicable unless and until a finding under one of the cited sections had been made and then the claimant had failed to comply with such ruling*"); In re Ames Dept. Stores, Inc.*, 582 F.3d 422, (2d Cir. 2009) (§ 502(d) does not apply to administrative claim arising under § 503(b)(9*)); In re TI Acquisition, LLC*, 410 B.R. 742 (Bankr. N.D. Ga. 2009).

656. Fed. R. Bankr. P. 3007(c).

657. Fed. R. Bankr. P. 3007(d).

by a single objection. Under Bankruptcy Rule 3007, objections "to more than one claim may be joined in an omnibus objection."[658] Normally in an omnibus objection, the objecting party will lump claims together in a single pleading based on the specific objection, set forth a general legal basis for the reduction or elimination of such group of claims, and attach as an exhibit a list of claims to which the objection applies. With this type of objection, a creditor must carefully inspect the exhibit to determine if its claim is affected.

In 2007, Bankruptcy Rule 3007 was amended to place certain limitations on the use of omnibus objections to provide appropriate notice and ensure the protection of claimants' due process rights. Specifically, Bankruptcy Rule 3007, as amended, provides significant protections to a claimant from unknowingly failing to recognize that its claim is part of an omnibus objection. Under Bankruptcy Rule 3007(c), omnibus objections to claims are generally not allowed unless the omnibus objections are: (i) authorized by the court, or (ii) permitted by rules governing omnibus objections in Bankruptcy Rule 3007(d).[659]

1. Nonsubstantive or Procedural Objections

Under Bankruptcy Rule 3007(d), claim objections may only be joined in a single omnibus objection if the objection is based solely on the following grounds, often referred to as "nonsubstantive objections" or "procedural objections":

(1) They are duplicative of other claims;[660]
(2) They were filed in the wrong case;[661]
(3) They were later amended by another proof of claim;[662]
(4) They were not timely filed;[663]
(5) They were satisfied or released during the case;[664]
(6) They were presented in a form that does not comply with the applicable rules and the objecting party is unable to determine the validity of the claims due to the noncompliance;[665]
(7) They are interests rather than claims;[666] or

658. Fed. R. Bank. P. 3007.
659. Fed. R. Bankr. P. 3007(c).
660. Fed. R. Bankr. P. 3007(d)(1).
661. Fed. R. Bankr. P. 3007(d)(2).
662. Fed. R. Bankr. P. 3007(d)(3).
663. Fed. R. Bankr. P. 3007(d)(4).
664. Fed. R. Bankr. P. 3007(d)(5).
665. Fed. R. Bankr. P. 3007(d)(6).
666. Fed. R. Bankr. P. 3007(d)(7).

(8) They improperly assert entitlement to priority treatment in excess of the maximum amount allowed under Section 507 of the Bankruptcy Code.[667]

2. *Substantive Objections*

What is treated as a "substantive objection" varies amongst jurisdictions. That said, examples of "substantive objections" or claim objections that must, absent authorization of the court, be included in a single objection often include: (i) litigation claims, (ii) claims that must be reclassified to the proper priority, (iii) claims that should be asserted against a different debtor, (iv) claims that should be reduced to an amount consistent with the debtor's books and records, and (v) claims that have no basis for liability based on the debtor's books and records.[668]

3. *Procedural Requirements*

Bankruptcy Rule 3007(e) governs the procedural requirements for an omnibus objections to be valid.[669] Specifically, an omnibus objection must: (i) conspicuously state that claimants receiving the objection should locate their name and claims in the objection; (ii) list the claimants alphabetically, cross-reference the claimants to the claim numbers, and, if appropriate, list the claimants by category of claims; (iii) state the grounds of the objection to each claim and cross-reference the pages in the omnibus objection pertinent to the stated grounds; (iv) contain the identity of the objector and the grounds for the objections in the title of the objection; (v) number the omnibus objection consecutively with any other omnibus objections filed by the objector; and (vi) object to no more than 100 claims.[670]

Since Bankruptcy Rule 3007(c) authorizes omnibus objections as "otherwise ordered by the court," a debtor may establish its own claim objection procedures depending on the type of the case and composition of the parties, and seek court approval by motion of such proposed procedures. Furthermore, local bankruptcy rules and general order may deviate from the federal requirements regarding the filing of omnibus objections.[671]

---

667. Fed. R. Bankr. P. 3007(d)(8).
668. *In re Food Mgmt. Group, LLC*, 484 B.R. 574, 584 (S.D.N.Y. 2012).
669. Fed. R. Bankr. P. 3007(e).
670. *Id.*
671. *See* D. Del. Rev. Local Bankr. R. 3007-1 (effective Feb. 1, 2009); *see also* General Order Regarding Applicability of Rule 3007(c) of the Amended Federal Rules of Bankruptcy Procedure (Bankr. D. Del. Nov. 27, 2007) (deviating from Fed. R. Bankr. P. 3007 and specifying additional requirements for the filing of omnibus objections). Delaware allows the filing of omnibus objections on grounds other than those set forth in Rule 3007(d) as long as certain requirements are satisfied.

I. Reconsideration of Objections

"A claim that has been allowed or disallowed may be reconsidered for cause" and "[a] reconsidered claim may be allowed or disallowed according to the equities of the case."[672] "A party in interest may move for reconsideration of an order allowing or disallowing a claim against the estate."[673] If the motion is granted, "[t]he court after a hearing on notice shall enter an appropriate order."[674]

If a disallowed claim is reconsidered and allowed, it will not affect the distributions already made to holders of other allowed claims. On the other hand, holders of allowed claims that are of the same class as the reconsidered and allowed claim will not receive any future distributions until the holder of the reconsidered claim receives payment that is "proportionate in value to that already received" by the holders of the other allowed claims.[675] If a claim is reconsidered and it results in the holder of the reconsidered claim having received "excess payment[s] or transfer[s]," those excess payments can be recovered by the trustee.[676]

672. 11 U.S.C. § 502(j); *In re Consolidated Pioneer Mortg.*, 178 B.R. 222 (B.A.P. 9th Cir. 1995), aff'd, 91 F.3d 151 (9th Cir. 1996); *In re Resources Reclamation Corp. of America*, 34 B.R. 771, (B.A.P. 9th Cir. 1983); *In re Arden Properties, Inc.*, 248 B.R. 164 (Bankr. D. Ariz. 2000).

673. Fed. R. Bankr. P. 3008.

674. *Id.*

675. 11 U.S.C. § 502(j).

676. 11 U.S.C. § 502(j).

15

Dischargeability

A. Overview

The end game for debtors is usually discharge of debt. The Bankruptcy Code defines "debt" as "liability on a claim."[677] But certain types of debt are excepted from discharge and it is also possible for a debtor to either be denied a discharge altogether or have their discharge revoked. Dischargeability overlaps with the claims process in several ways. The chapter and type of case inform whether the creditor (or even the debtor) should file a proof of claim in the case. Further, either the debtor or the creditor may need to initiate an adversary proceeding to determine the dischargeability of a debt. This chapter focuses on the dischargeability of certain debts through the lens of the claims resolution process.

B. Section 523: Dischargeability of Certain Debts, Including Unscheduled or Unlisted Debt

Section 523 is applicable in all chapters and excepts specific debts from discharge as opposed to Section 727, which contains provisions that can either prohibit debtors from receiving their Chapter 7 discharge or result in the revocation of their discharge. Chapters 11, 12, and 13 also contain analogous provisions providing for the revocation or denial of discharge in certain circumstances.[678]

Section 523 excepts nineteen categories of debt from discharge, including certain tax debt, debts arising from fraud, embezzlement, or willful and malicious injury, debts arising from domestic support obligations, and

677. 11 U.S.C. § 101(12).
678. 11 U.S.C. §§ 1141(d), 1228(d), 1328(e). Chapters 11, 12, and 13 also contain provisions permitting revocation of plan confirmation. 11 U.S.C. §§ 1144, 1230, 1330.

debts arising out of certain tortious conduct. Importantly, creditors asserting a nondischargeability claim under Section 523(a)(2) (fraud); (a)(4) (fraud or defalcation, embezzlement, or larceny); or (a)(6) (willful and malicious injury) must assert those claims in an adversary proceeding complaint brought not later than 60 days after the first date set for the meeting of creditors.[679] A complaint under any other subsection may be brought at any time and a case may even be reopened for the purposes of bringing such complaint.[680]

Additionally, a debtor's failure to list or schedule the debt with enough time to permit the creditor to timely file a proof of claim, or in the case of a debt specified in Section 523(a)(2), (4), or (6), with enough time to both timely file a proof of claim and timely request a dischargeability determination could result in the debt not being discharged.[681] But Section 523(a)(3) states that such debt is excepted from discharge "unless such creditor had notice or actual knowledge of the case in time for such timely filing." Thus, a debt is not excepted from discharge under Section 523(a)(3) if the creditor either had notice or actual knowledge of the bankruptcy case, even if the debt has not been scheduled, was listed or scheduled improperly, or was not timely listed or scheduled.

Such notice or knowledge cannot be constructive or imputed,[682] with the exception that knowledge of an agent authorized to receive notice for the principal may constitute knowledge of the principal.[683] The debtor bears the burden of establishing adequate notice, and may present facts pertaining to events occurring either pre or post petition.[684] Filing a responsive pleading in a suit against debtor that advises the creditor of the bankruptcy filing has been found sufficient to convey actual knowledge.[685] Written notice is not required and knowledge obtained from verbal communications or reading a newspaper publication has been found sufficient.[686] But when a creditor is unsecured, a publication is not itself notice.[687] Notice to a creditor's attorney representing the creditor in enforcing its claim against the debtor

---

679. Fed. R. Bankr. P. 4007(c). This deadline may be extended by the court for cause if the movant files a motion prior to the expiration of the original deadline. Fed. R. Bankr. P. 4007(c).
680. Fed. R. Bankr. P. 4007(b).
681. 11 U.S.C. § 523(a)(3).
682. *E.g.*, Small Bus. Ass'n v. Bridges, 894 F.2d 108, 22 C.B.C.2d 674 (5th Cir. 1990).
683. Ford Motor Credit Co. v. Weaver, 680 F.2d 451, 6 C.B.C.2d 1173 (6th Cir. 1982).
684. *E.g.*, Massa v. Addona (*In re Massa*), 187 F.3d 292 (2d Cir. 1999).
685. *E.g.*, Eagle Fin. Corp. v. Duhon, 216 So. 2d 367, 369 (La. Ct. App. 1968).
686. *In re Hunt*, 146 B.R. 178 (N.D. Tex. 1992).
687. Michigan Consol. Gas Co. v. Wilson, 4 Mich. App. 188, 144 N.W.2d 682 (1966).

is usually sufficient,[688] but notice after representation has ceased is not[689] and representation in state court proceedings alone is not sufficient.[690]

The operation of Section 523 and consequently whether and when a creditor (or debtor) should or must file a proof of claim is affected both by the chapter the case was filed under and the individual facts of the case, such as whether there are assets to distribute.

C. Discharge by Chapter

Chapter 7 discharges the debtor from all prepetition debts, regardless of whether a proof of claim has been filed.[691] Section 727(b) is also specifically subject to Section 523, so a discharge under § 727(a) does not cover a debt referred to in Section 523.[692]

Chapter 13 provides for a discharge "of all debts provided for by the plan," after the debtor completes all payments under the confirmed plan.[693] Not all provisions of Section 523(a) apply to a Chapter 13 discharge: notable exceptions include torts related to property (as opposed to personal injury) and obligations arising from a property settlement that is part of a divorce decree (as opposed to obligations for a child or spousal support). Chapter 12 contains a similar discharge provision but incorporates Section 523(a) in full.[694]

Chapter 11 is slightly different: generally, plan confirmation results in the discharge of debts arising prior to confirmation, regardless of whether a proof of claim has been filed, unless the debtor is an individual—in which case discharge is not obtained until completion of the plan payments—or the plan liquidates substantially all of the debtor's assets, the debtor does not engage in business after consummation, and the debtor would be ineligible for discharge under Section 727(a).[695] Additionally, debts of a kind specified in § 523 are excepted from this discharge for individual debtors.[696] Last, small business debtors proceeding under subchapter V of Chapter 11 may obtain a discharge on the date of confirmation if the plan is consensual, or after the completion of plan payments under a cramdown plan.[697]

---

688. *E.g.*, *In re Saltzmann*, 8 C.B.C.2d 9, 25 B.R. 125 (Bankr. E.D. Wis. 1982).
689. *E.g.*, Mizrahi v. Miscione, 60 Cal. Rptr. 680 (Ct. App. 1967).
690. *E.g.*, Lampe v. Kash, 735 F. 3d 942 (6th Cir. 2013).
691. 11 U.S.C. § 727(b).
692. 11 U.S.C. § 727(b).
693. 11 U.S.C. § 1328(a).
694. 11 U.S.C. § 1228(a).
695. 11 U.S.C. § 1141(d).
696. 11 U.S.C. § 1141(d)(2).
697. 11 U.S.C. §§ 1181(a), (c), 1191(b), 1192.

Why does all of this matter from a claims filing and management perspective? The timing and type of discharge inform the actions both debtors and creditors could, should, or must take with respect to the claims against debtor's estate.

1. Is a Proof of Claim Necessary?

Section 501 governs the filing of proofs of claims or interests. The language of Section 501 is permissive, stating that a creditor "may file a proof of claim,"[698] meaning there is no requirement under the Code that a creditor file a proof of claim. But a proof of claim is the vehicle through which a creditor establishes its right to share in distributions made during the case,[699] either through liquidation or payments under a plan of reorganization. For that reason, creditors generally timely file their proofs of claims in asset cases.

Section 501 also permits debtors or trustees to file a proof of claim on behalf of the creditors if the creditor fails to timely do so.[700] Debtors will often utilize this provision to file proofs of claims for nondischargeable debts they wish to pay through their Chapter 13 plan of reorganization. This is so because without a proof of claim, the debt is not paid during the pendency of the case, but the debtor still remains liable on the claim after the discharge is entered, impeding debtor's fresh start.

In a no-asset Chapter 7 case, there is no distribution for creditors to share in and therefore no reason for a creditor to file a proof of claim.[701] Further, Section 523(a)(3)(A) does not prevent the discharge of unscheduled debts unless the debt falls under Section 523(a)(2), (4), or (6) because no deadline is set for the filing of claims and therefore the creditor has not been deprived of the opportunity to timely file a proof of claim.

Chapter 11 also operates a little differently: the debtor's schedules are deemed to constitute evidence of the validity and amount of the scheduled claims, unless the claim is listed as disputed, contingent, or unliquidated.[702]

---

698. 11 U.S.C. § 501(a).

699. *See* Fed. R. Bankr. P. 3002(a) ("[a] secured creditor, unsecured creditor, or equity security holder must file a proof of claim or interest for the claim or interest to be allowed . . .").

700. 11 U.S.C. § 501(c). Such claims must be filed within 30 days after the deadline to file proofs of claims. Fed. R. Bankr. P. 3004.

701. *See* Kipp Flores Architects, L.L.C. v. Mid-Continent Cas. Co., 852 F.3d 405, 407 (5th Cir. 2017) ("In no-asset Chapter 7 liquidation cases, the filing of a proof of claim serves no practical purpose since there will be no distribution from the estate in which to participate. In such cases, the notice of the meeting of creditors may include a statement that it is unnecessary to file claims.").

702. 11 U.S.C. § 1111(a).

But a filed proof of claim supersedes the scheduled claim.[703] Accordingly, the creditor should assess whether its claim has been properly scheduled and file a proof of claim if it is not scheduled, is improperly scheduled, or is scheduled as disputed, contingent, or unliquidated so that the creditor can be treated as a creditor for voting and distribution purposes.

2. *Strategic Reasons Not to File a Proof of Claim*

It is not necessary to file a proof of claim in order to initiate an adversary proceeding alleging the debt is nondischargable: recall Section 523(a) specifically refers to "debts" and not "claims." Thus, it is possible to adjudicate the dischargeability of a claim without engaging in the claims allowance process. There are therefore some strategic reasons for creditors not to file a proof of claim.

First, filing a proof of claim constitutes a party's consent to the bankruptcy court's jurisdiction to adjudicate matters pertaining to the claim itself and related to the claim, such as claims the debtor may have against the creditor. Thus, a proof of claim can bring a claim the debtor would otherwise have to pursue in another forum into the jurisdiction of the bankruptcy court.[704] This is of particular concern for a foreign creditor because the filing of a proof of claim may prove a significant factor in determining whether the court has personal jurisdiction over it.[705]

Additionally, the filing of a proof of claim could deprive a creditor of the right to seek a jury trial. This is so because the filing of a proof of claim can bring a claim within the ambit of the claims allowance process, which is squarely within the equitable jurisdiction of the Bankruptcy Court.[706] One court has determined this is so even with respect to claims a debtor brings against the creditor in an adversary proceeding challenging the proof of claim and alleging counterclaims against the creditor.[707]

Last, filing a proof of claim could constitute a waiver of sovereign immunity because by filing a proof of claim, the state has voluntarily

---

703. Fed. R. Bankr. P. 3003(c)(4).

704. Langenkamp v. Culp, 498 U.S. 42, 45, 111 S. Ct. 330, 331 (1990).

705. Lykes Bros. Steamship Co., Inc. v. Hanseatic Marine Serv. (*In re Lykes Bros. Steamship Co., Inc.*), 207 B.R. 282, 286 (Bankr. M.D. Fla. 1997) ("Having voluntarily filed its proof of claim in this reorganization case, Andrea purposefully submitted itself to this Court's jurisdiction and was obligated to comply with its orders and with its procedures.").

706. *See* Langenkamp, 498 U.S. at 44; Granfinanciera, S.A. v. Nordberg, 492 U.S. 33 (1989).

707. MCI Worldcom Comm., Inc. v. Comm. Network Int'l, Ltd. (*In re WorldCom, Inc.)*, 378 B.R. 745 (Bankr. S.D. N.Y. 2007) (finding the creditor was not entitled to a jury trial because the resolution of the debtor's claim bore directly on the claims allowance process, for which there is no right to jury trial).

invoked federal jurisdiction and therefore submitted to the jurisdiction of the bankruptcy court.[708]

In addition to deciding whether to file a proof of claim, creditors and debtors must also decide whether to commence an adversary proceeding to determine the dischargeability of a debt.

3. Whether to File an Adversary Proceeding

As discussed above, debts falling under Section 523(a)(2), (4), or (6) are discharged unless a timely adversary complaint is filed. But there is no deadline to file a complaint objecting to the dischargeability of a debt falling under any of the other enumerated subsections of Section 523 and perhaps no need to file an adversary complaint at all unless the parties disagree on the dischargeability of the debt. In instances where the parties agree, the claim can be addressed through the claims resolution process instead.

Common areas of disagreement outside of Section 523(a)(2), (4), and (6) include tax claims where the taxing authority argues under Section 523(a)(1)(C) that the debtor either made a fraudulent return or willfully attempted to evade or defeat the tax obligation; and in a Chapter 13 case, claims where there is a disagreement over whether the debt arose from a property settlement under Section 523(a)(15) or domestic support obligation under Section 523(a)(5).[709] Additionally, debtors have increasingly opted to challenge the dischargeability of student loan debt under Section 523(a)(8) by filing adversary complaints against the student loan creditor.

Prior to filing the complaint, potential plaintiffs should consider the costs involved. In addition to attorney's fees, there is also a filing fee to file an adversary proceeding.[710] On the other hand, an adversary proceeding could provide valuable leverage needed to reach a favorable settlement agreement. This is especially true with respect to student loan and tax debts.

D. Conclusion

Nondischargeable debt can either be addressed through the claims resolution process or through an adversary proceeding. The optimal path depends on the chapter and type of case, the nature of the debt in question, and whether the parties agree as to the dischargeability of the debt in question. Debtors and creditors alike should assess these factors thoroughly before deciding whether to file a proof of claim or initiate an adversary proceeding.

---

708. *See* Arecibo Cmty. Health Care, Inc. v. Commonwealth of Puerto Rico (*In re Arecibo Cmty. Health Care, Inc.*), 270 F.3d 17, 26-27 (1st Cir. 2001) (citing College Sav. Bank v. Fla. Prepaid Postsecondary Educ. Expense Bd., 527 U.S. 666, 675 (1999)).

709. Recall that § 523(a)(15) is not applicable in Chapter 13, such that debts resulting from a property settlement in a divorce are dischargeable. § 1328(a)(2).

710. That fee is currently $350 but is not charged when the debtor is the plaintiff or the plaintiff is a child support creditor. *See https://www.uscourts.gov/services-forms/fees/bankruptcy-court-miscellaneous-fee-schedule.*

ABOUT THE EDITORS

Brett D. Fallon has practiced bankruptcy for 35 years and is a partner in the Wilmington, Delaware office of Faegre, Drinker Biddle & Reath LLP. He represents debtors, secured and unsecured creditors, unsecured creditors committees, asset purchasers and trustees in a broad range of bankruptcy matters including claim resolution, asset sales and acquisitions, plan confirmations, avoidance actions, directors and officers litigation, and a wide variety of other bankruptcy litigation matters. Brett is a graduate of Duke University and the Duke University School of Law.

Paul R. Hage is a partner in the Insolvency & Reorganization Practice Group at Jaffe Raitt Heuer & Weiss, P.C. in Detroit, Michigan. He represents debtors, secured and unsecured creditors, unsecured creditors' committees, asset purchasers and trustees in reorganizations, liquidations and other insolvency proceedings nationwide.

Monique D. Hayes is a partner at Goldstein & McClintock, LLLP in Miami, Florida. She has successfully represented clients in a broad range of bankruptcy matters including claim prosecution, asset sales and acquisitions, finance transactions, bankruptcy plan confirmations, avoidance actions, directors and officers claim litigation, Ponzi scheme and other fraud litigation. Prior to entering private practice she clerked for Judge Laurel M. Isicoff, United States Bankruptcy Court Southern District of Florida.

CONTRIBUTORS

Megan Adeyemo
Gordon Rees Scully Mansukhani, Dallas, Texas

Luis Casas
Akerman, Miami, Florida

Ashley D. Champion
Law Clerk to Hon. Sage M. Sigler, United States Bankruptcy Court Northern District of Georgia

Brett D. Fallon
Faegre Drinker Biddle & Reath LLP, Wilmington, Delaware

Paul R. Hage
Jaffe Raitt Heuer & Weiss, P.C. Southfield, Michigan

Daniel Halperin
Salazar Law, Miami, Florida

Monique D. Hayes
Goldstein & McClintock, LLLP, Miami, Florida

Freddi Mack
Jones Day, Miami, FL

Annie Matthews
Gordon Rees Scully Mansukhani, Dallas, Texas

Nicole McLemore
Law Clerk to Hon. Mindy Mora, United States Bankruptcy Court Southern District of Florida

Grace Robson
Markowitz, Ringel, Trusty & Hartog, P.A., Ft. Lauderdale, Florida

Lisa P. Sumner
Nexsen Pruet, Raleigh, North Carolina